Alexander Somek, at the height of his powers, has already enjoyed a long and distinguished career. He is, unlike most of us, altogether at home in both worlds – the Anglophone world with its myopia and the Continental European world with its vast perspectives but, all too often, with analysis that falls short of the mark. Alexander Somek brings the best of both worlds together, and his manuscript is a welcome effort to redress the balance in favor of, as he puts it, a post-legal positivist theory of law.

Stanley L. Paulson, Washington University in St. Louis

A mature masterpiece equaling Hart's Concept of Law or Dworkin's Law's Empire in jurisprudential ambition, originality, and sophistication, *The Legal Relation* is the most important continental European contribution to jurisprudence in the new millennium.

Mattias Kumm, Inge Rennert Professor of Law at the New York University School of Law and Professor of Global Public Law in the Berlin Social Science Center

With this bold and provocative book, Somek brilliantly reimagines legal positivism. Every legal philosopher must read this book. The argument is imaginative, penetrating, and ultimately convincing.

Dennis Patterson, Board of Governors Professor of Law, Rutgers Law School, Camden, New Jersey

THE LEGAL RELATION

What is law? The usual answer is that the law is a system of norms. But this answer gives us at best half of the story. The law is a way of relating to one another. We do not do this as lovers or friends and not as people who are interested in obtaining guidance from moral insight. In a legal context, we are cast as "character masks" (Marx), for example, as "buyer" and "seller" or "landlord" and "tenant." We expect to have our claims respected simply because the law has given us rights. We do not want to give any other reason for our behavior than the fact that we have a legal right. Backing rights up with coercive threats indicates that we are willing to accept legal obligations unwillingly. This book offers a conceptual reconstruction of the legal relation on the basis of a critique of legal positivism.

Alexander Somek is Professor of Legal Philosophy at the University of Vienna and Global Affiliated Professor of Law at the University of Iowa, where he previously held the position of the Charles E. Floete Chair in Law. He has been a Fellow of the Institute for Advanced Study in Berlin, a LAPA fellow, and visiting professor at Princeton University and at the London School of Economics. He is the author of eleven books.

CAMBRIDGE INTRODUCTIONS TO PHILOSOPHY AND LAW

Series Editors

Brian H. Bix
University of Minnesota

William A. Edmundson
Georgia State University

This introductory series of books provides concise studies of the philosophical foundations of law, of perennial topics in the philosophy of law, and of important and opposing schools of thought. The series is aimed principally at students in philosophy, law, and political science.

Matthew Kramer, *Objectivity and the Rule of Law (2007)*

Larry Alexander and Emily Sherwin, *Demystifying Legal Reasoning (2008)*

Larry Alexander, Kimberly Kessler Ferzan, and Stephen J. Morse, *Crime and Culpability (2009)*

Robin West, *Normative Jurisprudence (2011)*

William A. Edmundson, *An Introduction to Rights, 2nd edition (2012)*

Gregory S. Alexander and Eduardo S. Peñalver, *An Introduction to Property Theory (2012)*

Brian H. Bix, *Contract Law (2013)*

Liam Murphy, *What Makes Law (2014)*

Pablo E. Navarro and Jorge L. Rodríguez, *Deontic Logic and Legal Systems (2014)*

Alexander Somek, *The Legal Relation: Legal Theory after Legal Positivism (2017)*

The Legal Relation

LEGAL THEORY AFTER LEGAL POSITIVISM

ALEXANDER SOMEK
University of Vienna and University of Iowa

CAMBRIDGE
UNIVERSITY PRESS

CAMBRIDGE
UNIVERSITY PRESS

University Printing House, Cambridge CB2 8BS, United Kingdom

One Liberty Plaza, 20th Floor, New York, NY 10006, USA

477 Williamstown Road, Port Melbourne, VIC 3207, Australia

4843/24, 2nd Floor, Ansari Road, Daryaganj, Delhi – 110002, India

79 Anson Road, #06–04/06, Singapore 079906

Cambridge University Press is part of the University of Cambridge.

It furthers the University's mission by disseminating knowledge in the pursuit of education, learning, and research at the highest international levels of excellence.

www.cambridge.org
Information on this title: www.cambridge.org/9781107198012
DOI: 10.1017/9781108182096

First published 2017

Printed in the United States of America by Sheridan Books, Inc.

A catalogue record for this publication is available from the British Library.

Library of Congress Cataloging-in-Publication Data
NAMES: Somek, Alexander, 1961– author.
TITLE: The legal relation : legal theory after legal positivism / Alexander Somek.
DESCRIPTION: Cambridge [UK] ; New York : Cambridge University Press, 2017. | Series: Cambridge introductions to philosophy and law
IDENTIFIERS: LCCN 2017020501 | ISBN 9781107198012 (hardback)
SUBJECTS: LCSH: Law – Philosophy. | Legal positivism. | Law – Political aspects. | BISAC: LAW / Jurisprudence.
CLASSIFICATION: LCC K235 .S625 2017 | DDC 340/.1–dc23
LC record available at https://lccn.loc.gov/2017020501

ISBN 978-1-107-19801-2 Hardback
ISBN 978-1-316-64800-1 Paperback

Contents

Preface

In the face of the eventual demise of legal positivism, *The Legal Relation* offers an attempt to rebuild legal theory. The work of reconstruction is informed by viewing law as a morally significant relation among people.

In the intellectual format in which legal positivism persists in the Anglo-American world, it no longer possesses any critical edge; oddly enough, some of its proponents have even made it their intellectual game to incorporate elements of its sworn opponent, natural law theory, into it.

A return to natural law theory, however, is not in the cards. The belief in one morally right answer to legal questions not only reveals embarrassingly bad aesthetic judgment, it also ignores the fact that law is designed to address a predicament of morality.

A new beginning is needed. But where would one go when both legal positivism and natural law theory drop out of the picture? *The Legal Relation* proposes to return to the broader theoretical perspective from which modern legal positivism originated in the early work of Hans Kelsen, namely, constructivism.

Legal constructivism has a negative and a positive dimension. Negatively, constructivism is about stripping the law of unnecessary idealizations. Its view of the law is not intended to be morally uplifting. Positively, constructivism construes the law from the type of relation that the law constitutes among people. Roughly stated, the emphasis shifts from law as a norm to law as a relation. This relation gives rise to sources of law. From these sources, then, "flow" various legal norms.

Constructivism, like legal positivism, accords to sources of law a central role. In contrast to positivism, however, sources are not just constitutive rules designed to capture law-creating social facts. Each source lends to the law a new appearance. The legal process involves sources talking to sources. Indeed, legal knowledge itself must be regarded as a source of law.

Both constructivism and natural law theory recognize the relevance of morality to the resolution of legal questions. The former insists, however, that, within a legal context, morality changes its mood. Within the context of the legal relation, morality can no longer be dead serious. Consequently, a major theme of *The Legal Relation* is the relation between legality and irony.

While the first half of *The Legal Relation* speaks to contemporary legal positivism, it also returns to a way of thinking about law that we associate with nineteenth-century German legal philosophy. While the book aspires to be faithful to this legacy, it does not adopt any particular thinker (*e.g.*, Fichte, Hegel, Savigny, or Puchta) as its revered master.

Owing to its focus on the legal relation, the book rediscovers, in the exploration of alienation, an element of the Marxist critique of law. *The Legal Relation* is based upon a certain view of the purpose of jurisprudence. Legal theory does not invest future lawyers with supreme abilities to resolve hard cases, nor is it about enhancing our technical understanding of the structure of the legal system. Rather, legal theory ought to explain why and how the law matters to our lives.

Living our life we carve out a presence for ourselves in this social world. The inescapable means thereto is agency. Constructivism, ultimately, approaches the law from the conditions of autonomous agency.

Acknowledgments

I would like to thank Brian Bix and Bill Edmundson for accepting this book for publication in their distinguished series.

The text benefited from the critical and editorial comments provided by my research assistants Jakob Gaigg and Raphaela Tiefenbacher.

Work on this book commenced, unwittingly, during my time as a visiting professor in the Philosophy Department of the University of Vienna in 2014. I would like to thank Herlinde Pauer-Studer for having been such a gracious and generous host.

The largest debt of gratitude, however, I owe to my favorite American law school. Most of the work on the book was done while I was still a regular faculty member in the College of Law of the University of Iowa. It is with immense gratefulness and fondness that I recount its uniquely congenial atmosphere. I, for one, do not know of any other place where shared academic ambition and mutual benevolence create such a perfect environment for unimpeded scholarly growth. If I have accomplished anything of significance in my life, it is the result of the good fortune I have had as a part of an intellectual culture of friends.

Introduction
The Pursuit of Theory

KNOWLEDGE AND EXISTENCE

There would be no legal system if nobody could say what the law is. This is painfully trivial. The existence of law is mediated by knowledge that claims to know what the law is. Knowing the law is a business. Dispensations of legal expertise are services. They can be bought and sold. It should not come as a surprise that the deck is notoriously stacked in favor of those who can afford to mobilize more.

When service providers are widely immune to contestation (*e.g.*, judges, law professors, international arbitrators), they begin to develop their own idiosyncratic ideas. They have the power to do so.

Law is mediated by legal knowledge. Legal knowledge arrives in this world encumbered with both money and power. It is tainted by the very conditions that account for its existence. And so is law.

THE REVERSAL

Reflecting on what validates, rather than causes, its existence, legal knowledge claims to have a different constitution. Neither in legislatures nor on the pages of court opinions would the law, if it could speak, ever say that it follows the highest bidder or is ancillary to bosses. Law may *de facto* be borne out of money and power; *de jure* it presents itself as rising above them. The production of new law has to be based upon knowing the law, even if all that is known is an alleged "right to rule over others."

This coincides with what we expect the law to accomplish. It has to constitute authority in which is vested the task to control the treacherous voyages of money. This is how we ordinarily conceive of the integration of society.[1] The hierarchy of control ought to run from law via power to money. Money is constrained by (political) power; power is constrained by law.

De facto, however, legal knowledge exists by virtue of a reversal of this hierarchy. This creates a predicament. Law that is merely known by virtue of money and power is just money and power wearing the vestiges of law. Saying what is legal cannot *simply* be a matter of auctions or voting. Legal expertise needs to be validated with recourse to what the law *really* is.

OBJECTIVITY

Hence, the solution appears to be simple. Since legal knowledge has to say what the law is, it needs to be objective. This means, quite simply, that legal propositions, in order to be valid, need to give a true account of the legal situation. Only by virtue of truth can legal knowledge emancipate itself from the undue influence of money and power. And so can law.

LEGAL POSITIVISM AND NATURAL LAW THEORY

The problem is straightforward. Legal knowledge, in order to make the law possible, necessarily has to lay claim to objectivity. At the same time, as a social fact, it is likely to be caused by less auspicious forces than the quest for truth.

Consequently, in any of its more advanced forms, legal knowledge needs to embrace at least a modicum of suspicion.[2] One has to reckon with arguments that wish to pass as objective while they actually just serve some special interests. The pursuit of a political agenda may be wearing the mask of a theory of legal interpretation (*e.g.*, the mask of "originalism"). Its proponents may be legitimately censured for hiding the ball.

Unsurprisingly, therefore, in any of its more advanced forms, legal knowledge aims at exposing the idealizations with which money and power purport to pass as sound legal doctrine. The respective challenges would be futile, however, if the promise of objectivity could not be kept. Objectivity is possible only by developing an idea of what the law really is – as opposed to, say, kicking people around; buying oneself influence; or the persistence of mere habits, religion, morality, or best practice.

1 See Talcott Parsons, *Sociological Theory and Modern Society* (New York and London: Free Press, 1967) at 297–328.

2 On the hermeneutics of suspicion, see Paul Ricoeur, *Freud and Philosophy: An Essay on Interpretation* (New Haven: Yale University Press, 1970).

Answering the question of objectivity correctly has been subject to the seemingly perennial controversy between legal positivists and advocates of natural law. They were not the only contestants in this debate, but for the purpose of introducing the problem it is quite accurate to focus on them.

Legal positivists would have us believe that someone lays down law.[3] Law is a social fact that can be read off, in a value-neutral way, the face of law's sources, such as legislation, regulations, or precedents. Describing accurately what has been laid down, as law, by either insurmountable or merely presupposed authority is what it takes to arrive at a legal knowledge that is true.[4]

As is well known, modern natural law theory embraces an alternative version of objectivity.[5] It claims, basically, that finding the right answer to a legal question is fully continuous with finding the morally right answer. The objectivity of legal knowledge is, thus, of a piece with having a correct moral justification.[6] Actually,

3 This view is at least officially sustained by John Gardner, *Law as a Leap of Faith: Essays on Law in General* (Oxford: Oxford University Press, 2012) at 20.

4 The most famous exposition of this view is Hans Kelsen, *Pure Theory of Law* (2d ed., trans. M. Knight, Berkeley: University of California Press, 1967) at 1.

5 In a highly perceptive essay, Brian Bix distinguished between traditional and modern approaches to natural law. While the traditional approaches tried to identify, and to appeal to, some law that is "higher" than humanmade law and amenable to rational insight, modern natural law theory is a reply to legal positivism and insists on the relevance of morality to legal reasoning. See Brian Bix, "Natural Law Theory." In *A Companion to Philosophy of Law and Legal Theory* (ed. D. Patterson, Oxford: Blackwell, 1996) 223–240 at 231, 237.

6 Admittedly, the contours of "natural law theory" as a position in legal philosophy are far from clear. This book is following Kant's lead. He characterized natural law as law that is, without being supported by external law giving, recognized on the ground of practical reason alone. It is the law that ought to be positive law. See Immanuel Kant, Die Metaphysik der Sitten, *Werkausgabe* (ed. W. Weischedel, Frankfurt aM: Insel, 1968) vol. 8 at 345–346. On Kant's views of natural law, see most recently, Christoph Horn, *Nichtideale Normativität: Ein neuer Blick auf Kants politische Philosophie* (Berlin: Suhrkamp, 2014) at 131–135. See also Nigel Simmonds, *Law as a Moral Idea* (Oxford: Oxford University Press, 2007) at 12. According to John Finnis, *Reason in Action: Collected Essays: Volume 1* (Oxford: Oxford University Press, 2011b) at 200–201, the phrase "natural law" refers to "standards of right choosing." They are normative because of their truth, "and choosing otherwise than in accordance with them is unreasonable." In a manner similar to Kant, Finnis explains that the principles and standards of natural law are relevant prior to any "positing" by individuals or groups and provide the backbone for any critical evaluation of posited norms. The standards are also objective in that a person who fails to observe them commits an error of judgment. For the most part of the history of natural law theory, this elemental idea has been used to address the demands of "higher law" to the legislature. See Brian Bix, *Jurisprudence: Theory and Context* (7th ed., Durham: Carolina Academic Press, 2015) at 69–72. Arguably, this has been the case not only for natural law theories speculating about the *nomos* (Stoa) or a *lex aeterna* (Augustin and Aquinas), which were supposed to be manifest in the ordering of the world but also for the modern strand of natural law theory that focuses on rights (from Grotius to Locke). See Ernst-Wolfgang Böckenförde, *Geschichte der Rechts- und Staatsphilosophie: Antike und Mittelalter* (2d ed., Tübingen: Mohr

natural law is about having the morally right answer to the core legal question: under which condition may we coerce you into doing what we want you to do? We make arguments to this effect as participants in moral controversies. We, the good people, coerce you because we believe, firmly, that doing so is morally right. Natural law is an extension of moral claims to the domain where we have to decide over questions of coercion.[7]

THE POST-POSITIVIST SITUATION

At the beginning of the twenty-first century, however, things no longer look terribly good for these different claims to objectivity. The *descriptive* rendition of objectivity, which is epitomized by legal positivism, is no longer convincing. Law is not an array of semantically stable abstract entities. It is, as it were, permanently under construction.[8] There is nothing outlandish, let alone radical, about this view. Every student of hermeneutics knows that understanding is a process in the course of which the horizons of the author and the reader engage with each other productively.[9] Puzzlingly, therefore, as a position in legal theory, legal positivism can survive only at the price of its irrelevance for legal knowledge and, *a fortiori*, for the legal system. The late legal positivism of our age subsists in splendid isolation from its object – at any rate, in Anglo-American circles.[10]

By contrast, the rendering of objectivity in terms of moral justifiability is definitely on the right track. But it is also flawed when pushed up to the hilt. It is claimed, then, that there is one and only one substantive right answer to any legal question even in the face of initial moral disagreement among people who regard one another as reasonable persons.[11] Disturbingly, at the

Siebeck, 2006) at 138–139, 204, 234. See Sean Coyle, *Modern Jurisprudence: A Philosophical Guide* (Oxford: Hart Publishing, 2014) at 59–62. Once natural law theory becomes directed at the judiciary, however, its orientation changes. The institution to which the precepts of reason are addressed is not in charge in laying down good general laws but tasked with adjudicating specific legal questions. Consequently, the emphasis shifts from what constitutes "good laws" to what constitutes "right answers."

7 See Ronald Dworkin, *Law's Empire* (Cambridge, Mass.: Harvard University Press, 1986) at 93.

8 See, for example, Stanley Fish, *Doing What Comes Naturally: Change, Rhetoric, and the Practice of Theory in Literary and Legal Studies* (Oxford: Clarendon Press, 1989) at 511–513.

9 See, for example, Roland Dworkin, "Law as Interpretation." In *The Politics of Interpretation* (ed. W.J.T. Mitchell, Chicago: Chicago University Press, 1982) at 249–270.

10 This observation has been aptly made by Ronald Dworkin, *Justice in Robes* (Cambridge, Mass: Harvard University Press, 2006) at 213.

11 See Ronald Dworkin, A *Matter of Principle* (Cambridge, Mass.: Harvard University Press, 1985) 144–145. On different versions of the right-answer thesis, see Brian Bix, *Jurisprudence: Theory and Context* (6th ed., Durham: Carolina Academic Press, 2012) at 98–99.

same time, claims to moral objectivity in law are trailed with concessions regarding "burdens of judgment"[12] or "reasonable disagreements."[13] Insisting on one morally right answer for legal disputes in the face of concededly imperfect moral insight must appear strangely fanatical and perhaps even morally wrong.

SALOME

The first chapter of this book will address the problems of late legal positivism. At this point, it pays to examine briefly why we sense that the one-right-answer thesis is misguided.

The one-right-answer-thesis is cast into doubt, for it cannot accommodate aesthetic experience. Art and fiction invite us to see stories and situations in colorations that we necessarily ignore when we are engaged in action. This is true not only of the dreary genre of jury dramas but also of any piece of literature that suspends morality and is, therefore, capable of capturing life's perplexity. Good fiction does not preach. It reveals the elusiveness of our dealings and abstains from passing judgment. Art gives us the goodness of wicked schemes and the sinister side of righteousness without attempting to clarify which is which. It reminds us of a state of innocence to which we have no access in practice because of the existence of morality.

Aesthetic experience enables us to suspend responsibility. When we follow a story, there is no pain of having to pull ourselves together and to arrive at a moral perspective on it. We know that Salome is a horrible kid; but when she exclaims joyfully that she has finally kissed the lips of beheaded Johanaan, we cannot but join her in her triumph.[14] If one were to sum up Oscar Wilde's drama and Richard Strauss's music by saying that they confront us with the question whether there can be circumstances under which sexual desire can outweigh a man's right to life, one would have demonstrated, conclusively, that one is not amenable to the appreciation of art.

SUSPENDING JUDGMENT

Art reconciles us with life because it reconciles us with moral complexity. We are affected by it without being smushed by its grip. We do not need to pass

12 See John Rawls, *Political Liberalism* (New York: Columbia University Press, 1991) at 56–57.

13 See Jeremy Waldron, *Law and Disagreement* (Oxford: Oxford University Press, 1999) at 105–106.

14 On aesthetic freedom as freedom from practical freedom, see Christoph Menke, *Die Kraft der Kunst* (Berlin: Suhrkamp, 2013) at 150.

judgment on whether Hannah Schmitz, the fictional character in Schlink's *Reader* who became a prison guard in a desperate effort to hide her illiteracy, was an evil person.[15] On the contrary, we realize how stultifying morality is compared with life in narrated form. The pros and cons are part of the picture. But the scale of justice does not incline into one or the other direction. The reconciliation is *in* the narration. It defies being summed up into a moral lesson. The perceived reconciliation mitigates the impossibility of its conceptualization. Hannah Schmitz is convicted and commits suicide while serving her prison term. Undeniably, she gets what she deserves. But it does not strike us as right.

A steadfast belief in a right answer would deny this type of experience a place. The perception of innocence within guilt and guilt within innocence would disappear. The legally right answer is that in her capacity as a prison guard, Hannah Schmitz is guilty of a terrible crime. But how narrow-minded must that determination appear against the broader background in which being ashamed of her illiteracy figures along with her obliviousness to the politics of her time?

There can be no life without action. Why would what suspends guidance from morality and rationality be closer to life than socially useful experience? The explanation lies in a promise of transcendence. The perception of life transcends the vagaries of its evaluation from within. It reveals life in the state in which it does not have to be stamped with approval or disapproval to go on. Art does not give us heaven. It gives us earth beyond explanation and justification. It gives us truth, not in the sense of a better description, but as revealing the truer life that is eclipsed by our ordinary practice of judgment.

If the quest for the one-right-answer made sense, the suspension of judgment would not. If a moral controversy concerning the blameworthiness of Hannah Schmitz had to arrive at a right answer, art would not redeem us from judging. This explains why the idea that there has to be a one-right-answer is obnoxious owing to its moralistic embrace of banality.

THE QUESTION OF LEGAL THEORY

Legal knowledge cannot leave its labor to art, let alone grow into it. Storytelling is not a manner of giving each his or her due. The question before us is how one is to conceive of legal knowledge given that both legal positivism and modern natural law theory have run their course.

[15] See Bernhard Schlink, *The Reader* (trans. C. Brown Janeway, New York: Vintage Books, 1999).

The latter is embarrassing, at any rate in hard cases from the perspective of aesthetic experience. The attempt to come up with the one-right-answer is boorish. All the same, legal positivism can survive only at the cost of its irrelevance for legal knowledge.[16] Against this background, the core question of legal theory must be how one can conceive of legal knowledge once legal positivism no longer appears to be an option. More precisely, the question is how legal knowledge can still legitimately claim to rise above money and power and say what the law truly is without suggesting, as legal positivism did, that the law is out there, amenable to a value-neutral description.

SOURCES AND THE LEGAL RELATION

The answer to this question given in this book is threefold. First, sources of law lend expression to a particular relation between and among people. They are manifestations of the legal relation. We construct and sustain it to pass as socially recognizable agents. The law mediates our presence in this world. It does so in a manner that replies to a predicament of morality. The reply is the legal relation and the sources to which it gives rise.

Second, sources of law are not just rules used to constitute legally significant facts. What is constituted, in the form of sources, is something subjective, namely knowledge of the law. Customary law is a way of knowing the law, and so is legislation (which is at least a way of making up our mind). Both are based upon subjectivity, even if in different forms. Since sources ordinarily give rise to law while drawing on other sources, it is fair to say that all legal knowledge is self-knowledge, that is, knowledge *of* the law *by* the law. Its point is to attain clarity in singular cases.

Third, law is a background relation among people that can be pushed to the foreground when things turn sour or when people want to be guarded against harm. We invoke the law, for example, in order to end some more personal or amiable interaction. With an appeal to law, we become all of a sudden faceless. From then on, we interact as instantiations of "spouses," "employers," "employees," "parents." Relationships become cold and distant when they are perceived as exemplars of the legal relation.

The remaining sections of this introduction offer a sketch of the book's fundamental ideas. This sketch is followed by brief summaries of each chapter of the book.

16 See note 10.

EXPLICABILITY

The point that the law mediates our presence in this world merits some elaboration. Essential to constituting our presence *as agents* in this world is, first and foremost, the explicability of our actions.[17] *Explicability* means demonstrating responsiveness to reasons, that is, being amenable to what a person can conceivably be persuaded by. The relevant contrast is madness or loss of rational control. I would not succeed at coming across as a responsible agent and, hence, as the author of my acts if I merely said that I did what I did because I am I. If I said that what triggers my actions is the fact about me that I am I, I would fail to make myself explicable as an agent. Used in this manner, the "I" that is supposedly authoring actions – in spite of serving as an indexical that identifies me as the speaker – would not designate agency. I am present as an agent in the social world only if I can pass as being responsive to reasons. Otherwise, I would be perceived as thrown around by some strange force, which I would merely, and falsely, call my own because I happen to be driven by it.

"Why did you kill your baby?"
"'Cause that's who I am."

Only a crazy person would say that. In order to be an outgrowth of agency, our acts have to pass the threshold of explicability.[18]

"Here is why."
"I did it because . . . "

Hence, we encounter reason-responsiveness even where we find people acting on the wrong balance of reasons or for a defeasible reason.

"Why did you kill your baby?"
"He was screaming all night."

In the case of responsiveness to moral reasons, I claim that anyone would have done what I did had he or she been in a similar situation and burdened with similar commitments. If I am right about what I claim, I am present in my acts as an agent who is responsive to the *right* reasons. I am thus not only explicable but also universally justified in doing what I do. Under this condition, I am

[17] Explicability is not the whole story. As we shall see, what matters eventually is the realization as self-determining (autonomous) beings. Explicability, however, is an elementary condition thereto.

[18] On explicability, see J. David Velleman, *How We Get Along* (Cambridge: Cambridge University Press, 2009) at 16.

definitely elevated above a state in which I am merely a pinball thrown around by natural causation.[19]

As will be explained in Chapter 4, the social practice of moral justification reveals that the fixation of moral beliefs depends on diverse and particular evaluative outlooks. Some people, for example, attribute greater weight to protecting human health than others. This explains why they support more risk-averse policies and arrive, when it comes to the control of substances, at moral beliefs that betray their evaluative outlook. Others see things differently.

Universalization – the claim that one adopts as a binding rule what everyone would have reason to do – is of no avail when it comes to determining the right attitude toward risks at least as long as people are willing to put themselves into the shoes of others and claim readiness to face the consequences. When hypothetically taking the positions of others, the risk-averse and the risk-takers universalize differently. Moral universalization, therefore, confronts us with our particularity. What we may have intended to amount to a justification turns out to be mere explication. Instead of experiencing the sweet harmony of universal agreement, people end up attributing to others views bearing the imprint of evaluative outlooks ("I can see that a Puritan would want that"). It is the prevalence of outlooks that renders explicable why justifications may fail for a good reason.

In the face of particularity, only readjusting the focus of justification can restore universality. It has to be determined under which conditions it is right – justified – to accept mere explicability.

"I did it because I am a guy."
"I know that you are."

The *legal relation* holds out the promise that various manifestations of particularity can be universalized by virtue of conditional yielding to what might be the explications of others. In the first place, the legal relation is the attempt to universalize the failure of straightforward moral universalizabililty. In the second place, by mutually conceding to one another our particularity we construe a relation in which we are rendered as *choosers*, more precisely, as persons having various rights to make choices. The focus of justification shifts from the assessment of the overall appropriateness of action to the observance of the conditions under which we legitimately exercise a right. The authorship of action is thereby rendered as an exercise of free choice. Rightful choosings represent justified explicability.

[19] Concededly, this is a very Kantian perspective.

With that one enters the realm of legality.[20] It is the world where we relate to demands, choices, and norms only "externally." Without endorsing them, we merely adapt to their existence.

FROM BELIEF TO THE FACT OF BELIEF

The core of the typically legal distance toward normative demands resides in how we relate to reasons for action. Within a legal relation, I yield to demands made by others and enjoy the power to make others yield to mine. More precisely, I yield to what others want, but I do so not for the reason that I accept or share their reasons for choosing the chosen course of action. In contrast to communications with a friend, a colleague, or a spouse, I allow others to go forward without further discussion and without giving them approbation or rebuke.[21] I simply respect what they take to be their practical knowledge, that is, knowledge guiding their action.

Leaving the practical knowledge that gives rise to choices unexamined and unchallenged involves a simple but remarkable transformation of its ontological state. Instead of involving a claim to validity, this knowledge is rendered as a social fact eventuating in a "choice," which is yet another social fact. Yielding to the practical knowledge of others involves waiving or bracketing its claim to validity. Viewed from the perspective of the believer, any belief that concedes that it suspends its claim to validity represents the mere fact of believing. Students not infrequently preface their remarks by saying "in my view." Unsure about their ability to take responsibility for their claims, they prefer to report their beliefs as facts about them. Reporting the existence of a belief is, of course, different from making a claim.

If the change of the ontological state from a deontological claim to validity to the social fact of believing takes place in an interaction, the practical knowledge underpinning choices is put into brackets. In this form, it is incapable of grounding these choices, for it does not even claim anything. You have reason to eat if you need food. You have no reason to eat if it is a fact about you that you happen to believe you do not need food (while you constantly overindulge because of this misguided belief). The choices that are made by people whose choices are based upon bracketed practical knowledge are "mere choices."

[20] Throughout this work, "legality" is understood in the Kantian sense to mean morally uninvolved conformity with law. This is not consistent with the usage prevalent in Anglo-American circles where "legality" designates the quality of being law. See Chapter 1.

[21] The legal relation is what Darwall would call "second-personal." See, for example, Stephen Darwall, *Morality, Authority, and Law: Essays in Second-Personal Ethics I* (Oxford: Oxford University Press, 2013) at 151–153.

The legal relation demands that we respect such choices. Arnold believes that his skills as a driver are sufficient to warrant his ownership of a Porsche. Alas, he is sorely mistaken about that. I, for one, could do better justice to his ferocious motor. Nevertheless, Arnold – gray-streaked fellow that he is – has chosen to own a Porsche. The choice is all that matters, legally speaking. My respect for his ownership entitles him to live his conceit.

A REASONABLY UNREASONABLE WORLD

If someone believes to have reason to intrude on a public gathering that I have organized, I have to let this happen out of respect for the person's choice. Once I am making room, however, I am exposed to that person's beliefs. The reason for yielding confronts me with beliefs and attitudes that are not mine. Likewise, if my neighbor believes in the beauty of a building that he erects adjacent to my home, I am demonstratively affected by the reasons of another person. If all of my neighbors find it cool to drive SUVs, in spite of my dismissive attitude toward brazen demonstrations of bad petty bourgeois taste, I have to accept that they have them. I have to deal with it. I even have to accept that governments will legitimately address health and safety issues that arise from the use of these freaky vehicles.

A large part of the social world is being built on the basis of our indulgence of beliefs and desires that we regard as insufficient to give rise to reasons for action. Not only are the requisite beliefs, from my perspective, the beliefs of others; they may not at all be believ*able* for me. Many people believe that they are better off eating vegan food. I remain unconvinced. That I remain unconvinced shows that the reasons of others are the other of reasons, not reasons proper for me, but still reasons for someone else – no one in particular – whom I have to regard as reasonable (amenable to reasons, but in my view responding to the wrong ones). They are reasons in the state of otherness (*Veranderung*).[22]

INDIVIDUAL RIGHTS AND GENERAL SOURCES

Arnold's decision to own a Porsche is the source of my legal obligation to respect his property. Of course, it is not the only source. General sources of law, such as legislation, provide us with rules with which we determine the

[22] I first discovered this term in the work of Michael Theunissen but do not suggest that I am actually following his lead here. See Michael Theunissen, *Sein und Schein: Die kritische Funktion der Hegelschen Logik* (Frankfurt aM: Suhrkamp, 1980) at 237–242, and earlier in his *Der Andere: Studien zur Sozialontologie der Gegenwart* (2d ed., Berlin: de Gruyter, 1977) at 84.

circumstances under which Arnold's choice is generative of obligations for others, including myself. Hence, there are individual and general sources.

Remarkably, however, as a result of entertaining a legal relation with the institutions that wield political authority, we relate to general sources in the same manner in which we relate to individual sources. This explains why sources appear to be composed of practical knowledge wearing brackets. It is within these brackets that the law is known. More precisely, legal validity is composed of practical knowledge of which its own claim to validity is suspended and substituted with the demand to yield to what it says. Law is composed of knowledge that is only permitted to know subject to the condition that is does not really know. It is knowledge *in the state of revocation*.

Admittedly, at first glance, this may appear obscure. Upon closer inspection, however, the matter loses its seemingly mystical air. As is well known, *customary law*, as a source of law, is composed of general practice paired with the shared conviction that what is generally practiced is carried out rightfully. Thus stated, however, the relation between practice and conviction is only externally juxtaposed. One has to have one and the other. This view of the matter, however, does not unlock the secret of customary law. Custom needs to be seen as having its root in shared intuitions of law. The conviction that practice is law is practical knowledge, the seriousness of which has passed the test of time through practice.

One needs to be circumspect, however, to perceive clearly what it is that turns practical knowledge into a source. The relevant practical knowledge underlying customary law cannot seriously claim to be warranted, for it is merely based upon shared intuition. Therefore, it has to present itself as a social fact. It just posits that it counts. In a sense, it disclaims its claim to validity by answering any potential question about the ground of its knowledge with the tautological assertion that "we know what we know." Just like students disclaim their knowledge claim by adding a cautionary "in my view" and thus switch to reporting their state of belief, customary law abdicates all responsibility for commonly intuited demands by positing them as mere and sheer beliefs. The relevance of intuition suggests that what would otherwise count as a reason for believing is reduced to seeing matters in a certain way. "Seeing that . . . " is a belief stated as a social fact. The reasons for belief are *substituted* with the fact of belief.[23]

[23] If one were to anchor the source of custom in the reciprocity of practice ("As long as all others do the same, I regard doing so as law"), the shared belief in reciprocity would be the relevant fact.

VERANDERUNG

Claims to validity are "deontic" in the sense that they commit whoever is raising them to give reasons and thus to shoulder responsibility for their content.[24] Practical knowledge gives rise to such responsibility. What is remarkable about sources is that they insulate what is claimed from the deontological commitment of reason giving. Sources intrude on reason by positing that practical knowledge counts regardless of its merit. It is through the transformation of the deontological strains of validity into something factual that the subjectivity of knowing is rendered in the form of an object. Sources are objectifications of subjectivity, that is, knowledge that has left the sphere of "deontic score keeping" within which people are expected to defend their claims. It is knowledge that has descended into the netherworld of the matter-of-factual.[25]

Admittedly, such a transmutation involves a second-personal reaction to a first-personal claim. A disclaimed claim is a claim that is not taken seriously. The reaction of another is necessary for that. Sources, however, anticipate this reaction in the way of their constitution. Practical knowledge becomes stripped of its claim to validity and demoted to the level of explicability. In this shape, knowledge does not have to convince in order to command respect. Accepting a substantively disclaimed claim means regarding it as a source.

The concept of a "content-independent" reason for action[26] captures the relevant act of yielding without substantive engagement. What it does not capture, however, is that by virtue of yielding one is bound to observe expressions of practical reason in the state of *Veranderung*.[27] This state designates beliefs that one could have if one were another person. Legal sources confront us with the practical knowledge *of others*. This knowledge is, in the form of sources, in principle severed from underlying reasons. This explains the "literalness" of law. Law is rigid for the reason of being source based. It is thereby initially insulated against the broader background of practical reasoning.

DECISIONS AND POLITICS

Legislation is also knowledge of what we have to do. This knowledge is based upon a decision. Decisions are important forms of practical knowledge. A true

[24] The obligation is actually "deontological" in nature, for it arises regardless of the potential consequences of the claim.

[25] See Robert Brandom, *Making It Explicit: Reasoning, Representing and Discoursive Commitment* (Cambridge, Mass.: Harvard University Press, 1998).

[26] See Joseph Raz, *Practical Reason and Norms* (2d ed., Princeton: Princeton University Press, 1990) at 99–101.

[27] See note 22.

decision severs us from the tie that exists between competing insufficient reasons. Such a tie is pulling us down and inhibits action. Decisions emancipate from the standstill. They allow us to overcome the paralyzing effect of competing reasons that would be, if unaided by a decision, too weak to give rise to action.

It would be wrong, therefore, to view decisions as acts of recognition that kowtow to reasons of greater weight. According to such an understanding, decisions would still be conclusions. It may well be the case that many acts that we call decisions are in fact conclusions. But this is irrelevant to their legal form. We rely on decisions in order to be guarded against a situation in which practical reasoning may end in an impasse. It would also be wrong, therefore, to read decisions only in light of the reasons that appear to have prevailed over others. In principle, a decision would not have been necessary had the reasons counting in its favor been sufficient to warrant a conclusion.[28] The decision, rather, suspends or brackets the claim of validity of the reasons counting in its favor. It is the epitome of subjective practical knowledge that posits itself as an objective social fact.

Both customary law and legislation are forms of practical knowledge – legal knowledge in that case. They render political authority explicable. The legal relation determines the conditions under which we are required to put up with explicability.

No yielding is unconditional. If others vote to put you to death, your obligation to yield comes to an end. Hence, yielding to what others take to be practical knowledge is subject to *substantive* constraints. Fleshing out these constraints, however, is a matter of engaging political reason, which is always historically contingent. Again, decisions have to be made as to what these limits are, and these decisions are in turn arrived at against a backdrop of "common understandings." Politics has to put up with historical circumstances and existing institutions, at least as long as it must seem unwise to undo them. They may even command respect qua human achievements. Of course, "putting up with" is but another name for "yielding."

LEGAL SCHOLARSHIP

The legal knowledge that is produced in scholarship and manifest in court opinions and administrative decisions is also a source of law, for it rests on its own form of disclaiming. In the case of custom, the disclaimer is manifest in

28 This explains, incidentally, that those supporting a historical approach to interpretation do in fact side with the prevailing party. They read the decision as though it had been a conclusion.

the appeal to sheer intuition, which cannot ground anything. Decisions disclaim the force of practical knowledge that informs them. The justification for the relevance of sources lies, in both cases, in the necessity to get on and to move forward.

Legal scholarship embraces its own disclaimer. Understood as the systematic elaboration of law, the point of scholarship must be to guarantee the like treatment of like cases for a whole body of law. Only in this form can it bear the approval of the law, which is nothing but the relation among equals that seek to identify the conditions of justified explicability. Only when it is geared to the task of making the law known among equals can scholarship legitimately claim to speak for the law.

To accomplish its task, scholarship has to construct an array of conceptual distinctions to relate norms stemming from various sources to certain facts. In disposing of this responsibility, scholarship has to develop interpretations of the legal materials that enhance its explicatory appeal ("This is how German law conceives of the licensing of software").

Evidently, sources such as legislation cannot develop such constructive interpretations themselves. First, the legal materials (statutes, court decisions) do only occasionally ascend to the level at which they look at themselves and ask where their place might be in the larger scheme of things; if they do, they may well be mistaken. Second, sources are, by virtue of being sources, practical knowledge in a suspended state. They are insulated against the practical reason from which they emerge and require re-embedding. Borrowing Coke's venerable language, one could say that such a recontextualization is the work of an "artificial" practical reason. The artificiality is not least manifest in the single-minded orientation toward systematizing norms and differentiating factual situations. Arguably, to carry this task out properly, sources have to be made sense of in the best possible way. Legal scholarship invariably rationalizes a hodgepodge of norms into some *volonté générale*.

The whole business is strange. The raw material that legal scholarship works with is practical reason in the state of *Veranderung*. It is principally the practical reason of another. An array of contingent decisions is rationalized into coherent schemes or systematic bodies of law. Legal scholarship needs to reflect that what it knows is someone else's knowledge and that it is constructed anew for the single purpose of treating like cases alike. Serene irony, therefore, most adequately captures the mood with which legal scholarship emerges as a source of law. *Intuitions, decisions*, and *serene irony* are the three forms in which practical reason is encountered as the practical reason of another. In the case of custom, when I intuit law, my reason is even the other of itself.

Most remarkably, the legal relation is relevant to our inner freedom, too. It allows us to supersede the dictates of conscience and to regard desires as facts about us that are worthy of recognition. Viewing myself as a legal person I become an abstract anybody cut loose from the constraints of my concrete social roles and biographical shackles. I am free, for example, to disregard my own Puritan inner voice and to hang out in bars with friends instead of meditating on what I could do to become a better person. I can regard it as a fact of normative significance that I desire to hang out with friends: no questions asked, no justification necessary. The legal relation allows me to be a stranger to myself.

It can barely become more liberating than that. This liberty is, actually, redolent of how the burden of sensemaking is lifted from us through art.

OVERVIEW OF THE CHAPTERS THAT FOLLOW

The legal theory developed in this book, even though confronted with legal positivism's demise, seeks to preserve much of its original critical thrust. The latter is manifest in the attempt to retain only those idealizations of legal materials that are necessary to perceive law as law. This attempt is most clearly reflected in the work of Hans Kelsen, in particular in his critique of various forms of dualism in legal thought (*e.g.*, private law/public law, natural person/legal person, state/legal order, domestic law/public international law). These parts of Kelsen's project have forever set modern legal positivism against "common sense."

As will be seen in the first two chapters, the Anglicanization of Kelsen's *Pure Theory* reintroduced some common sense – and with it, unnecessary idealizations – through the back door. To vindicate the critical spirit, which is even older than legal positivism,[29] these chapters offer a critique of examples of currently prominent analytical legal positivism. Such positivism embraces the conventional foundation of law and has no qualms about accommodating morality or endorsing law's moral purpose. It has grown old and lost its edge.

The rapprochement toward morality avoids confronting the perplexity of legal validity. It is argued that the latter can only be resolved by changing the conception of law from viewing it as a system of norms to a specific relation among people.

Chapter 2 advances the critique of late legal positivism further. Modern legal positivism tries to preserve the normativity of law while abstaining from

[29] It is arguably part of the constructivist tradition of legal scholarship. See Stanley L. Paulson, "Hans Kelsen's Earliest Legal Theory: Critical Constructivism" (1996) 59 *Modern Law Review* 797–812.

generally viewing positive laws as reasons for action. This effort is epitomized, in particular, in Raz's idea that the substance of positive law can be imparted from the detached perspective of the "legal man." The first part of the chapter demonstrates that the problem that the introduction of the legal man is supposed to solve originates from an assimilation of Kelsen's legal positivism to common sense. The embrace of common sense, however, divests modern legal positivism of its critical edge. In the second part, the chapter offers both a *reductio ad absurdum* of a conventionalist understanding of the legal man and an analysis of legal knowledge that abstains from exploring its claim to validity. Legal knowledge of that type is bound to embrace bitter irony. This type of irony represents normativity that is too powerless to change anything and therefore vanishes in symbolic gestures of disengagement.

Chapter 3 develops an alternative account of legal knowledge. It reinvigorates a tradition of legal thinking that is closely associated with the philosophy of German idealism. While a great deal of inspiration comes from the historical school of jurisprudence – particularly from the theory of Georg Friedrich Puchta – the chapter also draws on ideas of the school's sworn opponent, Hegel, and on the work of the sworn opponent's major philosophical opponent, Schelling. This may smack of syncretism. Nevertheless, the analysis is self-standing and not indebted to any authors in particular. It is a style of thinking that is reintroduced into legal theory, rather than an exercise of worshipping of a master thinker revered by some self-nominated disciple. In the attempt to make itself understood to twenty-first-century legal positivists, the chapter relies heavily on conceptions of the Viennese school of legal positivism (Kelsen, Merkl, Sander).

The major point of the third chapter is to elaborate the point that has already been hinted at. Knowledge of the law, to be truly objective, requires approbation by the law. Knowledge of the law bearing the approval by the law is knowledge that is embodied in a source of law. The legal system can be shown to be a sequence – in fact, a circle – of sources. Moving through the circle, the law is rendered ever more clearly in that every new source on the sequence rectifies a deficiency of its predecessor. Customary law leaves undecided how many instances of practice one has to have seen before one identifies law. The rules for the adoption of legislation remove this indeterminacy. Positive laws, however, do not apply themselves to situations. They require mediation by systematic legal knowledge, which thereby also advances to the level of a source of law. Sources are not *just* law-creating social facts. They are also various gestalts of legal knowledge.

With a first rendering of a post-positivist theory of legal knowledge in place, Chapter 4 turns to the legal relation. It begins with a review of Puchta's claim that the law permits doing either good or evil. Taking this apparent puzzle as its point of departure, the chapter then develops the relation between law and morality on the basis of distinguishing between a basic and a reflective level of moral universalization. The reflective level moves from passing moral judgment to the mutual recognition of rights the exercise of which creates obligations. While the legal relation represents morality growing beyond itself, legal reasoning nonetheless has to resort to morality in order to determine rights and obligations. The mood of morality changes, however, once it becomes relevant for the legal relation. The raising of legal claims infuses moral thinking with serene irony.

The equivalent of moral universalization in the legal setting is the equality principle. Chapter 5 proposes that the meaning of equality is most convincingly drawn out by conceiving of equality as a norm that protects against discrimination. Also rights are equal if the system of rights does not permit discrimination. What is wrong with discrimination can be best understood by examining what a person would have to do to avoid unequal treatment. If such preemptive action involves self-denial – the hiding or repairing of who one is – we are at least *prima facie* confronted with a case of discrimination. At the same time, any lively participant in a market society is legitimately expected to adjust his or her practical identity and life projects to what is feasible in light of overall demand. The relevance of individual agility and adaptability rules out that a case of discrimination can ever be fully established with reference to individual idiosyncrasies. It must seem, therefore, that what remains for the protection of discrimination is the focus on characteristics that agile and adaptable individuals cannot alter. The protection from discrimination would hence have to be limited to discrimination on the grounds of characteristics that individuals cannot control. Yet, what individuals, aside from physical immutability, may legitimately regard as inalienable and unchangeable is not subject to a prior determination but rather a question of social struggles. The equality principle and the principle of equal rights are in and of themselves historical.

The final chapter turns to the problem posed by the legal relation from the perspective from which the distinction between law and morality originated, namely, that of creating presence through agency. It turns out that the horizontal realization of the legal relation poses an obstacle thereto. Among individuals who enjoy the rights to private property and freedom of contract, the legal relations give rise to alienation. Individuals, to be able to engage in trade and barter, have to generate economic power, which is the social power to make others want what they are able to offer in exchange. If, in such a context, people are confronted with choosing between a greater and a lesser evil, then alienation results from the social coercion that such a system of private transactions permits.

In a situation of widespread alienation, people develop conceptions of their agency that indirectly reflect their disempowerment. This can be shown for two forms of "despair" discussed by Kierkegaard. The end of the chapter sketches how relations of social freedom might offer a reprieve by moving beyond the legal relation proper.

The analysis in this book thus triangulates the legal relation with the broader context of autonomous (reason-responsive) agency. The law emerges from the necessity to extend moral universalization to a reflective level. This gives us the legal relation, which ceases to be the solution for the quest for agency if it is not superseded by structures of social freedom. The result is an old Rousseauvian wisdom. Each can be free only if he or she is interested in the freedom of each other.

These six chapters illustrate the arch of a post-positivist legal theory. They variously reinvigorate the long forgotten tradition of constructivism by abstaining from idealizing the legal system and rebuilding our conception of law from the legal relation. It actually joins those authors, such as Marx, who have criticized law as a social institution. It parts company with legal positivism in that it ascribes subjectivity to law. The law is not an abstract object amenable to description. Sources of law are forms of legal knowledge that alter the law. In a sense, they enhance its self-understanding. A value-neutral description of law, even if possible, would be pointless. Nonetheless, the post-positivist theory does not embrace natural law theory. It regards the one-right-answer thesis as an outgrowth of bad taste. Nevertheless, the theory does not draw a sharp line between law and morality. Rather, it regards the emergence of the legal relation as self-correction of moral judgment. Both law and morality are part of a continuum in which reason-responsiveness and its normativity are linked to the problem of agency. Moral beliefs and substantive law are concrete historical achievements.

Vis-à-vis these moral facts, a constructivist legal theory occupies a position similar to metaethics in moral theory. It simply wants to reconstruct how such achievements are best understood and what they mean to ordinary people.

CONCEPTUAL ANALYSIS

The philosophical exploration of a concept is the attempt to arrive at a reflective equilibrium with regard to various intuitions of its meaning.[30]

30 On the following, see John Rawls, *A Theory of Justice* (Cambridge, Mass.: Harvard University Press, 1971) at 48–51. In the context of legal theory, see Scott J. Shapiro, *Legality* (Cambridge, Mass.: Harvard University Press, 2011) at 13–18.

On the basis of considered judgments, one tries to make out, constructively, what lends coherence to a set of conceptual criteria. Such an understanding is then tested in certain cases and compared with other considered judgments. If a divergence arises, one revises either these judgments or the set of criteria until equilibrium has been reached.

If writing philosophy qua conceptual analysis invariably involves matching considered judgments concerning the meaning of a concept with constructive efforts to arrive at a better understanding of what lends coherence to these judgments – regardless of whether "better" must also mean greater moral appeal – then what this book is up to must necessarily fall into this category.

All the same, and at the risk of sounding immodest, the book claims to offer nothing short of a change of perspective. The path toward a reflective equilibrium involves altering the picture. It invites readers to view existing beliefs through a new lens. For authors such as Hart and Dworkin, the law is some socially constituted object, that is, either some unity of primary and secondary rules or a practice of adjudication that is ultimately guided by the ideal of integrity. Both views obscure the nature of law. Law is first and foremost a relation between and among people. This relation can be understood as the resolution of an antinomy of moral judgment (along the social and the substantive dimension). Only an adequate understanding of this relation explains why the law has to have sources. Only the antinomy of moral judgment helps us understand what legal positivism failed to comprehend clearly, namely, that law can only be endorsed by keeping it morally at arm's length.

To hit the mark of reflective equilibrium, the approach needs to be able to reconstruct what we already believe to know. It does so by claiming to cast everything into better light. In particular, the approach claims to elucidate intuitions of legal positivists in a more plausible way, for example, by pointing out that the detached attitude toward law is morally warranted and is best understood as expressing various forms of irony.

CONCLUSION

In an interview conducted in 2001, Mickey Spillane, who deserves to be immortalized for creating the character of Mike Hammer, described his doings with graceful humility: "I'm not an author, I'm a writer, that's all I am. Authors want their names down in history; I want to keep the smoke coming out of the chimney."[31] It is fair to say that the great majority of legal

31 www.wallacestroby.com/writings_spillane.html

writing is written to keep the smoke coming out of the chimney. In fact, it can actually generate quite a bit of smoke when we think of the writing that is done for a corporate clientele. Writing legal theory does not fall into this category. In contrast to the majority of legal writing, its value is usually not manifest in the houses that can be built of its revenue.

One might suspect, bearing Spillane's contrast in mind, that legal theory is written with the intent to have one's name engraved on the lintels of a museum of ideas. This, at any rate, is how it may seem in a culture in which shining brightly matters more than anything else. In this vein, Ronald Dworkin, one of the finest legal philosophers of late, raised – on the very last page of his last major book – the question of how we can make our lives into "tiny diamonds in the cosmic sand."[32] It may seem as though even he, one of the most celebrated legal philosophers of the twentieth century, was asking himself whether his name would go down in history.

But fame cannot be the point, not least because no one can be reasonably assured of it. The type of legal writing that keeps the smoke coming out of the chimney is in demand simply because it is relevant to practice; and relevant to practice means that it is useful in some court of law or in some corporate office. By contrast, the legal writing that does not easily convert into smoke is often likened to an unprofitable art. It does not have a direct impact. It is debatable whether it might ever help students become "better lawyers." But it has something that relevant legal knowledge notoriously lacks. It is relevant to life, for it goes to the heart of why the law matters to all of us. It pays attention to the chilliness of the legal world. It points out that the reasons that we encounter in law are most often the reasons of others and therefore also the other of reasons. It tries to show, as Chapters 2 and 4 will attempt to do, why irony best captures the mood with which the law is elaborated. It encourages aspiring practitioners to sustain their intellectual self-esteem in the face of the unreason that they encounter in law. Finally, it reminds us of the fact that conceiving of ourselves from a legal point of view can be liberating. It can help us shed moral constraints that had been inculcated into us before we have become mature enough to make up our own minds.

[32] Ronald Dworkin, *Justice for Hedgehogs* (Cambridge, Mass.: Harvard University Press, 2011) at 423.

1

Late Legal Positivism

Legal positivism is nowadays mostly associated with the work of H.L.A. Hart and those scholars defending his theory against Ronald Dworkin's critique. This is quite paradoxical given that the scholarship that has adopted Hart as its champion is not at all animated by legal positivism's ambition to submit law and legal reasoning to demystification. Not by accident, this version of legal positivism embraces the conventional foundation of law and has no qualms about accommodating morality or endorsing law's moral purpose. It represents a positivism that has grown old and lost its edge. This chapter attempts to expose the shortcomings of this late legal positivism by submitting it to a critique that remains faithful to Kelsen's project of demystification. It turns out that conventionalism is a symptom of legal knowledge that no longer takes seriously its claim to truth. The rapprochement toward morality, by contrast, avoids confronting the perplexity of legal validity that can only be resolved by changing the conception of law from viewing it as a system of norms to a specific relation among people.

SEPARABILITY

Legal positivism's critical edge follows from its most salient precept. In the twentieth century, this precept was most famously defended by Hart who claimed that legal knowledge, to be possible, must draw a line between law as it is and law as it ought to be.[1] This prime directive has been often understood to amount to a "separability thesis."[2] According to that thesis, a legal

[1] See H.L.A. Hart, "Positivism and the Separation of Law and Morals" (1958) 71 *Harvard Law Review* 593–600, 615–621. John Gardner, "Legal Positivism: 5½ Myths" (2001) 46 *American Journal of Jurisprudence* 199–227 at 223, would likely put it differently and state in greater proximity to Austin that the source-based existence of law is one thing while its moral merit or demerit is another.

[2] The separability thesis is often rendered as the thesis that there is no necessary connection between law and morality. See Jules L. Coleman and Brian Leiter, "Legal Positivism." In *A Companion to Legal Philosophy and Legal Theory* (ed. D. Patterson, 2d ed., Oxford: Wiley-

norm can be right from the viewpoint of law even if it is morally wrong.[3] Moral correctness is no necessary condition of legal validity. Rather, the validity of law depends on social facts. The separability thesis extends, however, to other modes of evaluating norms on their merits, for example, to grounds of economic efficiency or comprehensibility.[4] Inefficient norms are just as legally valid as regulations that are too complex to make much sense. Positivism, most broadly understood, is the belief that the criteria of legal validity – of what constitutes law – are not merit based.[5] Rather, these criteria contain references to social sources.

Positivism's critical edge resides in the practical consequences of this general precept. The social phenomenon that legal positivism is critical of is how the law is rendered in quotidian and unenlightened legal knowledge. In this context, which is prominently encountered in the ruminations of courts, the law itself is given an obscure appearance, not least owing to a persistent entanglement with mere moral ideas.

Depending on how deep this enmeshment is suspected to run, the consequences of separability are spelled out in two ways. While one suggests that the *comprehension* of law must be merely insulated against murky forms of

Blackwell, 2010) 228–48 at 228; Jules Coleman, *The Practice of Principle: In Defence of a Pragmatist Approach to Legal Theory* (Oxford: Oxford University Press, 2001) at 151. Gardner points out correctly that it is flawed to read the separability thesis as a no-necessary-connection thesis. For, on their face, there are necessary connections between law and morality, at any rate from the perspective of various significant renderings of legal positivism. Law and morality are necessarily alike in that both contain valid norms. According to Raz and Gardner, the law necessarily claims to have moral authority. Positive law – again, according to Gardner – gives rise to moral questions and can be judged morally. See John Gardner, *Law as a Leap of Faith: Essays on Law in General* (Oxford: Oxford University Press, 2012) at 48, 142, 161, 221 (the no-necessary-connection thesis is "transparently false"). See also Joseph Raz, *Between Authority and Interpretation: On the Theory of Law and Practical Reason* (Oxford: Oxford University Press, 2008) at 178–180; and Leslie Green, "Positivism and the Inseparability of Law and Morals" (2008) 83 *New York University Law Review* 1035–1058 at 1044, 1047–1054.

3 There is an alternative rendering of the separability thesis saying that necessarily legal validity cannot depend on the moral merit of norms since the authority of law is possible only if it does not overlap with moral norms. See Joseph Raz, *Ethics in the Public Domain* (2d ed., Oxford: Clarendon Press, 1995) 210–237 at 226–230. For a critical analysis that perceives the issue unresolved in Raz's writings, see Ronald Dworkin, *Justice in Robes* (Cambridge, Mass.: Harvard University Press, 2006) at 202.

4 This may explain why Gardner, note 2 at 19, reduces the view of legal positivism to a sources thesis.

5 I add in passing that theorists of functional differentiation would say, at this point, that the autonomy of the legal system is manifest in the code legal/illegal. See Niklas Luhmann, "Law as a Social System" (1989) 83 *Northwestern Law Review* 136–150; "Operational Closure and Structural Coupling: On the Differentiation of the Legal System" (1992) 13 *Cardozo Law Review* 1419–1442.

moral talk, the other believes that *the law itself* needs to be construed in a manner that highlights its difference from ordinary moral reasons for action.

DESCRIPTION AND CONSTRUCTION

The first consequence of separability perceives only a problem of apprehension. It proposes the morally untainted description of normative legal materials as a remedy.[6] If social sources matter, then their sober apprehension gives us all there is to know about the law, regardless of whether we think, as a practical matter, that we have reason to go forward with what it is. This explains, contrary to what Gardner recently, but falsely, suggested,[7] that there is a necessary connection between the identification of sources and a preference for certain methods of legal interpretation. Legal positivism is composed of, if anything, not only the belief that someone always posits law[8] but also the further belief that there is something, however indeterminate, that can be identified as valid law once it has been posited. If such an identification were not possible, new law would be created in the course of developing legal knowledge. The creation of new law, however, would, by definition, engage another source and permit, for the purpose of knowing the law, the influence of considerations of merit. This is not what legal positivists believe. Therefore, they have to believe, contrariwise, that there are some not haphazardly chosen methods of knowing the law that give us what the sources themselves identify as valid law. This is a consequence of separability. It is not by accident, hence, that legal positivists lean toward methods of interpretation that, unless there is specific authorization by sources, do not invite the exploration of moral merit.

6 See, for example, Hans Kelsen, *Pure Theory of Law* (2d ed., trans. M. Knight, Berkeley: University of California Press, 1967) at 69.

7 According to Gardner, note 2 at 42, it is one of the myths about legal positivism that it favors certain methods of legal interpretations and rejects others. At the same time, even he has to concede (43, 45) that authorities that have the power to make the law intentionally have to have the power "intentionally to determine what law one makes" and must be given a chance to have their will respected. Turning promulgated legal rules into the best interpretations of what they mean from the perspective of morality would be a very bad way of drawing out the consequences of separability. Rather, it would be a way of reintroducing moral mushiness. While Gardner correctly observes that legal positivism has nothing to say where law making should end and law applying should begin (47), legal positivism has to pay heed to how the law can be grasped from sources. Gardner, however, seems to have an easy way out. In his view (24, 51), legal philosophy does not instruct practitioners. It is limited to identifying the necessary features of practices and not how these are to be conducted. But this way out is not available to legal positivism. The type of positivism envisaged by Gardner is irrelevant to legal knowledge. Since the law, qua legal system, depends on legal knowledge, this type must therefore be irrelevant to law.

8 This is recognized even by Gardner, note 2 at 20.

This internal link to descriptive accuracy is preserved even in those versions of legal positivism the point of which is not to guide legal practice but to account for the structure of concepts explaining the possibility of the existence of shared legal meanings. In this understanding, a positivistic jurisprudence explores the conditions under which law, as a social fact, can be represented as an object.[9]

The second consequence of separability actually perceives a distortion on the level of the object of legal knowledge. Consequently, it calls for constructive efforts that respond to, and actively counteract, the law's tendency toward self-idealization or self-obfuscation.[10] Arguably, this has been, in the terms of H.L.A. Hart, the "sane and healthy center" of Bentham's positivism,[11] and the same can be said of Kelsen's project as it is manifest in his critique of "psychologism,"[12] or, more generally, in the scrutiny to which he submitted central concepts of public law, such as statehood and sovereignty.[13] Bentham's imperative theory, for example, is an attempt to clarify in most sober terms that law, far from being an embodiment of reason, is an expression of the human will and only of the human will. Bentham asserted this view in opposition to how the legal materials are presented in the interpretations of judges, which, in his opinion, were to be mistrusted for the reason of notoriously giving rise to mystery and confusion.[14] Legal positivism treats the self-idealizing tendency of the legal materials with suspicion. Hence, as *constructivism*, it cannot merely describe the law in the boastful colors with which it claims to have authority.[15] Law is not readily available as an object of description. It must be brought to confess to the grounds and limits that are making it possible.

9 I concur, on this point, with Dworkin, note 3 at 214–215. See also his *Law's Empire* (Cambridge, Mass.: Harvard University Press, 1986) 33–35.

10 Legal positivists, such as Hart or Gardner, can account for this tendency not least because, in their view, the law claims to have moral authority. This is what Raz has in mind when he ascribes to the law *de facto* authority. See Gardner, note 2 at 142. Raz, note 3 at 215.

11 See H.L.A. Hart, "Bentham and the Demystification of Law" (1973) 36 *Modern Law Review* 2–17 at 8.

12 See, most famously, Hans Kelsen, *Hauptprobleme der Staatsrechtslehre entwickelt aus der Lehre vom Rechtssatz* (2d ed., Tübingen: Mohr, 1923).

13 See Kelsen, note 12; idem., *Der soziologische und der juristische Staatsbegriff. Kritische Untersuchung des Verhältnisses von Staat und Recht* (2d ed., Tübingen, J.C.B. Mohr, 1928b); *Das Problem der Souveränität und die Theorie des Völkerrechts. Beitrag zu einer reinen Rechtslehre* (2d ed., J.C.B. Mohr, 1928a).

14 I owe these observations entirely to Hart. See Hart, note 11 at 3.

15 No legal positivist who is not completely out of her mind would say that God is the author of a constitution whose preamble states that the constitution was adopted "in the name of God the Almighty from whom all law originates."

With regard to the negative task of constructivism, which requires removing unnecessary idealizations, legal positivism has much in common with American legal realism.[16] The difference, however, must be duly noted, too. Realists have no qualms about setting aside the normative appearance of legal directives owing to their keen interest in exploring how things work *de facto*. By contrast, the more appealing versions of legal positivism attempted, in one way or another, to retain law's normativity while lending it a form that marks either an absolute or a relative departure from the moral realm. Rendering law normatively intelligible by moving beyond its naïve, moralistic, or ideologically distorted self-presentation and replacing the latter with something that reflects accurately the legal relation has generally been the positive task of legal constructivism.[17] It is about getting the law straight. Legal positivism is a particularly sceptical member of this intellectual family. Accordingly, arriving at law "as it is" as opposed to "as it ought to be" is taken to require, for example, introducing conditions of legal validity of which the participants in legal practice may not even be aware, such as the *Grundnorm*. Most importantly, it involves identifying or developing what law is truly made of if only law is seen as separate from morality. The results of the relevant attempts are various ontological constructions of legal norms, such as the imperative,[18] (social) rules,[19] the claim to be an exclusionary reason for action,[20] the hypothetical judgment[21] or most recently the device for the implementation of plans.[22]

[16] For a classical statement of the demystifying mission of realism, see Felix Cohen, "Transcendental Nonsense and the Functional Approach" (1935) 35 *Columbia Law Review* 808–849. For a useful comparison, see Brian Leiter, "Legal Realism and Legal Positivism Reconsidered" (2001) 111 *Ethics* 278–301 at 301. Alas, the author's discussion focuses almost exclusively on the legal positivism of H.L.A. Hart. This ignorance of Kelsen's work (perhaps Leiter cannot read German philosophy in German?) is sadly reflected in Leiter's otherwise rather meritorious piece "The Radicalism of Legal Positivism," *University of Chicago Public Law & Legal Theory Working Paper* No. 303, 2010.

[17] See Rudolph von Jhering, *Der Geist des römischen Rechts auf den verschiedenen Stufen seiner Entwicklung*, vol. 2.2 (5th ed. Leipzig: Härtel, 1899) at 385. See also Stanley L. Paulson, "Hans Kelsen's Earliest Legal Theory: Critical Constructivism" (1996) 59 *Modern Law Review* 797–812.

[18] See John Austin, *The Province of Jurisprudence Determined* (Amherst: Prometheus Books, 2000) at 13.

[19] See H.L.A. Hart, *The Concept of Law* (2d ed., Oxford: Clarendon Press, 1994) at 8.

[20] See Joseph Raz, *Practical Reasons and Norms* (2d ed., Princeton: Princeton University Press, 1990) at 64–65.

[21] Kelsen, note 13 at 254–255.

[22] See Scott J. Shapiro, *Legality* (Cambridge, Mass.: Harvard University Press, 2011) at 194.

THE DISTINCTION BETWEEN LAW APPLICATION AND LAW CREATION

It is submitted that while legal positivism, as a project, fails along the descriptive dimension, its valuable and lasting legacy lies in its constructivist ambition.

The horizon of descriptivism has long been transcended by literary theory;[23] social system's theory;[24] and, not least, hermeneutics.[25] It is not necessary to recount this story here. Its common denominator, as it were, can be elucidated by examining briefly why it is so difficult to sustain the distinction between the application and the creation of law.

An application is not supposed to amend existing law. It merely draws out what it already says. Amendments, by contrast, are the domain of law creation.[26] The distinction between the two is standard repertoire of positivist theorizing. Kelsen believed that every "legal act," which is any act laying down a new norm, involves both the application of already existing and the addition of new law.[27] New norms cannot be created if they do not also apply or, more mildly stated, do not conform to[28] laws governing their creation. A judicial decision can be valid only if it applies correctly the procedural and substantive rules prerequisite for its adoption. The relatively higher level of law – rules the observance of which is a necessary condition for the creation of more law – determines what should be done so that law at the relatively lower level can be validly adopted. Yet, in response to the revolt perpetrated by the so-called Free Law Movement, Kelsen, drawing on ideas of his disciple Adolf Julius Merkl,[29] conceded that rarely ever is a new norm entirely determined by the law providing these necessary normative conditions. Rather, owing to indeterminacy and leeway left for discretion, the

[23] See Stanley Fish, *Doing What Comes Naturally* (Oxford: Oxford University Press, 1988).

[24] See, paradigmatically, Gunther Teubner, *Law as an Autopoietic System* (Oxford: Blackwell, 1993).

[25] See Joseph Esser, *Vorverständnis und Methodenwahl in der Rechtsfindung* (Frankfurt aM: Athäneum, 1970).

[26] Raz, note 2 at 166, characterizes the distinction between application and creation by distinguishing between establishing the content of norms and supplementing this content by means of "interpretation."

[27] See Kelsen, note 6 at 233–236.

[28] On the distinction between conforming with a reason without intentionally acting on it and complying with a reason intentionally, see Raz, note 20 at 179–180. In the case of conformity, it matters that the act for which the reason is a reason gets done.

[29] See Adolf Julius Merkl, "Das doppelte Rechtsantlitz. Eine Betrachtung aus der Erkenntnistheorie des Rechts" (1918) 47 *Juristische Blätter* 425–427, 444–447, 463–465, reprinted in *Die Wiener Rechtstheoretische Schule* (ed. H. Klecatstky, R. Marcic, and H. Schambeck, Vienna: Europaverlag 1968a) vol. 1, 1091–1113; idem., "Das Recht im Lichte seiner Anwendung" (1917), ibid., 1167–1201.

determination of the relatively lower level by the higher-level norm is not complete. Extralegal factors enter the determination of new law. The laws governing its creation actually confer power thereto.

Both Merkl and Kelsen believed that the determination by existing law becomes stronger the further down the process moves along the chain of the legal process. While much discretion is left to a legislature, which is merely constrained by the constitution, far less room is available to a correctional officer kicking inmates around, for the officer's behavior is heavily programmed by legislation and implementing regulations. Kelsen believed that the scope left open for law creation becomes ever narrower the further one moves down the chain.

Different persuasions of legal positivism put the core idea in slightly different terms. Gardner, for example, suggests that the application of laws is determined partly by sources and partly by merit-based consideration.[30] If the source is, for example, a norm saying that discriminations on the grounds of sex are prohibited and the result of its application is that women must not be discriminated against for the reason of their pregnancy, the application is mediated by the merit-based consideration that discrimination on the grounds of pregnancy is equal to discrimination on the grounds of sex. The source and the merit-based consideration complement one another in order to give rise to new law.

NORMATIVE BELIEFS INFORMING APPLICATION

But is not what Gardner presents us with an instance of legal interpretation?[31] "Pregnancy" is taken to exemplify "sex." If that is so, it follows that merit-based considerations (or "extralegal factors") also underpin what wishes to pass as an application, for settling what constitutes an application presupposes a view as to what counts as an interpretation of laws. The sober and morally unalloyed application of laws is supposed to rest on the interpretative elaboration, and only on such an elaboration, of their meaning. If, however, arriving at views concerning the plain meaning of laws is dependent on merit-based considerations, the purported application turns out to be "creative" since it is informed by extralegal factors.

Imagine, for example, a statute declaring null and void contracts that "offend morals" and that a judge finds the promise and provision of sexual services to be invalid under such a statute. If the judge is a sexual moralist, she

30 See Gardner, note 2 at 39–40.

31 Gardner, note 2 at 47, would most likely agree on that point.

likely believes that the invalidity of sexual service contracts follows deductively from the statute.[32] In her eyes, contracts of this type are an element of the set of agreements that offend morals. Indeed, if asked what in her view offends morals, she might even immediately reply that this definitely includes contracts over sexual services. She would grant that there is one law-creative element to her judgment, namely, the fact of her judgment itself is a negative norm; but this fact would not, in her view, amend the plain meaning of what offends morals.

If, by contrast, the judge initially has no idea whether contracts of that type offend morals and rules later only in this vein because she finds that in the face of reasonable disagreement a requisite case can be made, she may be inclined to describe what she has done as creating new law. The same observation can be made with regard to Gardner's example. If a judge believes that discriminating against pregnant women is tantamount to sex discrimination because pregnancy is intrinsically related to sex (joke intended), she will claim to have applied the law and the law only. If, on the other hand, she frames the meaning of the sex discrimination statute in the manner suggested by Gardner, namely as presupposing for its application a comparator from the opposite sex,[33] she may even fear not to have applied the statute at all but to have amended it by analogy.

In both cases, the use of the distinction between law creation and law application depends on what organs or parties believe to be law. The fixation of beliefs about law is a matter of interpretation. The examples show that beliefs about what amounts to an interpretation – for example, understanding the plain meaning of words – are informed by extralegal factors, for example, a certain firmness or indecisiveness of moral beliefs. The language of the law is afloat in a sea of moral beliefs. Indeed, the hypothetical example shows that whether or not one believes that an act of application even requires an interpretation – or at which point interpretation flows over into law creation – depends on the moral beliefs with which officials arrive at the scene of application.

32 Legal positivists are usually inclined in such a case to find the language of the statute to be quite vacuous and to observe that the judge is reading her moral beliefs "into" the statute. But this is not how she reads the statute. In her view, the plain meaning of the statute determines the result. Legal positivists will say that what the source merely says is that contracts that "offend morals" are void and that it does not say that sexual service contracts are. But they thereby mistake the signifier for the signified. How can legal positivists be so sure that these contracts are not signified by the statute? Could it be that their semantic intuitions are informed by "extra-legal" beliefs?

33 See Gardner, note 2 at 39.

Legal positivists would, of course, insist that the identification of reliable methods of interpretations is supposed to take the application of law out of the hands of fickle moral intuition.[34] But it is easily overlooked that methods of interpretation do not interpret themselves. Some believe that the interpretation of the constitution ought to unearth an original understanding. It is then posited that the constitution means what the ordinary person would have understood it to mean at the time of its adoption.[35] While such a move promises to anchor the normativity of law in the normativity of linguistic conventions,[36] the relevance of conventions rests on the requirement that the lawgivers make themselves understood in the language spoken by ordinary folk. Constructing legal interpretation remains a matter of political morality all the way down.[37] In Kelsenian terms, this means that to determine what it takes to apply the law, an interpretive theory needs to draw creatively on moral ideas. Law-applying officials already have to have certain extralegal normative beliefs to use, in the guise of views about interpretation, the distinction between application and norm creation. These beliefs reflect, first, what organs and parties already believe before asking the law for an

[34] Quite surprisingly, Raz, note 2 at 118–119, 121, not only disavows all belief in the availability of general theory of legal interpretation which would provide useful guidance to the perplexed, he also believes that interpretation involves, inextricably combined, elements of both reproduction and creativity. Here is how Raz states the matter (121): "This means that there is no point in a theory of 're-creative' interpretation which will identify interpretations which do no more than state the content of existing norms." It may be doubted whether this view is really consistent with legal positivism, not least because Raz underscores, at the same time, that the content of the law must be determinable without moral argument. One wonders how that can be possible if creative elements – among which loom large moral intuitions – cannot be severed from the recognition of valid law. What is more, in the context of Raz's theory of interpretation, the sources of law themselves become a moving target. According to Raz, a legislature can "lay down" law only if it successfully anticipates what a law will be taken to mean from the perspective of the organs in charge of its interpretive elaboration. Since the legislature, however, can never be entirely successful at this task owing to the invariable influx of creative elements, legislation must turn out to be, as Raz puts it, "a cooperative enterprise between legislators and authoritative interpreters of their legislation" (122). Raz also concedes that over time the authority underpinning laws may shift from the legislature to adjudicating institutions. Since in all of that we are talking about matters of degree, the sources, which legal positivism put at the center of law, become a moving target. The law can no longer be pinned down unless one participates in a creative process of interpretation. This view already marks taking the step leading beyond legal positivism, for the center of law can no longer be the sources but rather various processes of their interaction.

[35] See, for example, Lawrence B. Solum, "We Are All Originalists Now." In Robert W. Bennett and Lawrence B. Solum, *Constitutional Originalism: A Debate* (Ithaca: Cornell University Press, 2011) 1–64 at 10, 12.

[36] See Solumn, note 35 at 40.

[37] A point that is conceded by Solumn, note 35 at 38–49.

answer and, second, what they bring to bear on the law to obtain such an answer.[38]

FROM INTERPRETATION TO SOURCES

The interpretive identification of applicable law is the privilege of the act of application. This is the observation that Kelsen's rebellious disciple Fritz Sander made in more general form already early in the twentieth century.[39] The applicable norm that confers limited power to create another norm functions as such a norm only for, and from the perspective of, the act on which it confers power. The statute is the applicable statute only in the eyes of the court that applies it. The meaning of the applicable law is determined by the act that claims the statute to be law as applied to some fact.[40]

But Sander understood all too well that this is only half the truth. The act of application cannot even purport to be what it claims to be if it produces the applicable law. It would be internally contradictory. The contradiction can be resolved if the act of application makes itself dependent on what it determines. The paradoxical dependence of the meaning of the higher law on the attribution of meaning by the lower act must be extended into *interdependence*. This is only possible if the distinction between application and creation is dropped in favor of recognizing the lower act as a source.

The explanation is straightforward. First, viewing the act as a source clarifies that what is viewed as applicable law depends on extralegal considerations to have effect. After all, it is the magic of the source to transmute the extralegal into law. Second, the self-denying ordinance reverses the ascendancy of the later over the prior act. It says that the form of the next source in a sequence is determined by its function to let the previous source speak. Kelsen's idea of neatly separating quanta of law application and law creation has to be given

38 See Hans-Georg Gadamer, *Wahrheit und Methode: Grundzüge einer philosophischen Hermeneutik* (4th ed., Tübingen: Mohr, 1975) at 252–256.

39 See Fritz Sander, "Die transzendentale Methode der Rechtsphilosophie und der Begriff der Rechtserfahrung" (1920). *In Die Rolle des Neukantianismus in der Reinen Rechtslehre: Eine Debatte zwischen Sander und Kelsen* (ed. S.L. Paulson, Aalen: Scientia, 1988) at 75–114 at 102–103: "A ist nicht bloß Rechtsvoraussetzung der Rechtsfolge B, es ist vielmehr Rechtsvoraussetzung *für* die Rechtsfolge B. Nicht nur B als Rechtsfolge wird an A als Rechtsvoraussetzung bestimmt, sondern auch in umgekehrter Richtung bestimmt sich A als Rechtsvoraussetzung an B als Rechtsfolge. A und B bestimmen sich wechselseitig, vielmehr werden sie wechselseitig in dem nach Gesetzen höherer Ordnung sich vollziehenden Verfahren bestimmt."

40 In a way, the legal system appears to be entirely outside of itself. It seems to begin anew with every single act of law application. Every act involves simultaneously the negation of all prior acts and the recreation of the legal system from within its own parochial perspective.

up. Every act is both fully law creating and fully law applying. It is fully law creating in that it involves a self-interpretation of what constitutes an application. It is fully law applying owing to lending its own voice to another source.[41]

If every act is, however, both law creating and law applying, it is also neither one nor the other. It is a synthesis of both. This synthesis has been given different names in different theoretical traditions. While Sander spoke somewhat enigmatically of a sovereign legal process,[42] hermeneutics points to the manifestation of a larger tradition in which the signified (*die Sache*) supposedly reveals itself,[43] while social system's theory refers to it as autopoiesis.[44] These various conceptions do not matter. What matters is that taking this step marks the end of legal positivism since it fundamentally alters the ontological commitments of legal theory. The law is no longer deemed to be produced and subsequently to be just there. Rather, the law is in a permanent state of reproduction.

DROPPING ONE AND SALVAGING THE OTHER

What remains, hence, of legal positivism is its constructivist legacy. It is older than positivism itself[45] and the wellspring of much of its intellectual vigor. Amazingly, however, this legacy appears submerged in the family of versions of legal positivism that predominate in the Anglo-American world. Members of this family share paying reverence to the work of H.L.A. Hart.[46] The most salient feature of this positivism is its embrace of conventionalism and the rapprochement vis-à-vis morality. Compared with the work of the pioneer of modern legal positivism,[47] Hans Kelsen, this is a remarkable development.

First, this more recent positivism views legal systems as resting on conventional foundations. It abstains, in particular, from arriving at a construct that, as is the case for Kelsen's *Grundnorm*, enigmatically signifies that legal

[41] This is not to deny that internally, as a matter of presenting itself, any act has to draw some distinction between application and creation. But it thereby deflects attention from the fact that the framing of applicable law depends on external factors.

[42] See Sander, note 39. [43] See Gadamer, note 38 at 439.

[44] See Niklas Luhmann, *Social Systems* (trans. J. Bednarz Jr. and D. Baecker, Stanford: Stanford University Press, 1996).

[45] See Stanley L. Paulson, "Hans Kelsen's Earliest Legal Theory: Critical Constructivism" (1996) 59 *Modern Law Review* 797–812 at 799–800.

[46] At times, one encounters a critique. See Gardner, note 2 at 236, where Hart's treatment of morality is classified as "a mess."

[47] Modern legal positivism is defined by its attempt to preserve the normative quality of law without embracing natural law. This attempt is reflected in the works of both Kelsen and Hart.

officials use the law as though it possessed authority even though it can never do so.

Second, it makes much room for accommodating a deep entanglement of law and morality and is ready to perceive a moral teleology built into the law.[48] Again, Kelsen would have raised a red flag and expressed concern that legal positivism becomes subservient to legitimizing the social order.[49]

Consequently, legal positivism appears to have lost its youthful vigor and begins to look wise, possibly even somewhat old. Emulating a move from Werner Sombart, who memorably introduced the term "late capitalism" to economic historiography, one may want to call it "late" legal positivism to signify positivism that is still alive but already crumbling.[50]

Late legal positivism is epitomized in the thinking of scholars for whom the work of H.L.A. Hart is the benchmark of successful legal theory.[51] As an outsider, one can of course only speculate what it takes to be admitted to the informal club, but arguably membership to the circle of late legal positivism – or, put differently, such positivism as a genre[52] – is mediated by five beliefs. First, through following Hart one becomes a legal positivist. Second, Hart was the greatest legal philosopher of the twentieth century.[53] Third, the Hart-Dworkin debate is of central importance for legal theory (even though there

48 See Gardner, note 2 at 167.

49 See Hans Kelsen, "Recht und Moral." In *Die Wiener Rechtstheoretische Schule*, note 29, 797–810 at 809–810. When in the course of one of the heated debates of the 1920s, Hans Kelsen remarked that natural law theory merely disguises the "Gorgonian face of power" underneath all appearances of law (see Hans Kelsen (1927) 3 *Veröffentlichung der Vereinigung Deutscher Staatsrechtslehrer* at 54–55), he stated most drastically to positivism's sobering mission. Where participants in the legal system would have us perceive good reasons and sound judgment, it is the task of the positivist to unearth asymmetries of power and choices that are made, potentially, to the detriment of opponents. In this understanding, the thrust of separability is epistemological as well as sociological. In eliminating moral criteria from the construction of legal validity, the theory intends to bring to the fore what truly constitutes law, namely, either the legally authorized or merely the effective exercise of power. Positivists would not deny that moral justification is the requisite *accompagnato* thereto. But it needs to be turned off, as it were, to see what is really going on.

50 According to Dworkin, note 3 at 188, 198, it is not a version of positivism at all.

51 For a highly useful and authentic introduction into the outlook of Hartianism, see Jules L. Coleman and Brian Leiter, "Legal Positivism." In D. Patterson (ed.), *A Companion to Philosophy of Law and Legal Theory* (2d ed., Oxford: Wiley-Blackwell, 2010) 228–248.

52 The allusion is, of course, to John Gardner, "The Legality of Law" (2004) 17 *Ratio Iuris* 168–181, at 171, where law itself is characterized as a genre.

53 See, for example Matthew H. Kramer, "Introduction." In M. Kramer et al. (eds.), *The Legacy of H.L.A. Hart* (Oxford: Oxford University Press, 2008) xiii–xviii at xiii. Without denying Hart his share of greatness, this is a bold claim to make, given that Hart competes in such a contest, questionable as it is, with the likes of Hans Kelsen, Karl Llewellyn, or Carl Schmitt (dare I say Ronald Dworkin?).

has never been a written exchange between the main protagonists).[54] Fourth, the debate was eventually won by Hart, even though Dworkin would not learn about this defeat before the posthumous publication of Hart's postscript in the second edition of A *Concept of Law*. Fifth, intellectual progress in legal theory can only be made by standing on the shoulders of Hart.[55]

It seems that late legal positivism is not only a school of thought but also a bit of a movement[56] composed of many members.[57] For the purpose of identifying and criticizing conventionalism as an element of late legal positivism, the following discussion focuses on ideas of the American Hart scholar Jules Coleman.[58] The discussion of late positivism's rapprochement toward morality will turn to a more recent contribution by John Gardner. Coleman's ideas

54 See Scott J. Shapiro, "The 'Hart-Dworkin' Debate: A Short Guide for the Perplexed." In A. Ripstein (ed.), *Ronald Dworkin* (Cambridge: Cambridge University Press, 2007) 22–55; Matthew H. Kramer, *In Defence of Legal Positivism: Law without Trimming* (Oxford: Oxford University Press 1999) 128–192.

55 The latter is clearly reflected in Shapiro's attempt to arrive at a legal theory by answering questions that were only unsatisfactorily addressed in Hart's work. See Scott J. Shapiro, "What Is the Rule of Recognition (and Does It Exist)?" In M. Adler and K. Einar Himma (eds.), *The Rule of Recognition and the U.S. Constitution* (Oxford: Oxford University Press, 2009) 235–268 at 250, where Shapiro undertakes to amend the house that Herbert built by developing a theory of "plans." It is supposed to answer a number of objections that have been made against Hart. See now also Shapiro, note 22.

56 The movement is present in a variety of publications. The important periodical is *Legal Theory*. The monographs are virtually countless, and the flagship publication is J. Coleman and S. Shapiro (eds.), *The Oxford Handbook of Jurisprudence and Philosophy of Law* (Oxford: Oxford University Press, 2002). There is now even a student textbook that almost exclusively reflects the mind-set of the school. See Kenneth Einar Himma, *The Nature of Law: Philosophical Issues in Conceptual Jurisprudence and Legal Theory* (New York: Foundation Press, 2011).

57 Among the most distinguished members are Jules Coleman, Kenneth Einar Himma, Matthew H. Kramer, Scott J. Shapiro, and Wilfrid J. Waluchow. It is submitted, however, that it is difficult to apply the rule of recognition concerning Hart admirers as an outsider. The wider circle of Hart's admirers is not composed of legal positivists alone; even one non-positivist takes Hart as having formulated the most defensible version of this position. Brian Leiter believes that, in contrast to Hart's, Hans Kelsen's theory is out of step with developments in modern philosophy. See http://leiterlegalphilosophy.typepad.com/leiter/2007/10/michael-green-a.html. Whether Leiter is a legal positivist is not quite clear. In earlier works, Leiter highlighted the disagreement between legal realism and legal positivism as regards the *de facto* importance of rules of decision making (viz., their empirical rule skepticism). Now he appears to present realism as a subset of positivism. See Brian Leiter, *Naturalizing Jurisprudence: Essays on American Legal Realism and Naturalism in Legal Philosophy* (Oxford: Oxford University Press, 2007) at 73, 80; "Why Legal Positivism Again?" http://papers.ssrn.com/sol3/papers.cfm?abstract_id=2323013 at 15.

58 His work on inclusive legal positivism surely ranks among the outstanding contributions to the jurisprudence of our time. For an introduction, see, for example, Brian H. Bix, A *Dictionary of Legal Theory* (Oxford: Oxford University Press, 2004) at 123. See also Shapiro, note 54 at 53 footnote 39 for references to the literature.

demonstrate, however, how one is linked to the other. If positivism can accommodate morality, then separability loses its central role and can be easily replaced with conventionalism.

The following analysis proposes to demonstrate that for two reasons late legal positivism falls short of the constructivist legacy.[59] First, the conventionalist strand is not sufficiently brazen from a sociological point of view. This lack of brazenness explains, indeed, why it has to be regarded as a symptom of something else. Symptoms have the quality of revealing that something is amiss which is nonetheless also concealed by the symptom. Thus understood, conventionalism reveals and conceals the lack of substantive self-reflection of legal knowledge. Second, the accommodation of morality raises the question why positivists insist on separability in the first place if there is no problem with admitting morality to the determination of law. If legal positivism is compatible with the wholehearted embrace of moral objectivity, one must wonder why one would deem it necessary to be a legal positivist in the first place. Late legal positivism fails to confront the potential absurdity of legal validity. Even worse, it ignores that morality might indeed pose exactly the type of problem that the legal relation is supposed to solve.

The analysis that follows brings the constructivist legacy of legal positivism, namely, its power to expose dogma, to bear on its latest and last version. It uses the better part of its legacy as a trajectory for moving beyond it. Late legal positivism is positivism's last gestalt.

CONVENTIONALISM

Coleman's work has long revolved around making sense of the seemingly paradoxical claim that it is consistent with legal positivism to see the validity of at least some legal norms depend on moral criteria.[60] He has defended an

[59] Not by accident, late legal positivism neglects the critical import of constructions arrived at by more advanced forms of legal positivism. Repeatedly, Shapiro reprimands Kelsen for arriving at a counterintuitive concept of the legal norm that conceives of it as primarily addressed to the law-applying official whose duty it is to impose a sanction. See Hans Kelsen, *Introduction to the Problems of Legal Theory* (trans. B. Litschewski Paulson and S.L. Paulson, Oxford: Clarendon Press, 1992) at 26–30; Scott J. Shapiro, "The Bad Man and the Internal Point of View." In S. Burton (ed.), *The Path of the Law and Its Influence: The Legacy of Oliver Wendell Holmes Jr.* (Cambridge: Cambridge University Press, 2000) 197–210 at 199, 204. By insisting against Kelsen that Hart's "puzzled man" (Hart, note 19 at 40) is to be guided by legal rules, he ignores the demystifying potential of Kelsen's construction, which reveals that legal systems can and do operate with disregard for how laypersons understand norms.

[60] See Jules L. Coleman, "Negative and Positive Positivism" (1982) 11 *Journal of Legal Studies* 139–164. See also Coleman, note 2 at 67, 109–110. Dworkin, note 3 at 189, has duly noticed the paradox.

extremely accommodating version of "inclusive" (or "soft") legal positivism, which would permit as part of the sources of law even a stipulation saying that laws necessarily have to be defensible from a moral point of view.[61] It cannot come as a surprise, then, that Coleman does not believe the core of legal positivism to be captured by separability, however understood, but rather by the puzzling claim, incidentally attributed to all contemporary legal positivists,[62] that the criteria of "legality"[63] are a matter of conventional social facts.[64] Conventional criteria concerning the set of social facts that we call law lay the foundation for the law's existence. They are applied in a customary judicial test of legal validity.[65] It is these beliefs, according to Coleman, which define legal positivism.[66]

The criteria of legal validity are believed to be components of the so-called rule of recognition.[67] As a convention, this rule depends on being practiced in order to exist and to be authoritative for legal officials.[68] The normative point of conventionalism is to see emerge from already existing common activity an obligation to carry on with it.[69] But this should not detain us here,[70] for, in any event, the existence of this rule explains how legal systems

61 See Coleman, note 2 at 112, 126. Of course, Coleman needs to struggle at this point with reestablishing the authority of law vis-à-vis morality. He attempts to do so by reintroducing the power of someone to establish for ordinary folk what, according to moral standards, is law. He thereby likens his position again to "exclusive" legal positivism. (ibid., 130, 141). Legal positivists, who, like Gardner, note 1 at 200, believe that all legal norms are posited and hence come into this world as a result of acts, find it quite difficult to make sense of the idea that some laws might be void *per se*, regardless of whether the voidness is alleged to follow from immorality or illegality. See Kelsen, note 6 at 276–278.

62 See Coleman, note 2 at 68–69, 75. This claim says everything about the cultural boundedness of the late and last positivist enterprise.

63 By "legality" Coleman means what is to be counted as law and therefore partakes of legal validity or is accepted by law-applying officials. See also Shapiro, note 55 at 240.

64 Coleman, note 2 at 152, 161. It may bear emphasis that the criteria for what partakes of legal validity are different from the criteria that account for the existence of a legal system, such as the unity of primary and secondary rules or the existence of legal officials. See Gardner, note 52 at 170.

65 See Hart, note 19 at 256.

66 See Coleman, note 2 at 161.

67 See Hart, note 19 at 94.

68 See Coleman, note 2 at 77. Hart's (late) claim that the rule of recognition is a coordinating convention has been famously contested by Leslie Green. See his "The Concept of Law Revisited" (1997) 94 *Michigan Law Review* 1687–1717 at 1695–1697.

69 See Dworkin, note 3 at 197. Coleman believes the rule of recognition to be a duty-imposing rule, however, only for legal officials, whereby the duty itself is only incidentally related to law, for it arises from participation in a common enterprise and is a special case of an associative obligation (77, 85, 95, 97, 159–160). The duty imposed by the rule of recognition can therefore never be a legal obligation and is not addressed to "ordinary folk" (139).

70 For the view that does not view the rule of recognition as a coordinating convention but as a constitutive convention, see Andrei Marmor, *Philosophy of Law* (Princeton: Princeton University Press, 2011) at 82.

are possible while leaving open whether any such system is also desirable.[71] The rule exists, socially speaking, if and only as long as it is practiced. The rule is practiced if and only as long as it is applied from an internal point of view.[72] This means that those participating in its application adopt a critical reflective attitude toward instances of applying or following the rule.[73] Convergent behavior would be socially beyond recognition as rule following or rule application[74] if it were not perceived as implicitly constituting itself vis-à-vis the question whether it is a following or an application of the rule.[75]

71 See Coleman, note 2 at 71, 93, 118. See also Hart, note 19 at 257.

72 The sloppy characterization of a social rule as a combination of a pattern of convergent behavior *plus* internal point of view is flawed. But see Coleman, note 2 at 76, 86. The flaw goes back to Hart. See Hart, note 19 at 255. Broadly understood, one cannot, as a matter of judgment, ascertain convergent behavior without adopting *a* point of view in the most elementary sense of discriminating between and among instances of a pattern. This point of view is adopted vis-à-vis all others who may arrive at different accounts of the rule explaining the pattern. The difference between such a broadly understood point of view, which is manifest in the exercise of what Kant calls "reflective judgment," and the more narrowly understood *internal* point of view, which is relevant for commonly practiced rules, lies in the fact that in the latter case the elements of the pattern are treated as instances of rule following. They are distinct from mere occurrences for which one tries to reconstruct some pattern. Hence, the internal point of view is not adopted toward others who are also engaged in trying to make out a pattern themselves. Using Hart's language, the point of view, broadly understood, is also adopted toward those who arrive at competing accounts of what people "make it a rule," that is, mere regularities that are not composed of instances that claim to follow a rule. Only from the internal perspective are instances of the pattern interpreted as instances of rule following. The critical reflective attitude is directed at the claim that is attributed to them, namely, the claim to be cases of following a rule. Social facts are thereby read as involving implicit claims whose validity is put to the test. Only thus understood, the following statement by Coleman makes sense (ibid., 82): "A social rule exists when convergent behaviour is conjoined with a critical reflective attitude towards that behaviour. The critical reflective attitude is the internal point of view."

73 See Coleman, note 2 at 88–89; Hart, note 19 at 86. Even in the case of what Raz would call "conformity," it matters that the act gets done for which the rule is the reason, even if no regard is had to whether the act was in fact guided by the rule. Observing the rule as a constraint on action is sufficient to engage the critical reflective attitude. See, generally, Joseph Raz, *Practical Reason and Norms* (2d ed., Princeton: Princeton University Press, 1990) at 180.

74 In what follows, no distinction will be made between following and applying a rule even though it can be plausibly said that a norm can be hypothetically applied to a situation in order to conclude that it ought not to be followed. See Gardner, note 2 at 158.

75 See Coleman, note 2 at 83, 153, according to whom the social rule exists only if there is widespread acceptance of the internal point of view. It is a delicate question whether the reconstruction of social rules from an external perspective merely suspends the application of the critical reflective attitude toward what it treats as instances of the rule but nonetheless extends it to those engaged in the same hermeneutic exercise. The adoption of a critical

The rule of recognition is the ultimate rule[76] of the legal system.[77] As Coleman explains:[78]

> [. . .] [I]t makes determinate which rules bear the mark of legality [. . .] [and] [. . .] creates a duty for a certain class of individuals – officials – to evaluate conduct under the set of primary rules that bear that mark.

The social constitution of this rule is invariably circular.[79] The officials who apply it are ultimately constituted by it in their capacity. They must be already guided by it[80] in order to be subject to its authority.[81]

What the rule means in fact is affected by their understanding of the rule's meaning. At the same time, however, this understanding must be informed by something that is independent of, and distinct from, various individual interpretations or manifestations of the rule in single cases.[82] Authoritativeness as a rule is possible only if the rule is more than the sum total of its applications and therefore, in a sense, something over and above them.[83] In Coleman's words, this means that "[i]n order for [. . .] behaviour to constitute a *practice* in the relevant sense, it must reflect a shared grasp of the rule."[84]

reflective attitude on the part of those engaged in an external and theoretical description of a social practice is absent in the otherwise highly useful discussion by Scott J. Shapiro, "What Is the Internal Point of View?" (2006) 75 *Fordham Law Review* 1157–1170 at 1160–1161.

76 See Hart, note 19 at 105.

77 The belief that law is a system was most certainly held by Hart. See Gardner, note 52 at 170.

78 Coleman, note 2 at 139. See also Shapiro, note 55 at 246. The rule of recognition is only a necessary but not a sufficient condition for law, which also requires obedience by "ordinary folk" for its existence. See Coleman, note 2 at 76.

79 The matter is discussed in Marmor, note 70 at 78.

80 It is not infrequently said that the rule of recognition must be "accepted" by officials. See Shapiro, note 75 at 1159, note 55 at 245. But this broad formulation obscures an important difference. Officials must accept that their behavior has to be intelligible and defensible as "rule following." But it is not necessary that they accept the rule substantively. Hart, note 19 at 255, made this clear in saying that rules must be accepted (merely) *as* guides of conduct and criticism. See also Gardner, note 2 at 141. Shapiro, note 59 at 202, gets it right when he says that officials must be "committed to following" the rule. But they need not accept it as such and not, of course, on its merits. Participants in the practice are therefore able to answer questions about how one plays by the rules. They are not necessarily able to answer questions about whether playing by the rules is useful and good. See Shapiro, note 55 at 259. Nonetheless, Patterson insists correctly against late positivists that what has to be accepted as rules by officials to be in the position to arrive at judgments about rule following are "forms of argumentative appraisals," such as methods of interpretation. See Dennis Patterson, "Explicating the Internal Point of View" (1999a) 52 *Southern Methodist University Law Review* 67–74 at 73.

81 See Coleman, note 2 at 78, 82, 95, 134.

82 See Dworkin, note 3 at 198.

83 See Coleman, note 2 at 80.

84 Ibid. at 80.

TWO DIFFERENT CRITICAL REFLECTIVE ATTITUDES

If the rule of recognition is a conventional rule, any interpretation of it, even though invariably implicit in its application and evolution,[85] must be intrinsically self-effacing, for the rule is supposed to be just manifest in practice. Moreover, it is supposed to be just there in the case that disagreement arises over what is just there.[86] It can only exist, therefore, when it is possible to sever the convention somehow from interpretive accounts of its meaning. At the same time, it is difficult to understand how the severed convention could exist unless a critical reflective attitude were manifest in its practice. Otherwise, the internal point of view would disappear and the social rule would evaporate in Marx's and Engel's proverbial thin air.[87]

Conventionalism encounters an impasse here. The content of the rule of recognition, says Coleman, must emerge from a "pattern"[88] of behavior that one observes, as an official, in others and in oneself. But where is the shared critical attitude if it is not revealed and manifest in interpretative elaborations of this pattern?[89] Since the critical reflective attitude is essential for the "shared grasp of the rule," one can possibly distinguish between the conventional rule and its interpretive elaborations only by seeing this attitude directed at different matters. Whereas interpretive elaborations concern the substantive meaning and point of the rule in the case of a conventional rule, the critical attitude concerns the convergence of behavior. Whereas in the former case the interpretation seeks to get the rule "right," in the latter case the question is whether others will share one's "grasp" of the rule ("Will they agree?").

Hence, the question of conventionality admits of a satisfactory answer from a social point of view. One merely needs to distinguish between the substantive and the social dimensions of rules. What is of interest about rules, substantively considered, is what they require. This is drawn out in interpretive elaborations. Socially understood, what matters about them is whether their

85 Members of the Wittgensteinian right notoriously contest this point. See Dennis Patterson, *Law and Truth* (Oxford: Oxford University Press, 1999b).

86 See Coleman, note 2 at 116. For perceptive critical observations, see Dworkin, note 3 at 190.

87 I add in passing that on the basis of understanding customary law as a social rule, it is difficult to see why agency and intentionality are supposed to be absent in its formation. But see Gardner, note 2 at 72.

88 See Coleman, note 2 at 91.

89 Here is how Coleman states the matter: "It is the shared attitude toward the pattern of behaviour that constitutes the fact that the behaviour is governed by a rule." The formulation suggests that there is a pattern that is somehow joined by the internal point of view. But this cannot be the case. Elements of a pattern can only be relevant for the rule when it is integral to their meaning to be "followings" of the rule. See note 72.

application or observance is supported by consent.[90] The latter is the social equivalent of a correct interpretation.

If producing a pattern of agreement matters and not a shared interpretive grasp of what the rule requires, then all that is needed to hit the convention is to trigger nodding among one's peers. Vis-à-vis "ordinary folk" (Coleman's genteel characterization of laypersons), who might occasionally react with bewilderment, one stands vindicated as long as the peers nod and mutter "This is what *we* do." Isn't this, if anything, the point of having a convention? "This is what we do"[91] and "I do as all others do" comprise the form of stating the rule's social dimension from an internal point of view.[92] This pair of maxims is the

[90] See Niklas Luhmann, *Rechtssoziologie* (Reinbek: Rowohlt Taschenbuch, 1972), vol. 1 at 99, 105.

[91] Wittgenstein sensed correctly that what is signified by the indexial "this" may remain indeterminate. See Ludwig Wittgenstein, *Über Gewissheit* (Frankfurt aM: Suhrkamp, 1984) § 28, at p. 125.

[92] Such social perspectives are still consistent with the standpoint that Shapiro characterizes, misleadingly, as "rule acceptance" or "internalization" (see Shapiro, note 75 at 1159, and note 59 at 200, 208). It is misleading, for what matters for the internal point of view is one's performance as a competent rule follower. Even – or maybe even in particular – hypocrites can be perfect rule followers. The rule is accepted by officials as a social rule for a variety of reasons, among which might figure the interest in earning a living, the desire to impress one's spouse, or according to Hart "the mere wish to do as others do." See Hart, note 59 at 203, 257. I mention in passing that Hart's distinction between the external and the internal aspect of rules (note 67 at 55–56, 86) is remarkably difficult to square with his conventionalism. The external aspect of rules captures general regularity of conduct, which is discernible even for an outside observer. The internal aspect is something that can be had by a rule "in addition" to the external aspect (ibid., 55). It is manifest in people "having views" (ibid., 56) about what it takes to play by the rules. Since in the case of a convention, these views have to have observance of a pattern of conduct as their point ("Now, you do as all others do!"), the external aspect is of overwhelming relevance for engaging the critical attitude (ibid., 55) from the internal point of view. What would it take to "have views" as regards conventions? One would have to come up with educated guesses about how peers will be judging one's application of the rule, for if that were not decisive it would not be a convention ("This is what we do"). Conceivably, a lawyer with training in American constitutional law would approach an equal protection problem by first asking which level of scrutiny has to be applied. However, if she were to do so in the context of Austrian constitutional law, she would be reproached by her Austrian peers claiming correctly that this is not the way things are done around here ("This is not what we do"). The internal point of view states what can be observed from the external point of view and asserts it as a matter of right. The difference between the internal and the external aspect is not whether one anticipates reactions from a pattern or, even more intelligently, one anticipates how peers believe all other peers to believe the pattern to be projected into the future, but whether one does it as a member of the group or as an outsider. Only as an insider do you get away with saying "This is what we do" and do not have to worry much about doing as all others do. Then one is in a position to use as a reason for decision (ibid., 102) what one anticipates to be the reasoning of all others. This is exactly the conventionalism that had once been reconstructed by Carl Schmitt in his early *Gesetz und Urteil* (Berlin: Otto Liebmann, 1912).

essence of social conventionalism.[93] Had Coleman studied George Herbert Mead, it would have also occurred to him that, in this understanding, conventional rules are means of exercising social control.[94] Conventionalism has to embrace the conclusion, hence, that that determination is right at which any other official whose intellectual demeanor and status make him into "one of the boys" would arrive too.[95]

One may even think that this is the immediate and natural rendering of the internal point of view. Any interpretive elaboration, by contrast, would, for the reason of being an elaboration, be more artificial. But the contrast is misleading. Mere coordinating conventions, such as the convention to drive on the right side of the street, are not likely to be susceptible to much interpretative elaboration. Elements of a purported rule of recognition are. Hence, the conventionalism of nodding peers is possible only when broader interpretative or justificatory appeals are avoided or suppressed against the backdrop of some permissive consensus that signals to peers that peers will react with "yeah" to whatever is done by other peers simply because the doing comes from a member of the peer group. It would be wrong, therefore, to assume that peer-group conventionalism is logically or historically prior to the interpretative elaborations of any potential justificatory appeal to the rule of recognition; rather, conventionalism is based on denying them relevance for a practice in which peers benefit from being able to claim that what *they* do is endorsed by others as the epitome of what *we* do. This is a quite artificial arrangement.

BOYHOOD AND GOING WITH THE CROWD

If the "shared grasp of the rule" is spelled out as peer group behavior, the application of the internal perspective can avoid broader justificatory appeals. The internal point of view can remain indifferent to substantive reasons of universal acceptability. This is written on the face of statements of the "this is what we do" variety. Therefore, the criteria relevant for exercising the critical reflective attitude need to focus on something other than the meaning or point of the rule. What one *does* matters less than who one *is*. Therefore, the shared

93 See Coleman, note 2 at 91–92.

94 See George Herbert Mead, *The Philosophy of the Present* (ed. A.E. Murphy, Chicago: University of Chicago Press, 1932) at 190. Had Shapiro read Mead, he would have likely explicated his "planning" theory of legal practice in the terms of a "game." See Georg Herbert Mead, *Mind, Self, and Society from the Standpoint of the Social Behaviorist* (Chicago: University of Chicago Press, 1934) at 153–154.

95 See Schmitt, note 92 at 71.

practice is easily possible under asymmetrical conditions.[96] While one group – viz., the boys – calls the shots and gets away with saying "This is what we do," the up and coming or the weaker members of the group – viz., the pack – adapt, resort to ducking, and follow the maxim "I do as others do." Interpretations of the rule are determined by what members of the pack guess will trigger nodding on the part of the boys because it may coincide with the latter's intuitive grasp of the rule.[97] Consequently, the rule of recognition can be a conventional rule only as long as the pack does not speak up, at any rate not too frequently, and reacts to the boys' piqued rejoinders in an apologetic way ("Thank you, now we have got it!").[98] The type of normativity that goes into creating the obligation to go on reflects the desire to follow the crowd.[99] Going along may carry the reward of being one of the boys tomorrow and of occupying the position, eventually, where one is free to assert "This is what we do."

ADDITION AND QUADDITION

It is now possible to appreciate more fully what it means that the rule of recognition is a *social* rule. How one gets along with others is more important than what one does. Being a proficient member of the group that Hart and Coleman refer to as "officials" requires social skills, and they are what is relevant from the internal point of view. One does not openly criticize high courts for reasoning mistakes. One does not raise embarrassing "theoretical" questions to which no one has an answer. One tries to play along even when one cannot make sense of what others do. These matters reflect, at any rate, the

96 It is quite amazing that Hart and late positivists always imagined the "group" to be egalitarian. How can one assume that in the legal system – vis-à-vis courts – criticism is taken seriously or even considered to be legitimate (but see Shapiro, note 75 at 1164)? Dworkin, note 3 at 196, quite correctly hinted at the fact that it is empirically doubtful whether the relation among members of the U.S. Supreme Court could be described as a shared cooperative activity.

97 This is not to say that members of the pack take their guidance from boys directly. They apply the rule as they believe it to emerge from the boys' internal point of view. See Shaipro, note 59 at 206.

98 This desire may be grounded in the expected reward to become bigger than one is when one is going with the crowd. See Friedrich Nietzsche, *The Dawn of Day* (trans. J.M. Kennedy, New York: Russell and Russell, 1964) at 32–34.

99 It is quite remarkable that in his critique of Austin's concept of legal obligation Hart shifts the focus from avoiding coercion toward avoiding rebuke for not going along with the crowd. See Hart, note 19 at 86: "Rules are conceived and spoken of as imposing obligations when the general demand for conformity is insistent and the social pressure brought to bear upon those who deviate or threaten to deviate is great." It is consistent with this understanding of obligation that the internal aspect of rules rests on the complementary maxims of "This is what we do" and "I do as others do," respectively.

most elementary experiences that are made in the course of being socialized into a member of the pack. In the eyes of students, professors are boys (even if they are female). What students attempt to do, using their social internal point of view, is to imagine what conceptions of rule and doctrines the professors might have in mind when talking about cases. Thereby they arrive at guesses about the professor's *substantive* internal point of view from their *social* internal point of view. This is what they do, for they have chosen to do as others do. The only interesting part of this story is that they need to make sense even of professors who, using Kripke's famous example, mistakenly assume to carry out additions while they in fact perform "quadditions."[100] Professors who believe in their own brilliance indeed are often incoherent. Students, nevertheless, need to make sense of their conduct as instances of a rule and trail their conduct in order to perform successfully in front of them an operation having the form "This is what we do."

The undefeated champions of quaddition are courts. In fact, having them occupy this position is the essence of the common law. The idea of the rule of recognition as social rule matches this situation. The court says, for example, that among 28 states in a federal system two state constitutions suffice to constitute a common constitutional tradition.[101] What a fabulous quaddition! It would be wrong, in such a situation, to criticise the court for either having misapprehended the law or for engaging in judicial legislation. Once the decision has been made, it creates a new situation. The law is no longer what it had been before.[102] All efforts to come up with substantive renderings of the rule from an internal point of view are thereby thwarted from the social internal perspective.

IDEALIZATION

The internal point of view is, to repeat, the "important capacity [. . .] to adopt a practice or pattern of behaviour as norm."[103] The way in which the boys use the rule brims with self-confidence: "This is what we do"; "This is how it's done"; "Here you have it." The critical reflective attitude exclaims "Don't you

100 In his discussion of rule following, Kripke introduces the example of someone who adds numbers and instead of adding one after the other at a certain point begins adding more than one number. From the perspective of an observer who tries to infer the rule from behavior, this rule turns out to be not the rule of addition but of something slightly different, for example, "quaddition," which does not use "plus" but "quus" as its operator. See Saul A. Kripke, *Wittgenstein on Rules and Private Language: An Elementary Exposition* (Cambridge, Mass.: Harvard University Press, 1982) 9 footnote 8.

101 See Case C-144/04, Werner Mangold v Rüdiger Helm [2005] ECR I-9981.

102 See Gardner, note 52 at 175.

103 Coleman, note 2 at 88.

dare." Members of the pack, by contrast, are more cautious: "They are out to lunch, but perhaps that is what they mean." The critical question is "What would I say if I were one of them?" Of course, the relation between these forms is dialectical. Brimming self-confidence may be dampened by the concern that too much audacity risks losing one's boyhood. One must not create an opportunity to be easily dismissed as senile or weird and whacky. On the other hand, one could never advance from the pack to the boys if one never tried one's hand at acting like one of them.

Interestingly, Coleman's conventionalism hides from us these simple truths about how social conventions work. It misses important points about the conventional existence of law, for example, that it is empowering to play by rules that have been laid down by others and not to ask too many questions, in particular not those questions that the boys would be too embarrassed to answer; that it pays to be cooperative and to show off one's smarts, but not in an impudent way; that it is advantageous to profess belief in the greatness of the legal enterprise; that one had better dodge substantive constitutional issues in the course of Supreme Court confirmation hearings (the Bork problem).

Remarkably, Coleman's eventual rendering of the rule of recognition, qua practice, as a form of shared cooperative activity[104] does not include any discussion of the complementarity of "This is what we do" and "I do as others do." On the contrary, his account of practical activity, for which he draws on Michael Bratman, merely arrives at a more diffuse and *idealizing* characterization of what is essentially an asymmetrical relationship: "[E]ach participating agent attempts to be responsive to the intentions and actions of the other [. . .] Each seeks to guide his behavior with an eye to the behavior of the other, knowing that the other seeks to do likewise."[105] What is eclipsed here is that people go about doing things differently depending on their position within the legal system or scholarly discourse.[106] What this view ignores is that substantive applications of the rule of recognition are overdetermined by applications informed by social status.

NEGATIVITY AND SPIRIT

Once this conventionalism is fully spelled out in social terms, it can be seen that it is a symptom for a certain state of legal knowledge. A symptom reveals that

104 See Coleman, note 2 at 96. 105 Ibid.

106 I add, in passing, that had Coleman taken the non-idealizing description into account, he would have had more difficulty claiming that this practice is pregnant with obligation.

something is amiss by simultaneously concealing what it is. Conventionalism conceals that, substantively considered, legal knowledge comes into existence in a form in which it is encumbered and distorted by power. Coleman unwittingly trails practiced legal knowledge's tendency to produce idealized descriptions of itself. It is almost comical that theory thereby falls victim to its own object. It emerges from a situation in which theoretical reflection has been exiled from the practice of legal knowledge. The symptom even endorses its exile position.[107] The theoretical reflection of legal practice inadvertently and indirectly reflects the repression of reflection within that practice.

The symptom reflects, however, that the practice is not composed of claims to apply the rule substantively correctly. Rather, whoever practices wishes to get away with what he does without rebuke. Such behavior supposedly "fixes" the rule.[108] The rule is manifest in certain paradigmatic instances of agreement even if the participants find it impossible to account, from the substantive internal point of view, for the reasons underpinning an agreement. It is in this vein that Coleman suggests that concepts, to function as concepts, do not require criteria but just agreement on paradigmatic cases.[109] This is boyhood all over the place.

Late legal positivism thus eclipses the internal perspective relevant for the substantive elaboration of rules. If the critical reflective attitude toward patterns is interested in seeing the point of rules observed, these patterns are composed – in the case of adjudication – of implicit or explicit self-reflective claims about what it takes to be faithful to the rule.[110] What matters about patterns in the context of adjudication are these self-interpretations. This is the point of the substantive internal point of view from a substantive point of view. Whatever is conceived of as candidate of rule following is potentially susceptible to critique for being out of line.[111]

From the perspective of a common practice, therefore, elements of a pattern come to this world as self-critically concerned about fitting a practice of which they want to make sense. The basis of self-critique is that which cannot be articulated in propositional form because it is initially manifest only in practice. It is neither something nor nothing. It is *something*

107 See, most candidly, Gardner, note 1 at 203.

108 See Coleman, note 2 at 80–81.

109 See Coleman, note 2 at 155.

110 I am aware that Wittgensteinians would at this point say that Wittgenstein insisted that there is a following of the rule that is not an interpretation. See, for example, Joachim Schulte, *Wittgenstein: Eine Einführung* (Stuttgart: Reclam, 1989) at 160–161. It never occurs to them that Ludwig might have been wrong about this.

111 See Peter Winch, *The Idea of a Social Science and Its Relation to Philosophy* (London: Routledge and Kegan Paul, 1958).

indeterminate.[112] Its internal negativity gives room to "creative" attempts to develop the point of rules. Dworkin was right when he, unwittingly, recognized under the name of "interpretive practice"[113] what Hegel long before him had called "spirit."[114] The latter stands for a reflective form of life that arises out of foundational indeterminacy. Owing to its negativity, spirit is a product of itself.[115] Steeped into that which is neither something nor nothing, it gives rise to practices for reassuring and examining the authoritativeness of reasons that are taken to be authoritative by their participants. It builds itself, as it were, from the indeterminacy into which the practice will always flow out.[116]

By contrast, conventional legal practice, even though possible,[117] simply is mindless second nature. Reflection is limited to asserting "This is what we do" and to obeying the maxim "I do as others do." The question of authoritativeness does not arise, at any rate, not beyond exploring the virtues of coordinating conventions.

Coleman goes wrong in presenting mindless social practice as though it embodied spirit. Nowhere is this more obvious than at various points where Coleman replies to Dworkin's objection[118] that a controversial rule of recognition cannot be conventional.[119] In the course of his replies, the idea that it is a convention ultimately begins to unravel. The ultimate characterization renders the rule of recognition as a shared cooperative activity. Coleman characterizes such an activity as "a framework of coordination, planning, and negotiation,"[120] which leaves wide leeway for disagreement. Coleman states explicitly: "It is not surprising that in resolving such disputes, the parties offer conflicting conceptions of the practice in which they jointly participate, conceptions that appeal to different ideas of its point or function." [121] There is nothing left of conventionalism here.[122] It has finally disposed of itself.

112 For a profound analysis, see Gerhard Gamm, *Flucht aus der Kategorie: Die Positivierung des Unbestimmten als Ausgang der Moderne* (Frankfurt aM: Suhrkamp, 1994) at 140–142.

113 See Dworkin, note 9 at 48; note 3 at 11–12.

114 See Terry Pinkard, *Hegel's Phenomenology: The Sociality of Reason* (Cambridge: Cambridge University Press, 1994) at 64.

115 See Robert Pippin, *Hegel's Practical Philosophy: Rational Agency as Ethical Life* (Cambridge: Cambridge University Press, 2008) at 65.

116 In anticipation of purportedly Wittgensteinian objections, I hasten to add that even within a reflective practice all justifications come to an end. That justifications come to an end (in the sense envisaged by Wittgenstein) does not mean that they are arbitrarily cut off.

117 I guess this is what Dworkin has in mind when speaking of a "pre-interpretative" stage of practice. See Dworkin, note 9 at 65–66.

118 See Dworkin, note 3 at 198. 119 See Coleman, note 2 at 68, 100, 116, 153–154.

120 Coleman, note 2 at 157. 121 Coleman, note 2 at 157.

122 I, for one, think that Dworkin, note 3 at 198, is right in suggesting that Coleman "has wholly decamped from the philosophical heritage he undertakes to defend."

THE EMBRACE OF MORALITY

Conventionalism is spiritless and vapid. It is *geistlos* in being the symptom of a spiritless practice. Late legal positivism's rapprochement vis-à-vis morality is not anything like that. It poses, however, a different problem, for it misses the opportunity to view morality as the problem to which the existence of the law responds if only in the low-key formula of Waldron's second circumstance of politics, which points to the persistence of reasonable disagreement.[123]

The rapprochement comes in three forms. In its mildest form, the rapprochement views law generally from the perspective of reasons for action. This is most thoroughly reflected in the work of Joseph Raz,[124] who nonetheless draws a clear line between morality and the purported authority that the law claims for itself.[125] The law possesses moral authority only if those subject to it are likely to make morally better choices by doing as the law says instead of acting on their own judgment of the situation.[126] Whether or not this is the case depends on individual knowledge and abilities. Exceptions such as consent to a government or identification with the political community aside, there is no general obligation to obey the law.[127] This does not alter the fact that the law expresses, on the level of norms and decisions, its claim to authority in the form of exclusionary reasons for action.[128] Such reasons demand that one not reflect on the reasons underlying a decision but simply comply with the first-order reasons expressed in a norm.[129] The law claims to have authority regardless of whether anyone finds it to be (morally) correct on the basis of reasoning leading up to its adoption. Therefore, legal validity cannot depend on a moral judgment on the merits. Raz does not at all suggest that the law, even though raising the claim thereto, in and of itself has moral authority.[130] But it will be seen in the next chapter that anchoring the analysis of law in the analysis of reasons for action already excludes a view of legal

123 See Jeremy Waldron, *Law and Disagreement* (Oxford: Oxford University Press, 1999).

124 One cannot agree more with Raz who stated quite clearly that "[. . .] [c]larifying the relations between law and morality is rightly seen as central to the explanation of the nature of law." Raz, note 2 at 168.

125 See Joseph Raz, *The Authority of Law: Essays on Law and Morality* (Oxford: Clarendon Press, 1979) at 9. For an excellent introduction, see Brian Bix, *Jurisprudence: Theory and Context* (6th ed., Durham: University of North Carolina Press, 2011) at 186–189.

126 For a brief restatement of his own views, see Raz, note 2 at 136–137.

127 See Joseph Raz, *Ethics in the Public Domain: Essays in the Morality of Law and Politics* (2d ed., Oxford: Clarendon Press, 1995) 342–343; Raz, note 2 at 175.

128 In recent writing, Raz, note 2 at 178–80, explains that the law has by its very nature a specific moral task because it is a structure of authority. It is "in the business of telling people what they must do."

129 See Raz, note 20 at 47.

130 The decisive criterion for legitimate authority is whether it facilitates conformity to reason. See Raz note 2 at 178.

positivism that does not conceive of the normativity of legal norms from the perspective of such reasons.

In its most common form, the rapprochement is known and debated as inclusive legal positivism.[131] The position admits of variations and sophisticated expositions. At its core, however, it says that the law can incorporate morality either as a matter of positive law or even at the level of the rule of recognition.[132] Strangely enough, therefore, such an inclusive legal positivism may in practice not look different from natural law theory. In fact, as Dworkin himself noted, it may appear to be altogether indistinguishable from the approach to legal reasoning that he advocates himself. He is rightly sceptical of what the point of such positivism is.[133]

The most puzzling form of rapprochement, however, begins by suggesting – not puzzlingly, to be sure – that being responsive to moral demands is an integral part of being reason-responsive and, hence, rational.[134] While engagement with moral norms is just as necessary as the engagement with the norms of logic, the same is not the case for legal norms,[135] which "[...] do not form an inescapable part of rationality."[136] Whether or not a legal obligation is really binding on us and whether or not we ought to be guided by legal norms requires a further nonlegal, viz. moral, reason to explain. Hence, in contrast to morality, laws are not part of rationality but answerable to it. Gardner puts this point as follows: "An unjustified moral norm is an oxymoron; an unjustified legal norm is always a live possibility."[137]

It may be noted, in passing, that both claims are unconvincing. Moral norms can be substantively unjustified in spite of being formally dictates of conscience and, hence, moral norms. *Legally* unjustified legal norms are quite inconceivable. They are void unless their validity is sustained by other legal norms. Obviously, what Gardner has in mind is the existence of morally unjustified law. In his view, such law is possible since the law does not claim to be morally justified but only to possess moral *authority*.[138] The legal claim to

131 For great brief characterizations, see Marmor, note 70 at 93. Brian H. Bix, A *Dictionary of Legal Theory* (Oxford: Oxford University Press, 2004) at 123.
132 The latter is the position vigorously defended by Coleman.
133 See Dworkin, note 3 at 188, 198.
134 See Gardner, note 2 at 150.
135 See Gardner, note 2 at 160.
136 Gardner, note 2 at 161. Gardner puts the matter more starkly at 175, where he says that morality "is natural" in that engagement with moral norms is an inescapable part of human nature. Law, by contrast, is unnatural. From a Hobbesian perspective, one could formulate long rejoinders to this claim.
137 Gardner, note 2 at 161.
138 See Gardner, note 2 at 141–143. In his view, the study of the nature of law can and must begin with the central case of morally successful law (175).

moral authority says that whoever is subject to the law is more likely to act morally when not acting on the balance of moral reasons but rather doing as the law requires.[139] Generally, authority is supposed to serve individuals to enhance their reason-responsiveness. Only inasmuch as it accomplishes this task is it legitimate.[140] The existence of authority, which knows better or is able to organize better, precludes taking reasons into account on which the decision of the authority depends. As Raz puts it, "[...] [t]he law resolves the dispute by pre-empting it."[141] From that perspective, it is consistent to attribute to the law the claim to be morally binding.[142] Gardner goes even so far as to vindicate a teleology for the law according to which it aims to be morally successful.[143] Nevertheless, the legal claim to moral authority may occasionally give rise to the well-known conflict between one's own moral insight and the exclusionary reason demanding to set such insight aside.[144] Father knows best, or at least he claims so. As Gardner puts it: "[M]oral authority is such that abiding by it is morally correct even though the exercise of it was morally incorrect. Authority may bind one morally to do certain things that one should never have become morally bound to do."[145] This means that it is morally justified to abide by the moral authority of law even in the event that in one particular case it does not possess it. It is not easy to understand how this claim fits into the overall Razian framework. We shall see that the problem of fit, indeed, resides in the framework itself. The following discussion focuses exclusively on this third form of rapprochement.

THE MORAL AUTHORITY OF LAW

Why should one grant the law moral authority if it demands that one act immorally? Why should one assume that the law knows best if one firmly believes to know better?

[139] For a short introduction to this central theme of Raz's legal philosophy, see Raz, note 127 at 214–214; note 2 at 136–137, 173–174.

[140] See Raz, note 2 at 140; 178: "The law's task, put abstractly, is to secure a situation whereby moral goals which, given the current social situation of the country whose law it is, would be unlikely to be achieved without it, and whose achievement by law is not counter-productive, are generalized" (italics deleted).

[141] Raz, note 2 at 140.

[142] See Raz, note 125 at 8. The reasons that the law requires us to conform can lead to the same result as obtaining guidance from other reasons. The exclusionary reason embodied in legal rules or decisions does not "stop us from following the reasons on the winning side of an argument." So Raz, note 2 at 144.

[143] See Gardner, note 2 at 170. See also Raz, note 2 at 103, 178. According to Gardner (ibid., 172) the law is defeasibly morally obligatory.

[144] See Raz, note 20 at 42, 45. [145] Gardner, note 2 at 143.

Gardner addresses the emerging paradox head on with an eye to Kierkegaard's interpretation of the biblical story of Abraham who has been ordered by God to commit the utterly immoral act of killing his son Isaac.[146] Abraham is ready to do the horrible thing because he has been told to do so by God. There is no justification for doing what God has ordered him to do but his faith in God. This faith concerns, of course, the goodness of what he is about to do just because God has ordained it. This faith entails the belief in the goodness of what is manifestly bad if God wants it. From this follows that God has the power to override all rationally elaborated distinctions between good and bad and to reallocate goodness at whim. If God can arbitrarily, but validly, turn evil into good, all reasoning involving this distinction loses its point. What remains is blind followership. Since there can be no moral reason underpinning such followership, the reason cannot be shared with others. It must look absurd. Following God becomes an entirely individual affair between the God and a "knight of faith."[147]

Gardner, however, does not go down Kierkegaard's road. The *differénd*[148] between moral and religious perspectives is not raised to the level of perplexity. Rather, believing is approached from the perspective of reasons for action[149] and treated as a problem of authority. It is at this point where Gardner begins to expand the Razian framework.

According to the service conception, whoever follows the directives of legitimate authority is served well by it because followership maximizes conformity to reasons. The self-incapacitation is sustained for the sake of reasonableness. Nevertheless, the effect of authority to set aside the relevance of individual judgment is not easy to determine.[150] Authority is possible only if and as long as it is reasonable to follow authority just because authority says so. Authority is the right to rule.[151] But authority is not handed down by God's grace. It is earned by virtue of performance.[152] Any excellence in giving advice, in carrying out tasks, or organizing conduct is key thereto, and moral considerations have to play a role in identifying and empowering authority.[153]

146 See Soren Kierkegaard, *Fear and Trembling* (trans. S. Walsh, Cambridge: Cambridge University Press, 2006); Gardner, note 2 at 2–6.

147 See Kierkegaard, note 146 at 61.

148 See Jean-François Lyotard, *The Differend* (trans. G. Van Den Abbeele, St. Paul: University of Minnesota Press, 1989).

149 See Gardner, note 2 at 4.

150 For a critical perspective that highlights that the "normal justification thesis" does not and cannot create authority to hold a subject responsible and therefore cannot be regarded as true second-personal authority, see Stephen Darwall, *Morality, Authority, and Law: Essays in Second-Personal Ethics I* (Oxford: Oxford University Press, 2013b) at 147, 153, 155.

151 See Raz, note 2 at 135. 152 See Raz, note 2 at 142, 174. 153 See Raz, note 2 at 114.

At the same time, accepting an authority requires severing the reasoning for submission to authority from following its directives. If one examined each case on the merits of what authority has one do, authority would cease to be what it is.[154]

But it is difficult to separate the reasons for the existence of authority from observing its proven ability to identify first-order reasons for action superbly for those for whom it is an authority.[155] Owing to this difficulty, any single instance of bad advice, awful judgment, or bad law may make one wonder whether one already has sufficient reason to reconsider its legitimacy. Raising this question is consistent with the service conception of authority according to which performance is what matters. How can authority ever be possible then?[156]

Raz attempts to steal himself away from this problem of the service conception by asserting that even in the event that authority commits a mistake, we have reason to follow its directives as long as it is legitimate.[157] This would explain the existence of the Gardner-type-situation in which morally legitimate authority directs us to do immoral things. Supposedly, yet somewhat surprisingly, Raz and Gardner would say that we are *morally* obligated to obey. But it should not escape our attention that this assertion of the preemptive force of authoritative directives is already different from the standard situation addressed by the service conception. It is the situation of self-incapacitation owing to a self-ascribed lack of judgment or lack of ability to bring about a desirable situation in which different reasons for action would apply. In the case of the immoral law, there is no such lack, which is why one may duly wonder whether the service conception even applies to it.

154 I take this to be a major point of the "normal justification thesis."

155 See Raz, note 2 at 104.

156 Darwall, note 150 at 149, 152, 154, 162, 165, distinguishes two conceivable understandings of authority that might underpin the service conception. According to the first, the authority in question is manifest in a responsibility on the part of its subjects to be answerable to it. Raz's service conception does not reach up to this level because, at the end of the day, the subjects remain only answerable to themselves. The point of authority is to maximize their own reason-responsiveness. If one is answerable to another person only as part of a strategy to attain a certain objective, this represents responsibility for reasons of the wrong kind, for it would not reflect how the responsible agent has wronged authority's right to rule and can be blamed for it (ibid., 156). Darwall concedes, however, that according to a second understanding, an authority of the Razian kind might merely generate preemptive reasons without linking these with being answerable to authority. Unfortunately, however, one cannot make sense of preemptive reasons without making the subject of authority answerable to it. If one remains, in spite of surrendering one's judgment, only answerable to oneself, there is no reason not to take excluded reasons into account (ibid., 161–163). Never mind that Darwall uses a weakness of the will problem to prove this important point.

157 See Raz, note 2 at 145.

Such a difference in the situation notwithstanding, Raz supports complying with authority in a case of conflict with considered substantive beliefs on the basis of one of the notorious "on the whole" type of arguments. In his view, an authority that on the whole acts wisely and morally is legitimate.[158] Evidently, this condition has to be inserted into the service conception to make sure that authority is not permanently vulnerable to revocation in the event that those who are subject to it judge it to be mistaken. But this cannot rescue the service conception from being undercut by its decidedly non-authoritarian foundation. Ultimately, it is left to the subjects of authority to judge whether or not an institution or person legitimately exercises authority over them.[159] This implies, *a fortiori*, that it is up to them to decide how grave or slight a mistake must be for authority to lose its legitimacy. This implies that in the eyes of the adjudicating subjects, one substantive mistake may suffice to establish such a loss and one substantive success enough to regain it. After all, it is left to them to decide what reason-responsiveness is and what is required for its maximization. What counts, at the end of the day, is their own conception of reason-responsiveness.

According to the service conception, the legitimacy of authority ultimately is determined on the basis of individual judgment. This explains why, conversely, *true* authority is either authoritarian or derivative of something other than the maximization of reason-responsiveness. Unless it is mediated by identification ("right or wrong, it is my country"), authority is possible only if the recognition of authority is taken out of the hands of the subjects for the reason that they are too immature, too inexperienced, morally too debased, or not well educated enough to understand that "on the whole" authority is good for them. It is simply impossible for authority to be as nice as the service conception wishes it to be.

STATUS-BASED AUTHORITY

Not surprisingly, explaining the Gardner-type-situation requires a different approach, however, an approach that casts the moral authority of law in a different light. In the course of his discussion of Kierkegaard, Gardner presents us with an intriguing attempt at resolving the puzzle by taking a detour to social roles. While there may be various personal reasons for fitting a certain social role – the role of a friend, of a judge, or an engineer – these reasons are different from the reasons for action that arise from occupying such a role.[160] Typically, people marry other people to enjoy the exclusive privilege of

[158] See Raz, note 2 at 104. [159] See Raz, note 2 at 140. [160] See Gardner, note 2 at 6.

having sex with them. That's the point. Once they are married, however, they incur a variety of spousal duties that are intrinsically unrelated to satisfying their sexual urges. Likewise, one becomes friends with a person, for example, out of sharing a passion for art. Even though this reason has nothing to do with loaning money to that person, one is expected to do so once ties of friendship have formed. Indeed, while the strength of the relationship is thus put to a test, it proves that one identifies with being a friend.

Gardner transfers the mode of generating reasons for action by virtue of entering into a relationship and playing a role within it to Abraham's relation to God and our relation to the law. You pledge unconditional allegiance to God because you have seen that others have really done well after they had done so.[161] Pledging allegiance alters your status. You have made yourself into a follower and therefore God has authority over you. The God that makes life good for you may occasionally come up with exacting tests of your faith, such as the killing of your beloved son, but this does not alter the fact that you behaved rationally when you decided to become a follower. By analogy, being an obedient legal subject may really benefit you in the rational pursuit of your business interests. Owing to your self-chosen status, you have reason to oblige cringingly if the law requires you to report any suspicious activity by your Muslim neighbours to the police.

Such a conception of authority is, however, decidedly different from the service conception. First, the authority in question is no longer moral. Identification with being a law-abiding subject may be morally desirable (not least because one avoids alienation),[162] but it is not at all morally required. From this follows that identification with the law of a particular community cannot underpin the moral authority of law; it can merely lend expression to the fact that one identifies with one's political community. If the political community orders you to do morally reprehensible things and you oblige, it merely demonstrates *who you are* but it *does not serve you* in conforming to the precepts of morality. If the identification with law were expected from you, then political authority would be definitely authoritarian.

Second, the conception of authority that focuses on identification does not share what must be the service conception's central concern, namely, that authority observe limits with regard to the purpose that it is supposed to serve.[163] Not by accident, the authority that Gardner has in mind is mediated by interposing institutional arrangements, indeed, relations that a Hegelian would regard as part of *Sittlichkeit*. The obligations that Gardner sees arise stem from committing oneself to a role that defines one's

[161] Gardner, note 2 at 6. [162] See Raz, note 2 at 151. [163] But see Raz, note 2 at 173–174.

status.[164] People marry for an obvious reason, but once they are married they have to do the dishes. Friends help each other out financially even if a friend may begin to appear in different light once he is asking for money. The institution of marriage and the institution of friendship mediate the obligations. It is the status that gives rise to obligations. Similarly, the authority of God stems from Abraham's endorsement of unconditional followership with the faith that whatever might come from it will be good no matter how bad it may seem. Observing the law even if the law requires one to do awful things stems from endorsing the status of a law-abiding legal subject.

In both cases, the relation inherent in the service conception of authority is reversed. According to the service conception, you do as authority says to conform better to reasons that apply to you (or to have reasons for action that you have reason to have by virtue of the existence of authority). Even if the existence of authority gives rise to new reasons for action, these are based upon reasons that apply to you beforehand. In the cases discussed by Gardner, God says what is good and the law says what is right and the obligations arise because you have made yourself into a follower.

BEYOND ABSURDITY

Puzzlingly, Gardner sustains the idea that the law claims to have moral authority and concedes that it would lack it if it made us permanently do terrible things. No constitution would ever have authority that proclaimed, solemnly, to have been adopted to entrench injustice.[165] Yet, the only explanation that Gardner gives for the fact that abiding by moral authority is morally correct even if its exercise is morally incorrect are status-related reasons. The service conception, by contrast, would sustain a claim to authority only if the seemingly morally incorrect exercise of authority were justified because moral authority knew better. In a case of conflict, the subjects would have to yield to better judgment. This also looks rather authoritarian. It is, indeed, reminiscent of the critique of Hobbes, in which Schmitt suggests that Hobbes did not go far enough in conceiving of sovereign power by leaving to the subjects space *foro interno* for disagreement.[166]

164 Later it turns out that Gardner recognizes authority that is based on faith. See Gardner, note 2 at 14.

165 See Gardner, note 2 at 143.

166 See Carl Schmitt, *Der Leviathan in der Staatslehre des Thomas Hobbes: Sinn und Fehlschlag eines politischen Symbols* (Stuttgart: Klett Cotta, 2012) at 85–86, 91.

If one did not buy into the better judgment conclusion, one could still arrive at an all-things-considered conclusion saying that it is better to yield to morally incorrect exercises of (alleged) moral authority because acts of rebellion would threaten to undo well-functioning institutions (Kant's old maxim: "reason, but obey"). In this case, however, it would also be wrong to call the exercise of authority morally incorrect for it would be justified on the basis of the all-things-considered consideration.

The perplexity inherent in ascribing to authority the power to require us to commit immoral acts can be shown a way out by viewing the problem as cognate to the fascinating enigma that Kelsen bequeathed on us when he characterized in his later years the basic norm as a fiction in the "Vaihingerian sense." The reference goes to the Kantian philosopher Hans Vaihinger whose *Philosophy of the As-If*[167] accords to fictions a central pragmatic role. Fictions are action facilitating. They are, in the case of true fictions, not only untrue but also internally contradictory.[168] According to Kelsen, the basic norm falls into this category. Not only is the basic norm not a norm of positive law, its claim to establish the highest authority necessarily presupposes an even higher authority to issue this power-conferring norm.[169] But this higher authority does not exist.

A self-contradictory norm is also a norm that denies its own normative status. With that we can return to Abraham. If Abraham has a duty toward God and acting on this duty offends morality, this means, in moral terms, that his maxim cannot be universalized. A duty that does not stand the test of moral universalization is not a duty, but only the fiction of a duty in precisely the sense introduced by Vaihinger. It is internally contradictory. Hence, the term "duty" can in this case at best only be a simile chosen for expressing the personal bond to a personal God. This type of duty is different from the moral realm. It is entirely personal and, as regards its ground, strangely incommunicable.

If Abraham's duty is not a duty in the moral sense, the same absence of normativity can be observed for the question-begging basic norm. Add Gardner to Kelsen and Abraham and you get the obligation to conform to immoral law. The law somehow suspends morality.

Legal positivists, with the exception of Kelsen qua a moral sceptic, never explored the suspension of morality. More precisely, they did not ask what it

[167] Hans Vaihinger, *Die Philosophie des Als Ob: System der theoretischen, praktischen und religiösen Fiktionen der Menschheit aufgrund eines idealistischen Positivismus* (9th and 10th ed., Leipzig: Felix Meiner, 1927).

[168] Ibid at 24.

[169] Hans Kelsen, *General Theory of Norms* (trans. M. Hartney, Oxford: Oxford University Press, 1991) at 256.

might be about morality that makes its suspension necessary. The story of Abraham, however, already offers the clue. It is the encounter with a moral duty that really is not one. A duty that really is none is a universalization that remains particular and personal. If one yields to a universalization that really only seems to be what it is, one simply makes room for what someone merely wants. One concedes rights and thereby suspends morality, however, subject to a condition that is itself significant from a moral point of view, namely the condition of reciprocity. The suspension of morality is thereby revoked, however, only to be introduced again when it comes to spelling out the conditions of reciprocity. It is along this path that an understanding of the legal relation can be developed that will hopefully overcome the quandary of late positivist legal theory. We pick up this theme in Chapter 3.

CONCLUSION

This chapter distinguished two consequences of positivism's separability thesis: descriptive accuracy, on the one hand, and constructivism, on the other. The ethos of sober description reflects a feature of positivism in general. Constructivism aims at arriving at a demystified and sober perspective on the law, stripping it of unnecessary idealizations that arise from attempts to cast it in a morally most favorable light. The promise of descriptive accuracy cannot be kept. The law invariably draws on merit-based consideration in the course of its reproduction.

Constructivism is absent in the late legal positivism that is currently held in high regard, at least by its adherents. This late legal positivism declares conventionalism to be its defining mark and does not draw a sharp line vis-à-vis morality. This conventionalism unwittingly reflects legal knowledge in a vapid state.

The greater proximity toward morality never even imagines that, potentially, moral reason poses a problem for which law provides the solution. It ignores, that is, the somewhat sceptical insight driving all more ambitious attempts to distinguish law from morality.

Overcoming both conventionalism and the rapprochement toward morality involves exploring the point of law. In this context, one encounters, not by accident, exactly the conflict of moral reasons that the discussion of authority cannot adequately grasp because it fails to view it from the perspective of moral reciprocity.

2

Legality and Irony

Modern legal positivism tries to preserve the normativity of law while abstaining from generally viewing positive laws as reasons for action. This effort is epitomized, in particular, in Raz's idea that the substance of positive law can be imparted from the detached perspective of the "legal man." From that perspective, it is not stated what one ought to do, all things considered, but merely what one ought to do from the legal point of view. The first part of this chapter shows that the problem that the introduction of the "legal man" is supposed to solve originates from an assimilation of Kelsen's legal positivism to "common sense." The embrace of "common sense," however, divests modern legal positivism of its critical edge. The second part of the chapter offers both a *reductio ad absurdum* of a conventionalist understanding of the "legal man" and an analysis of legal knowledge that abstains from exploring its claim to validity. Legal knowledge of that type embraces bitter irony.

REINING IN THE BAD MAN

Modern legal positivism has distinguished itself from its predecessor by complementing the "bad man's perspective" on the law with the recognition that those who busy themselves with knowing the law rightly attribute normative significance to it. From their point of view, the meaning of the law is adequately captured in statements using the language of obligations and rights.[1]

The "bad man's perspective" was most clearly and prominently stated in Holmes's "The Path of Law." The first paragraph of this work informs the reader that all that the legal profession is essentially up to is predicting what the courts will do in fact.[2] Studying the law amounts, as far as that goes, to the

[1] See H.L.A. Hart, *The Concept of Law* (2d ed., Oxford: Clarendon Press, 1994) at 84.

[2] See Oliver Wendell Holmes, "The Path of the Law" reprinted in (1997) 110 *Harvard Law Review* 991–1009.

sociology of legal behavior.[3] Similarly, what within the Anglo-American context passes as "old" legal positivism views the law as commands that are effectively enforced by the sovereign.[4] The force of the law is thereby reduced to some overpowering factual force.

Kelsen's legal theory became famous for avoiding the reduction of normativity to a matter of facts. The first edition of the *Pure Theory of Law* asserts boldly that the "ought" of the law cannot be reduced to "a regularity of a certain pattern of human behaviour."[5] Kelsen claims, and he will be joined by Hart,[6] that doing so would not adequately capture how the law appears to whoever obtains guidance from the legal system.[7] What Kelsen did not explicate – and this task was to be left to Hart – is that the legal system, as a social fact that is amenable to "external" description, necessarily involves the effectiveness of an "internal attitude."[8] Those adopt it who critically assess and answer questions of compliance. Indeed, an external observer might merely observe patterns of behavior. But such a radical objectification would miss the efficacy of the internal point of view. In the case of rule-guided conduct, patterns of behavior have to be read as manifestations of a critical reflective attitude on the part of those concerning themselves with following and applying rules.[9] As Hart famously put it, for those adopting the internal point of

3 See, for that matter, Felix S. Cohen, "Transcendental Nonsense and the Functional Approach" (1935) 35 *Columbia Law Review* 809–849.

4 See Hart, note 1 at 83.

5 See Hans Kelsen, *Introduction to the Problems of Legal Theory* (trans. B. Litschewski Paulson & S.L. Paulson, Oxford: Clarendon Press, 1992) at 32.

6 See Hart, note 1 at 88–90.

7 See Kelsen, note 5 at 34, where Kelsen equates the "normative meaning of the law" with "the law as it represents itself to the organs that make and apply the law and to the law-seeking public."

8 A reader of this chapter reminded the author correctly of Finnis's criticism of how Hart casually amalgated a variety of attitudes into one internal point of view. See John Finnis, *Natural Law and Natural Justice* (2d ed., Oxford: Oxford University Press, 2011a) at 13–14. According to Hart, the internal attitude can range from a moral concern for the observance of legal rules to the mere wish to pass as one law-applying official among others. Finnis explains quite perceptively that Hart's transition to the legal system from an assemblage of primary rules would not be conceivable if the rule-guided application of primary rules did not involve a serious concern with the integrity of law. Hence, Finnis insists on distinguishing between core and peripheral cases of the internal point of view and views an attitude of moral approbation as a characteristic of the first.

9 According to Marmor, Hart retained the reductivist approach to normativity by claiming that the normative point of view, which is manifest in internal statements, is itself amenable to empirical observation. This is Hart's more sophisticated version of the external point of view from which normativity is rendered as a social fact that is manifest in certain attitudes and beliefs. See Andrei Marmor, *Philosophy of Law* (Princeton: Princeton University Press, 2011) at 53–55.

view, the violation of a rule is not "merely a basis for the prediction that a hostile reaction will follow but a *reason* for hostility."[10]

Consequently, Hart insisted that the legal officials (or legislatures) do not merely obey the law. *Mere* obedience does not involve "any view" with regard to how one's behavior actually fulfills a standard that is established within a group.[11] Whoever merely obeys the law adopts an external point of view, for he or she is conceivably only interested in not triggering negative reactions by the state.[12] In other words, the merely obedient comply in a manner that Kant called "external." They behave *legally*, that is, their conduct can be described as *de facto* conforming with what is required by rules.[13] Of ordinary people the law asks no more than to behave as "bad men." The law does not give them an exclusionary reason to adopt the law as a reason for action.[14]

DETACHED STATEMENTS

We owe an important amendment to this richer picture to Joseph Raz.[15] Internal statements are made from the perspective of those accepting legal rules as valid, either directly or indirectly on the basis of accepting a rule of recognition. Stating what the law is, therefore, seems to lend expression to what you ought to do, morally considered. Legal statements state legal rules, which, in turn, purport to be reasons for action.[16] They seem to tell you what you *really* have to do. But this, Raz reminds us with an eye to Kelsen,[17] does not capture the intention with which normative statements are often made in legal discourse.[18] Statements using ordinary normative

[10] Hart, note 1 at 90. [11] See ibid. at 115.

[12] See ibid. at 89. Both the bad man and an unaffected external observer are interested in the internal point of view only inasmuch as its existence makes the legal system predictable. A purely external observer, however, is not necessarily interested in observing predictability.

[13] See Immanuel Kant, Die Metaphysik der Sitten, *Werkausgabe*, vol. 8 (ed. W. Weischedel, Frankfurt aM: Insel, 1968) 324 (A 15).

[14] See Joseph Raz, *Between Authority and Interpretation: On the Theory of Law and Practical Reason* (Oxford: Oxford University Press, 2008) at 144.

[15] On the following, see Joseph Raz, *The Concept of a Legal System: An Introduction to the Theory of Legal System* (2d ed., Oxford: Clarendon Press, 1980) at 236; *Practical Reason and Norms* (2d ed., Princeton: Princeton University Press, 1990) at 170–177.

[16] See *Practical Reason and Norms*, note 15 at 171.

[17] On the Raz-Kelsen relation, see Stanley L. Paulson, "A 'Justified Normativity' Thesis in Hans Kelsen's Pure Theory of Law? Rejoinders to Robert Alexy and Joseph Raz." In *Institutionalized Reason* (ed. M. Klatt, Oxford: Oxford University Press, 2011) 61–110 at 67–68.

[18] For a helpful elaboration of Raz's view, see Luís Duarte d'Almeida, "Legal Statements and Normative Language" (2011) 30 *Law and Philosophy* 167–199.

vocabulary, such as "duty" or "claim," are not intended to state reasons for action but only what one would have to *regard* as such reasons from a certain point of view,[19] namely, the viewpoint of the legal system or of the "legal man."[20] Such statements are not "committed," for they do not commit the speaker to the view that he or she expresses.[21] Rather, they are "detached." They state what one has reason to do assuming, hypothetically, that the law has authority. Statements of this type are neither uninformative nor pointless if the content of the assumption is part of what makes the statement true.[22] The content of the assumption is that the law provides reasons for action.[23] The statements do not report the views that some might harbor about what the law is on a certain question.[24] Instead of describing other people's normative beliefs, they articulate what the law is from the perspective of the law itself,[25] while leaving its authority open. They say, for example, "legally speaking, you have committed a crime," without thereby suggesting that you have indeed engaged in blameworthy conduct and do deserve punishment. They simply say that the law views what you have done in that way.

Modern legal positivists go to great pains to triangulate the illocutionary role of legal statements because it is the defining mark of their position to

19 See Joseph Raz, *Practical Reason and Norms*, note 15 at 175.

20 See Joseph Raz, *The Authority of Law: Essays in Law and Morality* (Oxford: Clarendon Press, 1979) at 142. See also *Practical Reason and Norms*, note 15 at 171: "The legal point of view (of system S), we could say, consists of the norms of S and any other reasons on which the subjects of S are required by the norms of S to act. The ideal law-abiding citizen is the man who acts from the legal point of view. He does not merely conform to law. He follows legal norms and legally recognized norms as norms and accepts them also as exclusionary reasons for disregarding those conflicting reasons which they exclude."

21 See Duarte d'Almeida, note 18 at 182.

22 See ibid. at 185. According to Shapiro, committed statements have normative truth conditions. They are true if there is indeed a moral duty or a right. Whether this is the case depends on some moral justification. Detached statements, by contrast, have "exclusively" descriptive truth conditions for they are true if there is someone from whose point of view something is required or prohibited. See Scott J. Shapiro, *Legality* (Cambridge, Mass.: Harvard University Press, 2011) at 415. This, however, suggests that detached statements report what someone believes to have reason to do. But this is not the case. They are about what appears to be right or wrong from a certain point of view.

23 Duarte d'Alemeida, note 18, at 186, contends that statements reporting what someone has reason to do on the basis of some doctrine or persuasion do not require adopting any point of view. I did not understand why and how d'Almeida reaches this conclusion, but I duly take note of it in spite of my puzzlement.

24 This is stressed in particular by Julie Dickinson, "Interpreting Normativity." In *Properties of Law: Essays in Honour of Jim Harris* (ed. T. Endicott, J. Getzler & E. Peel, Oxford: Oxford University Press, 2006) 22–42 at 37–38.

25 See Raz, *The Concept of a Legal System*, note 15 at 236.

retain the normativity of law without conflating it with morality. Detached statements are "morally uncommitted." They merely assume that the law is valid.[26] They are tantamount to saying, "assuming that the Ptolemaic view of the world is correct it is true that the sun is about to set momentarily"; if some people actually share this assumption, they do not state it and simply say that the sun is about to set.

What is assumed, however, by the theory of normative statements, is an "isomorphic" mapping of moral beliefs onto legal norms.[27] The core idea is that the normative nature of law, as revealed from the internal perspective, is the *same* as that of morality and thus gives rise to the same type of reasons for action.[28] Hypothetically, at any rate, the law says "You ought to" and if you do not do as you ought to, the law will regard you as having "failed" or as having behaved "badly."

It is submitted, with all due respect, that the basic isomorphism is mistaken. It is implausible for at least three reasons. The first is that Raz's isomorphism rests on a remarkable disregard of how Kelsen presented the normativity of legal norms.[29] The second concerns the fact that the elaboration of detached statements remains pragmatically stale. It ignores the essential performative element inherent in detaching oneself from the legal man. Enacting the legal man without identifying with what he believes in is tantamount to engaging in playacting in front of an audience that is composed of other players (and clients). Detached legal knowers are mutually engaged in behaving *like* the legal man. The third reason concerns, finally, the legality of law, not in the sense recently suggested by Shapiro,[30] but in the sense that the law does not give us an exclusionary reason to regard the law as a reason for action. While the last two issues cannot be explored at greater depth here, it is important to note that if the law merely requires legality of behavior, then this will be manifest also in how the law is publicly known. The following sections explore how Kelsen's conception of the normativity of legal norms eluded contemporary analytical jurisprudence.

[26] See Joseph Raz, "The Purity of the Pure Theory." In *Normativity and Norms: Critical Perspectives on Kelsenian Themes* (ed. S.L. Paulson & B.L. Paulson, Oxford: Clarendon Press, 1998) 237–252 at 247–248.

[27] See Paulson, note 17 at 68.

[28] See Raz, note 26 at 245: "Legal statements are normative statements in the same sense and in the same way that moral statements are normative."

[29] This point has been already made by Paulson, note 17 at 102.

[30] Shapiro uses the concept "legality" to designate the "property of law being law." This is a quite eccentric use of the term. See Shapiro, note 22 at 7.

KELSEN'S OBJECTIVE RENDERING OF THE DETACHED ATTITUDE

In the first edition of the *Pure Theory of Law*, Kelsen famously introduces the *Rechtssatz* or the "reconstructed legal norm."[31] Contrary to Kelsen's later usage,[32] the *Rechtssatz* is not the sentence reporting what the law requires but the type of object that legal knowledge is prepared to accept as its proper object, namely, as a legal norm. This is consistent with the task of pure legal science. The object needs to be presented in a manner that preserves normativity while holding it distinct from morality. Oddly enough, Kelsen presents the pragmatic dimension of morality in imperative form:[33]

> The Pure Theory of Law [. . .] completely sever[s] the concept of the legal norm from its source, the concept of the moral norm [. . .] The Pure Theory does this not by understanding the legal norm, like the moral norm, as an imperative – the usual approach of traditional theory – but by understanding the norm as a hypothetical judgment that expresses the specific linking of a conditioning material fact with a conditioning consequence.

The presentation of "full-blooded" moral normativity in imperative form is no obstacle to understanding the contrast that Kelsen intends to draw. Actually, one merely needs to view the imperative as a specification of a broader view of normative directives that are all about what people "ought to do," "should do," or "have reason to do." If maternal practical authority provides backing for an imperative that she directs at her child, then the imperative actually establishes what the child has reason to do. Morality, thus understood, is always about reasons for action.

Kelsen submits that the normativity constructed by the Pure Theory for legal norms is radically different from morality. A legal norm links a legal condition and a consequence in a manner analogous to how laws of nature link cause and effect. The requisite link, however, is not causation but "peripheral imputation." If the legal condition is met, the legal consequence ought to – or may – follow. The normative consequence follows with the same relentless necessity with which that happens which happens according to the laws of nature.

In Kelsen's view, such a "nomological"[34] understanding is all there is to the normativity of law. Or, put differently, the nomological construction of

[31] This is the translation chosen by Paulson and Paulson following Eugenio Bulygin. See Kelsen, note 5 at 23 footnote 20.

[32] See, for example, Hans Kelsen, *Pure Theory of Law* (2d ed., trans. M. Knight, Berkeley: University of California Press, 1967) at 71. This is, however, the usage that has become widespread in the literature. On this, see Duarte d'Almeida, note 18 at 175–176.

[33] Kelsen, note 5 at 23.

[34] See Paulson, note 17 at 106–109.

legal norms renders the detached view in objective form, that is, in a manner that can be read off the legal norms themselves. The legal scientist detaches him- or herself from morality by avoiding the language of duty and blame. This can be observed, indeed, for how those people talk about the law whom Raz believes to adopt the detached perspective, namely "a solicitor advising a client or a writer discussing a point of law."[35] They elaborate on the law by exploring the normative significance and consequences of certain acts without adding expressions of moral approbation or disapprobation. Indeed, doing so might be regarded as unprofessional. For example, when I revealed to my accountant my plan to import a German sports car into Austria via St. Petersburg in an effort to avoid Austrian taxes, he replied dryly that if I did that I would bring criminal responsibility upon myself. He did not imply that I had better be ashamed of myself. He did not speak about how the officials of the tax authorities would view the matter. He simply stated what the legal consequence of my conduct would be.

A statement of legal consequences, even if not a prediction of what the courts would do in fact, is detached from passing moral judgment on the matter. The detachment is possible by virtue of casting the legal materials in the form of Kelsen's reconstructed legal norm. As is well known, stating reasons for action is, according to Kelsen, the preserve of the "secondary legal norm," which is formulated from the perspective of addressees.[36]

It is for this same reason of drawing the line vis-à-vis morality that Kelsen observes that the law "cannot be broken." All talk of a "breach" of law moralizes its normativity. It suggests that doing what triggers legal sanctions is somehow bad. Against such an overdetermination of legal with moral meaning, Kelsen contends:[37]

> The unlawful act does not represent an interruption in the existence of the law (as the traditional view would have one believe), but exactly the opposite: it is by way of the unlawful act that the existence of the law proves itself, for this existence consists in the validity of the law, that is, in the "ought" of the coercive act as the consequence of the unlawful act.

35 Raz, *Concept of a Legal System*, note 15 at 236.

36 See Kelsen, note 5 at 29–30. While the primary legal norm is addressed to the organ of the state obligated or empowered to impose a sanction, the secondary norm is derivative of the primary norm and reflects the awareness on the part of the addressee that a sanction must be or may be imposed. The norm that "murder is to be punished with life-time imprisonment" is thereby rendered as "I should not murder."

37 Kelsen, note 5 at 28.

From this follows that the more deviant behavior one observes, the more law springs up from legal norms requiring the imposition of sanctions (a point to which we shall return later).[38]

Admittedly, Kelsen's nomothetical reading of the normativity of law presents the latter as a rather mechanical and lifeless contrivance. Without being driven by any reasonable purpose and without paying heed to whether what it reacts to is a social ill or not, the law responds to the condition of the legal norm by saying that a legal consequence ought to follow.

THE GREAT UNDOING

Arguably, this view of the law offends common sense,[39] not least because we take it for granted that the law is a purpose-driven endeavor and capable of being used as an instrument of rational social control. If this is indeed common sense, it proves that common sense does not as radically distinguish between law and morality as Kelsen suggested. Not by accident, Kelsen used to be highly suspicious of common sense, in particular if it translates into some purportedly sociological perspective on the law.[40]

Kelsen's project was about stripping the law of its moralistic or ideological veneer. Somewhat tragically, this achievement of modern positivism was undone in the course of its appropriation by analytical jurisprudence. Quite remarkably, this precipitated the assimilation of Kelsen's legal positivism to exactly the mind-set that Kelsen was up against in his Pure Theory.

Hart took the first step and Raz was to follow suit. Without anything further, Hart reintroduced the action-guiding significance of legal norms by suggesting that this was what was "ordinarily thought of as the content of law."[41] Are the laws not designed to guide the conduct of ordinary citizens?[42] The law speaks. Folks understand and comply. They know what it means to "breach" the law.[43]

[38] Kelsen's "objectivistic" view may be difficult to fathom for those unfamiliar with certain peculiarities of the civil law tradition in which it is quite common to assimilate the generation and transformation of legal claims to natural events. For example, it is assumed that within "the logical second" that a chattel is damaged, the claim to compensation comes into existence.

[39] This was famously conceded by James W. Harris, "Kelsen's Pallid Normativity" (1996) 9 *Ratio Iuris* 95–115.

[40] See Hans Kelsen, *Der soziologische und der juristische Staatsbegriff: Kritische Untersuchung des Verhältnisses von Staat und Recht* (2d ed., Tübingen: J.C.B. Mohr, 1928).

[41] Hart, note 1 at 36.

[42] See ibid. at 36. It does not come as a surprise that this form of legal positivism always has a hard time answering the question why it distinguishes between law and morality and that the distinction is notoriously difficult to draw.

[43] See ibid. at 39.

The "puzzled man" looks into the law in order to find out what he ought to do.[44]

As a view of the legal world, it can hardly get more straightforward and nicer. This is the lure of the great undoing. The problem that it creates at its tail end is, of course, that it has to wrestle with reintroducing the distinction between moral and legal normativity. This explains why from the fog of the analytical appropriation of modern legal positivism must emerge the legal man, who is no other than the avatar of Kelsen's *Rechtssatz*.

What is sacrificed here is modern legal positivism's anti-ideological stance. Hart gives us a morally idealized perspective on the law. The law is designed to guide the conduct of ordinary citizens.[45] Isn't that what the law is supposed to do? In the case of criminal law, Hart reproofs Kelsen for obscuring the "specific character of law as a means of social control." He claims that Kelsen is mistaken in viewing substantive criminal law as directed not at citizens but at officials only.[46] He appeals to common sense to expose as misguided Kelsen's views because were Kelsen correct, the intensional difference between fines and taxes could not be sustained.[47]

But all that Hart's critical observations demonstrate is that Hart is not faithful to the spirit of modern legal positivism.[48] First, it does not occur to him that he reintroduces a view of legal norms according to which these are, at any rate from the internal perspective and as applied to cases, full-blown reasons for action. Second, the critique does not consider whether the *Verfremdung* inherent in Kelsen's *Rechtssatz* is not of great heuristic value. Kelsen's *Rechtssatz* allows us to drop various fictions dear to those believing in the value of law and to open our eyes to the widespread social fact that, traffic regulations aside, ordinary people do not obtain direct guidance from legal rules. Their legal knowledge is mostly indirect and gathered secondhand. It is obtained by following the mass media or seeking advice from legal experts. Ordinary people are indeed guided by what Kelsen calls "secondary norms." What Hart presents us with, by contrast, are fairly idyllic idealizations of the legal system. It is quite audacious, in fact, to suggest that criminal codes are not indirectly absorbed by ordinary people on the basis of news concerning how the law is applied in fact. It amounts to a sugarcoating of social realities if a legal theory deflects attention from the fact that criminal norms confer powers to impose sanctions and that someone actually chooses to impose

44 See ibid. at 40. 45 See ibid. at 36. 46 See ibid. at 39.

47 See ibid.; see also at 720. H.L.A. Hart, "Kelsen Visited" (1963) 10 *UCLA Law Review* 709–728 at 720.

48 For a first elaboration of this point, see Alexander Somek, "The Spirit of Legal Positivism" (2011b) 12 *German Law Journal* 729–756.

these. Kelsen's normative take on criminal law invites attention to the fact that the criminal justice system would not work if it were not for people who do not at all mind being in the business of punishing and controlling others. Some get a kick out of kicking others around.[49] If that were not the case, the law would lack efficacy. That taxes are punitive and penalties excise taxes on behavior strongly suggests that the valuable purpose of a legal norm lies in the eye of the beholder. Libertarians and some conservatives do indeed believe that taxes penalize individual initiative. At the very least, Kelsen's theory of norms invites attention to these phenomena, whereas Hart is attuned to hiding them behind a curtain of commonsensical naïveté.

Admittedly, the Hartian persuasion would press Kelsen hard on the point of what the *Rechtssatz*'s conditional ought is about if it is not, at the end of the day, about reasons for action. What else might there be normative? An answer to this question can be found in how Kelsen may have replied to Hart's characterization of his view that the legal norm is "directed"[50] at the legal official. From the point of view of the Pure Theory, "directed" can only mean "p → Oq" (if it is the case that p then the sanction q ought to follow). The normative significance of the obligation to impose a sanction is spelled out in an obligation to impose a sanction if the sanction is not imposed ("p → Oq & -q → Or"). Backup sanctions come to an end within finite legal systems. What remains is a legal power to impose a sanction. This reveals that when legal norms – *Rechtssätze* – come to an end, any sanction is legally based upon a lack of immunity. This implies, as Kelsen must have realized later,[51] a gestalt switch. From the perspective of the ultimate power to impose sanctions (and a permission to enforce them), all other obligations to impose sanctions can also be rendered as powers to impose sanctions that are backed up by powers of the same type. One feels obliged to exercise the power if one has to reckon that one's superior will likely exercise the requisite power of control. At the end of the day, behaving legally means occupying the space where one is immune from sanctions because no one has a legal power to impose them. This is a view of normativity that reflects quite accurately how "subjects" approach the legal system. It is, more importantly, also a view that does not involve

49 The point here is not to suggest that the legal force is either equivalent or superior to nonlegal force. This question is of relevance to a different debate. See Hamish Stewart, "Incentives and the Rule of Law: An Intervention in the Kramer/Simmonds Debate" (2006) 51 *American Journal of Jurisprudence* 149–164.

50 See Hart, note 1 at 36.

51 See Kelsen, note 32 at 118. On Kelsen's turn to empowerment, see Paulson, note 17 at 83–85.

reasons for action. Legal powers create opportunities for the exercise of power and control,[52] but they do not tell anyone what to do.

If the Hartian persuasion were to find this resolution of the normativity riddle unconvincing, one could still offer a reserve explanation. Kelsen's *Rechtssatz* is a person-neutral and incomplete reason for action. It is person-neutral in that it does not depend on who the person is who has it; it is incomplete because it has to be combined with an extralegal reason to give rise to a complete reason for action. If dispensing legal expertise is paying my bills and if I happen to be a judge, I have reason to impose the sanction.

At any rate, in this vein modern legal positivism develops a perspective of the legal system by avoiding all unnecessary idealizations. Alas, this commitment to sobriety did not become part of analytical jurisprudence.

THE REVENANT OF THE MORAL MAN

We have spent much time on how analytical jurisprudence sidelined one of Kelsen's most important insights. Most remarkably, it thereby ended up endorsing rather idyllic views concerning the social functions of law. What we now have to turn to is the abstractness inherent in the idea of detached legal statements. Once more, it will be seen that doubtful sociological intuitions translate into a rather doubtful understanding of law's normativity.

Prefacing one's statements with "legally speaking" is a social act.[53] It determines the statement's illocutionary force ("I do not mean to say that you are a crook, but . . . "). Yet, its social significance is even greater. Shared knowledge of the law is necessary for legal systems to come into existence. This is one of Hart's most important insights. Legal systems are possible if valid laws are *de facto* generally identified.

Detached statements suffice to sustain the normative quality of law. Even if everyone prefaces statements with "legally speaking," the existence of the legal system is possible. The rule of recognition can be used as though it were accepted as a common standard as long as everyone tacitly argued from the

[52] See Shapiro, note 22 at 64.

[53] We have to discuss this point because Hartian legal positivists may well grant that nomothetical normativity renders the detached attitude in objective form. They may, however, still insist that to be used consistently, it also has to be used subjectively, that is, with an attitude of detachment. Instead of saying to the defendant "you can now be sanctioned," the detached statement needs to say "Legally, you can now be sanctioned." It is open to debate, of course, whether such a duplication of detachment is really necessary. But why should we not concede this point?

perspective of this rule.[54] Even if nobody participating in the legal system has a view, but only adopts a view, with regard to the validity of rules, the legal system does not suffer any harm.[55] Legal systems can exist as long as most are concurrently playing at being the legal man. As George Herbert Mead memorably put it, playing is "the simplest form of being another to one's self."[56]

The question must be, however, how one can know how to play the game without being assured of who of the participants actually is a detached embodiment of the legal man. Raz's idea suggests that the legal man follows the law with moral fervor.[57] The legal man is the revenant of the moral man. But this poses two problems. The first is that the legal man is supposedly a legal positivist and, consequently, draws a sharp line between law and morality.[58] Would such a line-drawing exercise make much sense if the law guided him morally? There is an inner resolve underpinning moral belief that may not be appropriately reflected in a more detached cognizance of legal rules. This blends into the second problem. Apparently, for the purpose of impersonating the legal man one would have to know what it means to be guided by rules morally. There is conceivably more than one answer to this question. Is the conclusion to be drawn that a man of the type of the legal man observes with moral zeal how legal rules are observed by others? But how is the moral zeal to play out? Does it have to manifest itself in legalistic pedantry?[59] This is far from obvious. More plausibly, the legal man would behave more like Dworkin's Hercules. He would perceive the law as embedded in positive community morality of which he has to provide the best account that he can possibly give.[60] Consequently, the line between law and morality would no longer be clear. This is the major problem posed by viewing the legal man as the moral man. Assuming his point of view does not solve the problem of what it takes to

54 It may be objected that the observations in the previous paragraphs read too much into acceptance. Acceptance merely means "acceptance as the relevant standard" and not "acceptance as good." But the point is precisely that "acceptance as a standard" is what is simulated by participants in the system. They behave as though they accepted the rule of recognition as a standard for the identification of valid laws.

55 Never mind that Raz stated that legal systems necessarily claim to have authority. Raz believed that to be the case because the law confronts us with normative language. But if this legal language is drawn out in detached statements, the law actually does not necessarily claim to have authority over us.

56 George Herbert Mead, *Mind, Self, & Society from the Standpoint of a Social Behaviorist* (Chicago: Chicago University Press, 1934) at 151.

57 See Raz, note 26 at 246. 58 See Harris, note 39 at 112–113.

59 See Judith Shklar, *Legalism: Law, Morals, and Political Trials* (Cambridge, Mass.: Harvard University Press, 1986).

60 See Ronald Dworkin, *Taking Rights Seriously* (2d ed., Cambridge, Mass.: Harvard University Press, 1978) at 127.

approach a set of standards with a moral attitude, even if only for the sake of making a legal argument. Rather, this is very much open to interpretive debate.

The major problem is, however, that the legal man as the moral man undermines the distinction between law and morality. It requires turning knowing the law into a moral matter. At the very least, it either revokes the distinction between legal and moral obligation or leads to a performative contradiction within the counterfactual point of view ("assuming that the law is valid . . . "). If the task is to take the perspective of the legal man as the moral man, one cannot do so by detaching oneself from this viewpoint. But would not it be immoral to simulate belief in law that ought to be believed in morally?

For this reason, construing detachment qua emulation of morally serious engagement with the law turns out to be untenable. Detachment has to be accounted for in a different way.

Apparently, legal statements have to embrace two forms of detachment. The first concerns the authority of law. The law is known only as if it provided reasons for action. The second concerns elaborate views of what it takes to know the law in a morally committed way. The statements also have to detach themselves from drawing out what that morally committed way of knowing the law really amounts to which they purport to emulate. Rather, the statements have to be based on an idea that is congenial to the reductionist thrust of legal positivism. It suggests that there has to be, as a social fact, something like the viewpoint of the law without which the legal system could have never come into existence. This viewpoint must be built into the law as a social phenomenon and, hence, conventionally given. Simply put, the legal man needs to be conceived of as a social construct that is of no one's making in particular.

PLAYACTING

Prefacing remarks with "legally speaking" has a signaling function. It says, "Let it be known that I am now speaking from the perspective of the legal man." By virtue of this signaling function, knowing the law is a variety of playacting. The participants in legal discourse do not carry out the real act – knowing the law – but demonstrate the performance of an action – the action of knowing the law.[61] Arguably, that is what is going on within the detached perspective. Knowing is put on a stage.

61 On playacting as the representation of an action, see Christoph Menke, *Die Gegenwart der Tragödie: Versuch über Urteil und Spiel* (Frankfurt aM: 2005) at 123.

The enactments of knowing or recognizing the law cannot take their cue from some real legal man providing a script. As we have seen, interpretative elaborations of morality are not only likely to be divisive but also irrelevant as they are giving rise to a performative contradiction in their counterfactual use. Consequently, all that participants in the legal system can do is to "play along" from the detached perspective. The legal man is normatively real only if enacted. It must seem, therefore, as though we could find out how to perform acts of legal knowing by attending to the conventions of saying and claiming "legally speaking, it is the case that . . . "[62]

Playing along is, however, intellectually enslaving, in particular when conventions substantively claim to be based upon something that is itself not conventional.[63] For example, it may be widely assumed that from the perspective of the legal man, the constitution means what the framers of the constitution intended it to mean. There are grave doubts over whether this idea is correct.[64] Nonetheless, conventional standards may well be observed with which members of the judiciary attempt to make sense of their misguided quest for a conventional understanding. If the legal knowers whose knowledge accounts for the efficacious internal perspective of a constitutional system

62 Knowing the law, thus understood, is essentially theatrical. It puts action on the stage that does not happen offstage. The counterfactual nature of knowing the law is thereby doubled. Not only is it counterfactually assumed that the law reveals authority from the perspective of the legal man, it is also counterfactually assumed that there are standards practiced that give each and every participant clues as to what it takes to impersonate that man. For the purpose of knowing the law, we assume that "this" is how you present a legal argument because all that matters from the internal perspective is to signal that you are assuming the perspective of the legal man. Both counterfactuals increase the distance from "distance toward the authority of law" to "distance toward what is supposedly conventionally given."

63 One may wonder how that can be the case. Conventions are arbitrary in the sense that any other could do the same job of providing a common standard for the sake of coordination or of providing a rule for a game. Nonetheless, rules can function as conventions in the sense of establishing a common standard even if people falsely believe the standard to be substantively correct. A rule that claims to have not merely a conventional foundation is nonetheless practiced as a convention if people disregard the alleged foundation and follow the rule for the reason of having some common standard. On the related distinction between agreements by convention and agreements in conviction, see Ronald Dworkin, *Law's Empire* (Cambridge, Mass.: Harvard University Press, 1986) at 136, 145.

64 See Ronald Dworkin, *A Matter of Principle* (Cambridge, Mass.: Harvard University Press: 1985) at 34–57. Today's widely established alternative – public-meaning originalism – is indefensible, too, for it rests upon a single-mindedly conventional understanding of language. For an elementary exposition, see Lawrence B. Solum, "We Are All Originalists Now." In Robert W. Bennett & Lawrence B. Solum, *Constitutional Originalism: A Debate* (Ithaca: Cornell University Press, 2011) 1–64 at 43. Against the view that all linguistic meaning is conventional, see Donald Davidson, *Inquiries into Truth and Interpretation* (Oxford: Oxford University Press, 1982) at 265–280.

collectively practice this false belief, it will give rise to a set of conventions for claiming what the constitution means (*e.g.*, study the common law of the eighteenth century). Consequently, whoever wants to speak legally has to enact common nonsense as if it were true. Indeed, since the conventional standards for elaborating the constitution are merely conventions if they *falsely* purport to be substantively right, no player can rely on his or her own judgment about what the standards really require,[65] for this would disable him or her from playing the game. All players have to look to the left and to the right and try to do as all others do.

This is an arduous task. Conventions are notoriously elusive. If you are supposed to follow conventions that are not clearly stated, you need to tell yourself: "I'll do as all others do." Once you have risen to the top of the pack, you may more self-confidently claim: "This is what we do." These two statements exhaust the pragmatics of conventions. You are on top of a convention if you are playing along. Therefore, even after you have become a champion among those playing the legal man and are considered to be "one of the boys,"[66] your boyhood would take serious damage if you repeatedly did not garner the support of your fellow boys. Lack of convergent behavior is embarrassing ("What? You looked into the private diaries of members of the constitutional convention? You are crazy!"). Not by accident, ducking is most in request among those playing by conventional rules.

Therefore, all internal statements are infused with an external component. As a newbie you want to make sure that you do as all others do to pass as a member of the in-group. Even once you have advanced to being one of the boys, you still have to be wary of being dismissed as a senile old fart. Hence, even if you speak legally from the internal perspective and say, artfully, "It is the law that . . .," you cannot but do so with a certain anxiety that your fellow boys may disagree because in their view you are not speaking from the viewpoint of the legal man. And since the business of dispensing detached statements is likely in one way or another essential to driving your Jaguar, what must matter the most to you is your standing as a legal expert. If a large part of the measure of recognition consists of your proven ability to predict or to

65 An elaboration of a standard involves what Dworkin called the "interpretive attitude." This attitude attributes to the standard a certain point and supposes that the practice of the standard is sensitive to how that point is best drawn out. See Dworkin, note 63 at 47.

66 The author begs forgiveness for using an American English idiom that captures in-group bias most adequately on the ground of its rather overt sexist connotation. Being male and belonging to a group with influence and power have long gone together in our civilization, also in the context of the legal profession and of professional training. See Lani Guinier, Michelle Fine, & Jane Balin, *Becoming Gentlemen: Women, Law Schools and Institutional Change* (Boston: Beacon Press, 1997).

influence court decisions, you have to be able to design "passing theories"[67] and to divine what courts will take to be the view of the legal man. The internal perspective invariably becomes invaded by the external. Instead of stating what the law is from the law's very own perspective, the detached statements have to be guesses of the beliefs that others harbor on legal issues. At any rate, those who have to be successful before or within a court (as a member of a panel or a bench) have to be concerned about inviting convergent behavior on the part of those who have the power to say what this law is.

This invasion of the internal perspective by the external must never amount to a total takeover. Otherwise the legal man would be replaced with the bad man.[68] But it explains why legal statements are strangely undecided with regard to their illocutionary role: "If you import your German sports car to Austria via St. Petersburg you'll go to jail." Would this happen? Should it happen? The statement does not clarify whether it means either or both. Actually, in not saying what it does not say, it steps outside of itself[69] and tells you, with a cunning smile, "This is what we do."

In spite of saying what the law is from the viewpoint of the legal man, the legal statement blinks. It celebrates a symbolic victory over both the intellectual embarrassment inherent in following conventional standards for speaking like the legal man and the reduction of the normativity of such standards to making out patterns of behavior.

SYMBOLIC VICTORIES

Elusiveness of its own meaning is a consistent feature of the concept of irony.[70] What irony denotes cannot be pinned down. Nevertheless, for the limited

67 Such "theories" are developed by speakers from situation to situation to account for the meaning of the utterances of others. See Donald Davidson, "A Nice Derangement of Epitaphs." In *Truth and Interpretation* (ed. E. LePore, Oxford: Blackwell, 1986) 433–446 at 442.

68 The "bad man" is the person merely interested in predicting the behavior of public officials. It was famously introduced into legal theory by Oliver Wendell Holmes. See his "The Path of the Law."

69 The formulation alludes to Friedrich Schlegel's famous characterization of irony as "parabasis." The latter designates an interception of the flow of events on a stage that is followed by mocking commentary. See Friedrich Schlegel, Philosophische Lehrjahre I (1796–1806), *Kritische Werkausgabe*, vol. 18 (ed. E. Behler, Munich: Verlag Ferdinand Schönigh, 1963), II 668, at 85. On Schlegel, see Ernst Behler, *Klassische Ironie – Romantische Ironie – Tragische Ironie: Zum Ursprung dieser Begriffe* (Darmstadt: Wissenschaftliche Buchgesellschaft, 1972) at 80.

70 See Paul de Man, *Aesthetic Ideology* (ed. A. Warminski, Minneapolis: University of Minnesota Press, 1996) at 164–165.

purpose of exploring the significance of detached legal statements, it is possible to make some progress with a few elementary ideas.

According to the classical understanding, an ironic statement insinuates the opposite of what it appears to say.[71] More accurately stated, the statement is ironic by means of suggesting this reversal. Irony is performed; it is not denoted by some symbol. Only sentences trying to capture irony attempt to denote it.

Whether irony is performatively successful depends on the context. The statement "Tony Blair was a great social democrat" is likely to be considered ironic if it is uttered by an old lefty among fellow old-fashioned lefties. The statement suggests, in such a context, that Blair was a defector in disguise. Conceivably, if the same statement were made among Tories, the greatness of Blair would insinuate "not great for them, but great for us."

Of course, irony does not always work in this way. Proclaiming in front of Tories that David Cameron is a man who cares may be understood as praise or as mockery. In this case, the irony lies in leaving open whether or not the statement is ironic. Nonetheless, one thing is accomplished by the speaker. The irony of irony allows her to rise, symbolically, above a slightly bewildered crowd.

In both examples, irony involves the gesture of rising above someone or something else.[72] By stating that Tony Blair was a great social democrat, one attempts to expose elite consensus as a sham. One chooses irony to reveal the pervasiveness and oppressiveness of this consensus. Actually, the literalness of the statement indicates that critique can be safely voiced only in the guise of conformity. The perception of oppressiveness becomes thereby enhanced. Conformity is used as a signal of distance. Through affirmation, irony disaffirms the affirming. It performs the disaffirmation in the act of affirming, thereby divesting any affirmation of its most straightforward means of symbolic expression. Irony makes it henceforth impossible to state simply that Blair was a great social democrat. Everyone would have a good laugh about this.

"How are you?"

"I am great!"

That it does not rest on arguments is irony's strength. It allows one to rise above falsehood while showing that one also needs to take cover. This is also true of saying that Cameron is a caring man. Ironizing the irony, one remains at a safe distance from one's symbolic victory over a befuddled crowd. One

71 See, for example, on Quintillian, Claire Colebrook, *Irony* (Abingdon: Routledge, 2004) at 1–3.

72 Rising above from below explains why irony is symbolically empowering only if it is intended. Involuntary irony is an embarrassment. This is true, in particular, of tragic irony or the irony of fate. If what you have planned is undone by forces that are beyond your control, then fate has put you into your place.

does not directly invite retribution. The disaffirmation of the affirming becomes disaffirmed without restoring a determinate meaning. What could have ever been serious is transcended into play. It is no longer clear whether one has said anything at all. The meaning shifts back and forth like waves of water lightly gusted by wind.[73] Nevertheless, the lack of voice – the inability to say something in the face of potential repercussions – is successfully put on a stage in conjunction with delivering the message that purportedly cannot be delivered.

Both instances show that irony is, at least in certain cases, part of the deportment of the weak. Not by accident, irony is deeply woven into the cultures of societies with lingering authoritarian or totalitarian legacies. Irony is what the weak understand by strength. It is all they have at their disposal.

TAMING THE INTERNAL PERSPECTIVE

Detached legal statements are made with the implicit awareness that it must be left open whether there exists even a conventional normative standard for speaking from the perspective of the legal man. But this must not be said, for this would establish the impossibility of legal statements. Consequently, no participant can escape the predicament of having to look to the left and the right to obtain cues as to what it takes to speak legally.

The only means available for rising above this form of practice is irony. It allows for symbolic victories in spite of pervasive disempowerment. In contrast to irony qua figure of speech, legal knowledge is ironic in virtue of various outlets for real parabasis,[74] that is, the disparagement of front-stage behavior through backstage commentary[75] that exposes the conventional existence of the viewpoint of the legal man as a counterfactual myth. Disaffirming commentary of this type concedes the relevance of the internal point of view while seeing it permanently displaced ("Your argument is entirely correct, but I do not think that anyone will buy it") and ranges from voicing frustration from below ("These judges are all bonkers") to the almost cynical juridical elaboration of law from above in spite of a patent lack of good

[73] See, on this image, Hans-Georg Gadamer, *Die Aktualität des Schönen: Kunst als Spiel, Symbol und Fest* (Stuttgart: Philipp Reclam Jun., 1979) at 29.

[74] See earlier note 69.

[75] On the distinction of the formal and the informal precinct of legal knowledge, see Pierre Schlag, "Normativity and the Politics of Form" (1991) 139 *University of Pennsylvania Law Review* 801–932 at 882. On the distinction between the "front" and the "back" of public role performance, see Erving Goffman, *The Presentation of Self in Everyday Life* (New York: Anchor Book, 1959) at 22–23.

reasons.[76] Everywhere what might be the viewpoint of the legal man becomes invaded by the external perspective on what it takes to know the law successfully. "Speaking legally" always requires speaking as others would (courts, boys, peers, professors). But this must not be said because of the pervasive expectation to sustain the (detached) normative mood and integrity of legal statements. Even the abstention from clarifying the merely predictive or normative import of legal statements is an ironic rebellion against the noble lie that conventions govern the outlook of the legal man.

"May I import my car via St. Petersburg?"
"You'll end up in jail."

This is how legal statements achieve a symbolic victory over the contextual constraints on their production. This is how they disaffirm the doubtful affirmation of the conventional viewpoint of the legal man.

Such a disaffirmation is amazingly consistent with viewing the law legally (and not morally). Legality means that conformity to law does not require adopting the law as an exclusionary reason for action.[77] The law permits what Hart would call mere obedience.[78] Surprisingly, this attitude of mere obedience is carried over into how the law is known. If the normative standards for knowing the law remain unexplored, their normative force is reshuffled with irony, for the latter sustains normativity in a form in which it no longer guides. The critical aspect of rules that transcends actual practice and allows for the identification of mistakes is then manifest in an ironic revocation of the authority of practice. But a mere ironic revocation does not change anything. It does not guide practice. It merely signals detachment and thereby, ironically, delivers what the detached attitude is supposed to accomplish.

This divestment of normativity's edge can be properly understood by examining what its proper investment is supposed to accomplish. Supposedly, the normative claims of law are revealed from the internal perspective of the legal man. The normative nature of speaking internally is manifest in the critical reflexive attitude with which norms are used to assess or to criticize behavior. Since the internal perspective is, as we have seen, practiced, the adequate standards for speaking legally must emerge for participants on the basis of "forming an explanatory hypothesis" about the rules governing practice.[79]

76 The "heroic" European Court of Justice is an example for that. See Alexander Somek, "The Emancipation of Legal Dissonance." In *Europe: The New Legal Realism* (ed. H. Koch et al., Copenhagen: DJØF Publishing, 2010) 670–713.

77 Or, as Raz, note 14 at 144, puts it: "The exclusionary reasons do not, of course, exclude relying on reasons for behaving in the same way as the directive requires."

78 See Hart, note 1 at 89.

79 Charles S. Peirce, *Lectures on Pragmatism* (ed. E. Walther, Hamburg: Meiner, 1973) at 226.

Once such a hypothesis has been formulated, instances of legal arguments can be understood to be cases of professional conventions. For if anything is internal about the internal perspective – in this case, applied to itself – then it is this synthesizing of what one takes to be instances of rule following into more explicit rules. Owing to such a synthesis, instances of behavior can be recast as cases of rules. In Dworkinian parlance, such a synthesis requires an "interpretation" of the requisite practice.[80] One needs to suppose that the practice has a point and is responsive to its elaboration. Plainly speaking, the critical reflexive attitude is manifest in this interpretive attitude.[81]

Any interpretive elaboration of normative standards requires moving beyond viewing them as concatenations of convergent behavior. Viewing x as a case of y ("This is the type of originalist argument that is accepted here") presupposes some explanation of the point of a convention.[82] A rule is only properly conceived by viewing it from the point of that purpose that explains why it has to be a normative standard. Following a rule from an internal perspective – even if this affects the conventions of the internal perspective itself – is possible only by moving beyond viewing the rule as a sequence of applications on which folks converge. If only convergence itself counted, it would never become clear on what it is that the folks converge. The critical standard for the identification of cases of a rule lies beyond observations or convergent behavior, since the construction of rules from a standpoint that is above and beyond convergence is a creative process.

Irony, by contrast, involves symbolic detachment from practice *tout court*. It does not infuse practice with a view of its point to identify mistakes. It is thoroughly negativistic. Since this negativism does not identify a point, it merely seeks to expose what is non-conventional at the bottom of allegedly conventional conduct.

CONCLUSION

Legal positivists have claimed that statements of law retain normative import while detaching themselves from the law's claim to authority. Such statements are made by assuming that the law provides reason for action.

80 In this case, one would arrive at an "abstract interpretation of legal practice as a whole." Dworkin, note 63 at 139.

81 See Dworkin, note 63 at 47.

82 In Dworkinian parlance, this means that the meaning of conventionalism needs to be drawn out in terms of a "soft" conventionalism that transcends the purview of conventionalism altogether. See ibid. at 124, 127.

This view of detached legal statements is oblivious to how Kelsen attempted to construe the normativity of law without assimilating it to the reason-giving force of morality. The key elements of this project were the "reconstructed legal norm" and the recalibration of legal systems from the vantage point of legal powers.

Kelsen himself, however, ignored the fact that legal systems are *de facto* constituted and sustained from a normative point of view. In this context, the theory of detached legal statements retains great heuristic value, for it is entirely plausible to assume that legal systems can exist even if everyone participating in their reproduction is making statements of this type. All that is required are conventions governing their use.

Raz's view is difficult to reconcile with this fact and generally scarcely compatible with legal positivism. If detached legal statements indeed rested upon the emulation of morality, they would explode the conventionalist picture, for everyone who intends to speak legally would have to arrive at some convincing conception of what it takes to observe the law, even if only hypothetically, from a moral point of view. Knowing the law would have to embrace a theory of morality, properly understood. It is questionable if it remains possible, under these auspices, to sustain the distinction between law and morality.

Hence, detached legal statements have to detach themselves not only from the authority of law but also from any interpretive account of what it takes to know the law in a committed way (*e.g.*, in a manner that makes it look particularly appealing in light of the principle of treating like cases alike). Rather, the standards governing the knowledge of the legal man have to be conventional. They have to be inferred from the common practice of enacting the legal man.

Yet, if one follows through with conventionalism, one arrives at an invasion of the internal standpoint with an external perspective. The latter is attentive and deferential to what it takes to pass in the eyes of concrete others as a capable legal expert. Consequently, detached legal statements vacillate between a normative and a descriptive mode. They claim to know what the law is by suggesting what relevant concrete others would agree on *de facto*.

Such wavering could only be avoided if participants arrived at normative conceptions of the legal man and invoked them to guide practice. The relevant interpretations would conceivably draw out the normativity inherent in speaking as a legal man. But interpretative accounts of what it takes to speak legally in the proper way are risky. They invite debate and dissent, which can be harmful to one's standing. It must appear to be safer to muddle through by developing educated guesses as to how relevant members of the peer group might react to one's own legal statements. Since convergence is then all that matters, the critical and interpretive element of normativity can be sustained only in a form in which it no longer feeds back into practice. The manner of rising above instances of convergent behavior shifts from confronting the practice with its ideal point to disaffirming the affirmation of its correctness through irony. In contrast to confronting the soundness of originalist arguments in constitutional interpretation head on, one succumbs to using them front stage and to belabor their idiocy backstage. The practice-transcending element of normativity is preserved in gestures that symbolically disaffirm that which socially affirms itself owing to each individual participant's lack of power to change it.

Thus understood, detached statements not only abstain from communicating the bindingness of law, they also do not communicate that they are genuine knowledge of the law. They speak about law while leaving open whether there is valid law and whether it is actually known. If these attitudes are actually manifested in the viewpoint of the legal system, socially understood, then the law exists by thoroughly detaching itself from itself. It becomes the embodiment of irony, that is, of the symbolic disaffirmation of its own existence. Owing to its commitment to moral sobriety, modern legal positivism should have every reason to embrace this conclusion.

3

Legal Science and the Common Law

The following analysis is an attempt to reinvigorate a tradition of legal thinking that is closely associated with the philosophy of German idealism. While a great deal of inspiration comes from the historical school of jurisprudence – particularly from the theory of Georg Friedrich Puchta – it also draws on ideas of the school's sworn opponent, Hegel, and on the work of the sworn opponent's major philosophical opponent, Schelling. What is more, in the attempt to make itself understood to twentieth-century legal positivists, the analysis that follows relies heavily on conceptions of the Viennese school (Kelsen, Merkl, Sander). To be reasonably accessible to the Anglophone world, the texts occasionally hint at the work of H.L.A. Hart.

INTRODUCTION

Constructivism

The first chapter attempted to explain that any grasp of the content of legal sources presupposes a view of how sources ought to be construed in light of what one takes to be knowing the law. For example, if an interpretation is expected to reconstruct the original understanding, such an expectation presupposes some view with regard to the study of which document is relevant to accomplishing this task. This view cannot be read off the sources themselves even if the sources said what the relevant materials were, for such a pronouncement would itself require construction in light of an interpretive agenda.

Legal positivism tried to sustain objectivity by supposing that the production of new law must be based on a correct account of existing law. But there is an alternative view of objectivity. It says that law is objectively known if the relevant knowledge has legal authority. Under this condition, knowledge of the law is objective inasmuch as it lays down the law (and therefore "is" law). Knowledge is a source of law. An application of law synthesizes views of sources with views of facts into new law.[1] It is knowledge *of* the law *by* the law, that is, of a prior source by a later source.

The established view of sources highlights their factual component: someone "said that ...," "ordered that ...," or "ordained that ..." The narrowness of this view makes us forget that sources are devices that permit us to know what the law is. Not least Hobbes's view of the sovereign indicates that the lawmaker is authorized to lay down the law, for this is how we become able to arrive at a common view of what is right or wrong.[2]

Before the next chapter will try to demonstrate how legal knowledge can take into account, and reflect, the legal relation – and thereby convert the bitter irony of conventional legal reasoning into something more serene – this chapter is interested in exploring the dynamic of sources. This dynamic presupposes only one objective, namely, the aim of the law to make itself known. It must be granted, however, that the title of this chapter uniquely and curiously combines two of the most tedious topics of legal theory. Hence, a brief explanation is in order.

Sources

Sources demarcate the Maginot line of hard-nosed "exclusive" positivists. They defend, proudly and publicly, a "sources thesis" according to which only that can be law which is caused by social facts that are amenable to description in value-neutral terms.[3] It is this type of claim that triggers, also as a social fact, skepticism and, worse still, yawning among more sophisticated legal theorists who know very well that knowing the law involves more than ascertaining normatively significant social facts. That is, it requires obtaining "a sense of appropriateness developed in the profession and the public over time."[4]

[1] For a similar perspective, see Christoph Kletzer, "Absolute Legal Positivism" (2013) 43 *Netherlands Journal of Legal Philosophy* 87–99.

[2] See Thomas Hobbes, *Leviathan* (ed. I. Shapiro, New Haven: Yale University Press, 2010) chap. 37 at pp. 266–267.

[3] See Joseph Raz, *Ethics in the Public Domain: Essays in the Morality of Law and Politics* (2d ed., Oxford: Clarendon Press) at 211.

[4] See Ronald Dworkin, *Taking Rights Seriously* (2d ed., Cambridge, Mass.: Harvard University Press, 1978) at 40.

Legal Science

The other topic, legal science, does not fare any better. Indeed, ever since the realist revolution the subject has become the laughing stock of Anglo-American jurisprudence.[5] It is forever associated with the false hopes of legal formalism according to which the law was supposed to be gapless and aligned along the paths laid out by a limited number of fundamental principles. Realists – and before them the members of the German Free Law Movement – had a great time of debunking these ideas.[6] We all know today that the study of law is not like biology and very much unlike physics. If mastering the law is anything at all, it is a "craft," a set of skills, or possibly an "art."

Is This the Point?

Against this background, causing boredom must appear not even to be the author's gravest intellectual sin. He seems to posit that something quite delusional – namely, legal science – is a normatively significant social fact. A social fact that is a delusion is a social fact only inasmuch as the delusion is a fact. Therefore, the author seems to suggest that *de facto* delusional beliefs about law are sufficient to constitute a source of law. This is not terribly convincing. Not that the existence of delusion preempts the genesis of law – under certain circumstances *communis error facit ius* – in this case it seems to be suggested that it is the false belief about knowing the law that maketh law. If anything, such an assertion, unfounded as it may seem, can do nothing to restore dignity and recognition to the much-derided "science" of law.

5 See, for example, Oliver Wendell Holmes, "Law in Science and Science in Law" (1899) 12 *Harvard Law Review* 443 at 452 (criticizing continental legal science, "a theological working out of dogma or a logical development as in mathematics … " as a false jurisprudence); Jerome Frank, *Courts on Trial: Myth and Reality in American Justice* (Princeton: Princeton University Press, 1949) 190 ("[W]e ought to put an end to notions of a 'legal science' or a 'science of law,' unless we so define 'legal' or 'law' as to exclude much of what must be included in the judicial administration of justice, because no formula for predicting most trial-court decisions can be devised which does not contain hopelessly numerous variables that cannot be pinned down or correlated"). One of the most pronounced indictments of legal science is to be found in Felix Cohen, "Transcendental Nonsense and the Functional Approach" (1935) 35 *Columbia Law Review* 809–849.

6 See Herman Oliphant, "A Return to Stare Decisis" (1928) 14 A.B.A. 71, 76; Karl N. Llewellyn, *On Legal Realism* (Birmingham, Ala.: Legal Classics Library, 1986) at 104–106; James E. Herget and Stephen Wallace, "The German Free Law Movement as the Source of American Legal Realism" (1987) 73 *Virginia Law Review* 399–442, at 411–417.

On Lowering Expectations

Obviously, unless the author has a special penchant for absurdity, he must have something else in mind. Indeed, the observations that follow aim to recover a *defensible* conception of the science of law. They claim that such a conception entails taking legal science to be a source of law. To prove this claim, the observations must alter our understanding of both sources and science.

This alteration can be introduced on the basis of the simple realization that originally "*scientia*," from which legal science qua "*scientia juris*" is derived, simply meant "knowledge."[7] Legal science is, thus understood, merely the proper manner of knowing the law.

An Alternative Picture

Hence, with regard to the claims of legal science, the observations invite readers to lower their expectations. "Science of law" means knowing the law and knowing nothing but the law. At the same time, the observations aspire to accomplish the reverse with regard to sources. Sources are not just facts. Of course – and undeniably – sources not only have their basis in facts and are, unmistakably, somehow "factual"; yet, the factual aspect is insufficient to explain what they really are. It is through sources that the law takes on different and specific appearances. They render the law from particular outlooks. It will be argued, too, that each source is a mode of recognizing – knowing – another source.

Confronting the Common Law

Finally, this chapter takes it upon itself not only to develop a defensible understanding of legal science, it also dares contrast this understanding critically with the common law. Challenging the common law has become pretty much unheard of in a globalized world. Not only does it violate the courtesy among the world's leading legal systems, it also tends to upset the sensibilities of postcolonial political correctness. Why, for example, offend India? Why aim at Sierra Leone?

But not only have former colonies and protectorates embraced the common law after the demise of the British Empire, legal systems all around the world

7 Science, *Online Etymology Dictionary*, www.etymonline.com/index.php?term=science (last visited December 24, 2014).

have become more and more common-law-esque, in particular also on an international scale. This common-law-ishness is manifest in the increasing importance of – and attention paid to – courts. Arguably, more adjudication means more rule of law and consequently a more effective protection of rights. Who would be opposed to that?

The Common Law Is a Mistake

Of course, taking issue with the common law might involve a variety of things. It can mean that one regards the substance of some common private law system appallingly business oriented and insufficiently sensitive to social issues; it can also mean that one regards a certain form of constitutionalism, which emphasizes tradition and the "living" development of the law, as inadequate to a free people. But this is not what is at stake here. Rather, for the purpose of our inquiry, the common law signifies a way of thinking that prioritizes the particular over the universal and cases over doctrine. As is well known, this way of thinking can have numerous adverse effects, in particular when knowing the law becomes the arcane business of "judge and company." Criticisms of this type have been around since the days of the Levellers[8] or since Bentham's indictment of the common law.[9]

The perspective developed here moves beyond a mere critique of the politics of the common law. It suggests that the common law is at best a highly imperfect version of legal knowledge proper. To demonstrate this point, the observations distinguish between genuine and false common law. Genuine common law is not a form of legal knowledge. Rather, as we shall see later (see p. 104), it is a mode of endorsement. False common law, by contrast, emerges from the attempt to turn genuine common law into the knowledge of the law. Since genuine common law is deeply defective, it is not by accident the case that false common law is a regular occurrence. Ordinary common law is false common law. It is a hybrid combination of genuine common law and legal science. It aspires to be legal science without eliminating the defining feature of genuine common law: *stare decisis*. It thereby aims at the impossible. For that reason, ordinary common law is both false legal science and false common law. Hence, this chapter submits that the world of the law

8 See Christopher Hill, *The World Turned Upside Down: Radical Ideas During the English Revolution* (London: Pelican Books, 1975) at 133–135, 269–276.

9 See Jeremy Bentham, *An Introduction to the Principles of Morals and Legislation* (Oxford: Clarendon Press, 1789) at 34, available at www.econlib.org/library/Bentham/bnthPML.html. For a useful introduction, see Gerald J. Postema, *Bentham and the Common Law Tradition* (Oxford: Clarendon Press, 1986).

would be a much better world if scholarship did not pay attention to the "holdings" of cases.

LEGAL SCIENCE

Knowledge and Existence

There would be no legal system if nobody could say what the law is. *Nullum ius sine juris dictione.* The existence of law is mediated by knowledge that claims to know what the law is. These bold statements seem to conflate "existence" with "effectiveness." To be effective, undoubtedly, law *may* have to be recognized by someone giving it effect; but this does not rule out that law might be unconsciously followed or even exist in a state of latency in which it remains hidden from the eye of recognition.

Indeed, the claim that there would be no law if nobody could say what it is is calibrated to fit legal systems and not law in a potentially more exalted state in which it remained beyond human apprehension and was revealed, if at all, only in oracular statements. Legal systems are "dynamic" owing to the interaction of primary rules of obligation and secondary rules of norm creation. In such a context, knowledge of norms – viz., knowledge of secondary rules – is required to produce other norms.

Natural Law

At the same time, the statements must strike one as accurate if the notion of "existence" is viewed more broadly. Then they comprise, in addition to efficacy, also the intelligibility of valid norms. Thus understood, the law exists also if it is merely accessible to cognition, but not (yet) practiced. There is still no legal system if nobody can say what the law is. The law exists only if we are able to state what it is.

It is debatable whether this concept of existence is capacious enough to include natural law. It is, indeed, so long as natural law is understood to be law that is amenable to rational insight. More to the point, law of that type claims that it would have to be known by every reasonable person. Being necessarily knowable is essential to what it claims to be. It exists, if it exists at all, in well-grounded beliefs concerning the validity of norms: no well-grounded beliefs, no natural law. What would perennially elude human insight might be law in some more cryptic proto-state, but it would not be natural law. In the case of actual legal systems, however, the secret to the existence of law is no secret. Law can exist only where claims to legal knowledge are *performatively* successful. In other words, there would be no legal system if legal knowledge were not a *social fact*. Since this assertion concerns the social dimension of knowledge, it suggests that law can exist only if legal knowledge claims are widely and largely accepted. Indeed, we seem to have known that at least since the publication of H.L.A. Hart's *The Concept of Law*.[10]

Forms of Recognition

In developed legal systems, the acceptance of such claims is mediated by the application of legal rules. They lay down, as a matter of law, under which conditions a legal knowledge claim is to be socially accepted. These rules are authority conferring. What the judge says is law because the judge has the authority to say what the law is.

Rules of procedure confer this power. Any outcome of a procedure bears the imprint of its origin. Borrowing the memorable conceptual innovation by Adolf Julius Merkl, one can say that what is known to be law is validated by the form according to which it has been constituted, or its *form of recognition* (the *Rechtssatzform* in Merkl's original parlance).[11] Such forms constitute *sources* of law.

Habermas's Tension and the Necessary Form

Legal knowledge claims necessarily involve a tension between "facticity" and "validity." This tension is a major theme of Habermas's legal philosophy.[12] *De facto* the law can exist within a legal system only if the legal knowledge claim is socially successful; *de jure*, however, the success of the claim ought to be based upon reporting accurately what the law truly is (*e.g.*, what a secondary rule really requires). With regard to the latter, the application of procedural rules is mediated by knowledge that does not avail of a deliberately posited (legal procedures), but of a necessary form of recognition (a *notwendige Rechtssatzform*, as it were).

This necessary form is manifest in various ways of legal reasoning and classifying legal materials. These ways epitomize what it takes to "think like a lawyer" and to do so properly. Even legally ordained forms of legal reasoning

10 Oxford: Clarendon Press, 1961.

11 See Adolf Julius Merkl, "Prolegomena zu einer Theorie des rechtlichen Stufenbaus." In *Gesellschaft, Staat und Recht: Untersuchungen zur reinen Rechtslehre* (ed. A.J. Verdross, Vienna: Julius Springer, 1931) 252–294.

12 See Jürgen Habermas, *Between Facts and Norms: Contributions to a Discourse Theory of Law and Democracy* (trans. W. Rehg, Cambridge, Mass.: MIT Press, 1996).

would have to be implemented on the basis of some preordained form governing their application.

For reasons of infinite regress, it would be pointless to inquire whether there might be some ultimate form of recognition. Whatever form there is, it has to be presupposed, that is, posited, even if contingently; or, in other words, it has to be necessarily posited without thereby lending expression to a necessary presupposition of law. One or the other method of reading the legal materials is necessary to let the law speak, but neither one in particular appears to be inevitable.

Not the Rule of Recognition

The necessary form of recognition is not to be mistaken for what Hart called the "rule of recognition," which represents his conventionalist rendering of Kelsen's *Grundnorm*.[13] Both the rule of recognition and the *Grundnorm* are *ultimate norms*.[14] That is, they supposedly provide legal knowledge with access to positive forms of recognition. They identify sources. But that is not the point of the necessary form of recognition. At issue is a whole style of apprehending the law, that is, of integrating the reading of legal materials into a strategy of analyzing legal questions. Such a style is usually sustained by conventions and shaped in the course of scholarly debates.

Money and Power

Scholarly conventions are often not as harmless as they may seem. Substantively, they might betray the influence of money and power on what wants to pass as a statement of the law. When such an influence prevails, the law is not known within a medium that plainly reports what it is. On the contrary, legal knowledge is then subject to manipulation and distortion.

Money and power are capable of bending the law into a shape that it would reject if it were able to speak for itself. The law is thereby transformed into an extension of the social force exercised by these media. Money can buy. Power can command (and work in more subtle ways). If these forces override the law, it no longer is what it would be of its own accord; rather, it amounts to a commodity or a pawn in the hand of some master. It appears, thus, that

[13] See Andrei Marmor, *Philosophy of Law* (Princeton: Princeton University Press, 2011) at 35, 51.

[14] See Hans Kelsen, *Introduction to the Problems of Legal Theory* (trans. B.L. Paulson and S.L. Paulson, Oxford: Clarendon Press, 1992) at 58–59: H.L.A. Hart, *The Concept of Law* (2d ed., Oxford: Oxford University Press, 1994) at 105.

the law can only be properly recognized within a medium that reveals what it truly is. The law, so it seems, has to be known by truth sayers.

Truth Saying

What truth sayers say has to be law. The exhortative "has" is grammatically ambiguous. The statements of truth sayers "have" to be law in the sense that they must reflect what the law is. Borrowing Montesquieu's parlance,[15] this means that such persons have to serve as the mouth of the law. But it also means that their statements have to convey the authority of law. Apparently, true truth sayers fulfill both requirements by being passive. In faithfully reflecting what the law says their statements also reflect the authority of law. The thinking of the truth sayers, while supplying the necessary form of recognition, is not authority conferring in the way in which positive forms of recognition are. It is as though the law recognized itself. The truth sayers do not contribute anything. They are not "truth makers." Their thinking is part of the picture only inasmuch as its function is to drop out of the picture. They are self-effacing.

Ideally, hence, the law effectively serves *as* its own necessary form of recognition. Conceptual mapping and matching rely on the object as form of recognition. The truth sayers simply abide by this form. This is how the law comes to reveal itself in their statements.

The Object as a Subject

It may now have become clearer what underpins the idea of legal science. There would be no law, properly speaking, if the law did not reflect itself in virtue of the necessary form of recognition. Of course, thus stated, the idea of legal science is cast in a strangely "objectified" form. Supposedly, the object makes itself known by using the truth sayers' statements as carriers of communication.

But the object is thereby also tacitly cast as a subject, for the object must somehow be able to shed claims that originate from money and power and to make the truth sayer state what it, the law qua object, truly is. The passivity on the part of the latter is the receptacle of the activity of the former. Put differently, the idea of truth saying presupposes a subject nesting in the object. The truth sayers serve as the screens onto which this subject casts projections. The subject is in the object. Being a subject is essential to what the object truly is.

15 See Montesquieu, *The Spirit of the Laws* (trans. A.M. Cohler et al., Cambridge: Cambridge University Press, 1989) at 163.

Action, Not Causation

Subjectivity is activity. It may seem, therefore, as though the story of truth sayers has been misleading all along. They are supposed to be passive. But the story was not terribly misleading. We simply need to understand that the object itself is active. It is active not in the sense in which objects are active when they are pinballs of causation; rather, the object is acting, not causing in the sense of being pushed and pushing others. There is a sense of purpose to what it does; this purpose is, plainly and simply, to make itself known.

Ordinary Sources and the Necessary Source

Positive forms of recognition constitute ordinary sources of law. A "statute" adopted pursuant to the constitution is law because the constitution recognizes that source. The necessary form of recognition, by contrast, allows these sources to be what they are. If it were not for the intervention of this necessary source, the positive sources would dry up completely. They would remain mute.

The necessary form mediates the recognition of instances of the positive forms. Hence, positive forms can function as effective sources only with the aid of the necessary form. Since sources account for what the law is as an object ("This is the law because the judge said so"), the objectivity of law is mediated by subjectivity acting as the necessary form. The object is essentially subjective.

Reply to a Positivist Objection

At this point, legal positivists may reply that the necessary form is after all nothing short of the ultimate norm that makes sources into what they are, namely, normatively relevant positive forms of recognition. But this would miss the point. The necessary form is ontologically subtler and more modest than any conceivable ultimate norm. Instead of validating positive forms it merely allows for their realization. It assists the law in making itself known. It cannot be denied, however, that the necessary form has to have some idea as to what counts as an ultimate rule in any given legal system.

The Object-Form

The traditional positivist understanding of law would also immediately inquire into what lends validity to norms. It would ask whether or not an ultimate rule or any other secondary rule identifies the relevant sources. Legal positivists thereby render the law in object-form. They want to know whether the source accounts for the normative mode of "existence" – that is, validity of norms – as if the source merely contained conditions the fulfillment of which triggered valid laws. This style of thinking relies on an *analogy to causation*. This analogy explains why legal positivism often renders the law in object-form (another example would be Kelsen's view of the "reconstructed legal norm").[16]

The Subject-Form

The alternative understanding of law presented and defended here renders the law in subject-form. To make itself known, the law has to engage in some kind of action the purpose of which is, trivially, to make itself known.

Therefore, the simple image of truth saying has to be altered after all. It is implausible to imagine that truth sayers are screens on which the law casts projections of itself. Rather, they are active knowers. Their activity, however, would still be tantamount to an accurate reflection of the law if it mimicked the activity the law would itself engage in for the purpose of making itself known. If what thruth sayers do were equivalent to this activity, they would possess authority.

This type of authority cannot be derivative of a positive form of recognition; rather, it must be, as the late Joseph Bochenski might have put it, "epistemic."[17] It is the authority inherent in that which allows the law to be manifestly known and practiced. Arguably, the rightfulness of this authority would be established if the law, were it asked and it could speak, approved of the pronouncements made by those investing themselves with epistemic authority. Indeed, approval by the law is the only criterion that we have in order to identify this type of authority. The law, if it could speak, would say to those in whom this authority has been invested: "You are spirit of my own spirit."

Sources Talking

As mystical as the previous statements might appear, we are nonetheless back on remarkably familiar ground. Any legal knowledge claim bearing the stamp of approval by the law necessarily flows from a source of law. This follows analytically, if anything does, from the concept of a source. To every utterance

16 See Kelsen, note 14 at 23–24.

17 See Joseph Maria Bochenski, *The Logic of Religion* (New York: New York University Press, 1965) at 168.

that claims to be legislation the source – the positive form of recognition – nods its approval if, in the eyes of that source, the piece of legislation meets the relevant constitutionally determined conditions (The constitution says: "Oh yes, this is legislation"). The norm flows from the source because the source recognizes it to be one of its manifestations. This is how, according to our original truth sayers' conception, subjectivity is built into the objectivity of sources. To its manifestation the source says: "You are spirit of my own spirit."

Sources Talking to Sources

What is true of any positive form must also be true of the necessary form of recognition. The necessary form intervenes to let the positive forms speak. It supplies the mode with which sources supposedly identify their manifestations. For example, to any serious contractual dealing can be attributed the implicit statement, "Hello, I am a contract." This statement is true if the positive form of contract law recognizes "I" as a contract ("Oh yes, you are! How do you do?"). The necessary form invests the positive form with the wherewithal to mediate such recognition. It tells the source to recognize the contract. The objectivity of sources is composed of, thus, sources talking to sources. The source, when rendering judgment on its manifestations, obtains guidance from the necessary source. The necessary form of recognition is a necessary source of law. It is the epistemic source of law that makes other sources possible.

Hierarchy Reestablished

A clarification is in order. The source approvingly identifying its own manifestations – contract law contentedly identifying valid contracts – speaks from within another source. It is, as it were, outside itself and can be with itself only in virtue of the necessary source.

This matter may seem dark, but, in fact, it is crystal clear. The constitution identifies something as valid legislation from the perspective of either the legislature or some court of law. A piece of legislation is applied to a set of facts in a judgment of a court. The source is active – the form of recognition activated – from within another one that is supposedly controlled by it. The hierarchy of control is thereby reversed. At the same time, the court's judgment can take the perspective of legislation only as a result of the necessary form. If it were not for the latter, judicial rulings would determine legislation and hence determine themselves. They would cease to be what they claim to be.

Each source realizes itself in another. This other form needs to embrace the necessary form to stay true to itself and not to overstep its bounds vis-à-vis the source from which it speaks.

A Circle and Its Resolution

In the context of the conversation of sources, the law could not recognize itself if it were not for the necessary form. At the same time, the necessary form would not possess epistemic authority if it were not recognized by the law, that is, if the law did not embrace it as spirit of its own spirit. The necessary form allows the law to speak. The law allows the necessary form to articulate the law. Evidently, we are confronted with a circle.

The circle can be resolved by removing an equivocation. The law that is articulated by the necessary form is law in particularized form. It is manifest in particular sources. These are positive forms of recognition. By contrast, the law that allows the necessary form to go forward is the law *as a whole*. Law as a whole makes its appearance in the necessary source of law. The necessary form enacts the law as a whole in every particular instance of it. It builds the whole into the particulars.

This is the essence of the idea that legal knowledge – the science of law – is a source of law. Just like a contract is a manifestation of contract law, understood as a source, every act of legal knowledge is a manifestation of the law as a whole. Legal knowledge is self-knowledge. It is knowledge of the law by the law. It is knowledge of the particular by the whole in particular cases.

Law as a Whole

We have already determined that the necessary form involves activity. Subjectivity integrates the particular into the whole. Apprehension of the particular by the whole is self-knowledge that, evidently, assigns to each particular its particular place. But what is the law as a whole? Again, the view of legal positivism provides a useful contrast.

Drawing on Hart's theory as a paradigmatic example, it is fair to say that for legal positivists the law as a whole is the "union"[18] of primary rules of obligation and of secondary rules of norm creation. Union implies the existence of some mode of establishing relations. To be the unity of primary and secondary rules, the law has to be composed of operations of relating, that is, purposive action.

[18] See Hart, note 14 at 94, 99.

Alas, legal positivists have never really accounted for this.[19] By default, positivism suggests that law is a set of rules ultimately validated by some basic norm. This is sorely mistaken. Law is more than rules. It is also manifest in decisions taken in singular cases. More importantly, law cannot be a "sum" of something. Confronted with novel factual situations, the law needs to be clarified and further developed. The law could not be what it is if it were static. Only if the law is capable of arriving at clarifications in the face of new sets of facts can the law be an object, namely, a knowable thing. The law as a whole – or even law if and inasmuch as it is whole – is the situation in which the legal significance of every social fact is clear. Such clarity depends on intelligibility at any point in time. This intelligibility is the work of a systematic elaboration of law.

Viewed from the perspective of subjectivity, the law is an activity of recognition exercised through various forms; viewed from the perspective of objectivity, the law is constantly transforming itself to reach the state in which the normative significance of every social fact can become clear.

Kenosis

Legal knowledge is possible in virtue of the necessary form of recognition. But what about a hypothetical incipient state in which there are no positive sources? In such a state, the necessary form has no positive form to lend a hand to. The necessary form of recognition is about truth saying. Yet, in the hypothetical incipient state, there is nothing to truth say about. There is nothing, that is, but truth saying itself. Yet, activity can turn on itself and become its own object. This is not the Fichtean act of intellectual intuition.[20] It is something simpler.

The only source there is in the hypothetical incipient state is the necessary source. If it turns on itself, it is thereby turned into an object. There it is. This means that inasmuch as the activity reflects on itself it becomes objective (admittedly, this is an old Fichtean trick), namely, the observable activity of knowing what the law is. Once the activity is objective – that is, a social reality, a social fact – it can become an object of itself. The necessary form can have itself as an object, which is, in a sense, the pure form of knowing the law.

[19] For a somewhat muted attempt, see Kletzer, note 1.

[20] See Johann Gottlieb Fichte, *System der Sittenlehre nach Prinzipien der Wissenschaftslehre* (ed. H. Verweyen, Hamburg: Meiner, 1995) at 46.

Belief in Law

This implies that law as a whole, active through the necessary form, can recognize law before there is any positive law because the necessary form, in turning on itself, externalizes itself into a socially positive form. This does not require extra effort or resolution. The necessary form is always and already positive.

This positivity involves, however, a certain forgetting of subjectivity. To realize its objectivity, the necessary form has to forget that it is about *knowing* something and to focus on its social face, which is plainly and simply *shared recognition*, which is believing that does not account of its status. The object-status of legal knowledge is then manifest in its social dimension, while the "internal" cognitive dimension is provisionally submerged.[21]

In the incipient state, legal knowledge exists as something that is shared, but without a warrant as to what it is about. It is knowledge in an uneasy state in which it is neither knowledge nor ignorance. It is simply belief, or, as stated in the Introduction, it is a disclaimed claim (see p. 10).

Arché

Every beginning is negation.[22] The beginning is negation of that from which it originates. Knowledge of the law begins with turning knowing into simple believing.

The origin of law is the self-negation of the necessary form. It can avail of itself as an object by *blindly* being objective. Simply put, the law begins with shared beliefs in law.

Believing Without Knowing

It takes belief and nothing but belief to get the law off the ground. At the same time, the incipient positive form involves the forgetting of knowledge. The believers believe what they believe without being able to say why. They know what they know without knowing why they know what they know. Their knowledge is a social fact. They merely say: "This is what we believe

[21] The previous sentences capture, even though they are not about the ultimate rule of a legal system, a step that is similar to the transition from a hypothetical basic norm that is devoid of any criterion of validation to a conventional rule of recognition. The transition is warranted by the fact that any basic norm, as Hart well understood, necessarily has to have a social dimension.

[22] See Wolfgram Hogrebe, *Prädikation und Genesis. Metaphysik als Fundamentalheuristik im Ausgang von Schellings "Die Weltalter"* (Frankfurt aM: Suhrkamp, 1989) at 114.

around here," and add, as though this were proof: "We have acted accordingly before."

The basic gesture is not "This is what we have done, and this is why it is right," but rather "This is what we believe to be right and we have exhibited this belief consistently and persistently in our conduct."[23]

Existentialism

The earliest form of existentialism confronts us with the proposition that incomprehensible being precedes and eludes all understanding. It is accessible only to intuition, not to thinking.[24] In a similar vein, it is suggested here that the origin of law lies in shared intuitions of law (*Rechtsanschauungen*). They are not underpinned by reasons. Only their existence is warranted by practice.

Custom

Socially shared truth saying gives rise to the first positive form of recognition, which is not quite yet a source of law. It will grow into it once the necessary form reawakens from its slumber (see p. 95).

Someone says "It is the law that . . . " Others agree. To make sure that the relevant statements are not blithe professions of moral sentiments, one wants to see a warrant for the existence of this belief. People have to live up to what they say to be law in their behavior. They have to impose sanctions on offenders and bite the bullet of compliance. Practice proofs the firmness of belief, not its soundness.

Prototypes

Such shared and practiced understandings are *prototypes* of the first positive form of recognition, but not positive forms proper because they are not aided by the necessary form, which still lies dormant in custom. The law is not really known. Its existence is intuitively grasped and practically projected. The law is "made," however, with the intent of recognizing something that is already there. But this something is elusive. It can only be intuited.

23 Gardner regards customary law as the incidental by-product of individual efforts to follow the law as it is. See John Gardner, *Law as a Leap of Faith: Essays on Law in General* (Oxford: Oxford University Press, 2012) at 74. I am wondering how that by-product is linked to *opinio juris*.

24 See Friedrich Wilhelm Joseph Schelling, *Philosophie der Offenbarung*, vol. 1 (reprint, Darmstadt: Wissenschaftliche Buchgesellschaft, 1955) at 160–161.

Endorsement

Custom nonetheless exhibits the form of knowledge: "We know that . . . " All the same, this form has fallen into a negative state. It is knowledge that does not really know. If the folks were asked why they believe what they believe, they would conceivably respond that they believe what they believe. They might add that they *want* to believe their beliefs because they do not intend to change who they are. They are fine with it. We believe in the death penalty. Such believing is – pun intended – wanting. It is an endorsement. Ultimately, it is an endorsement by, and of, the endorsing self. Knowledge that does not know anything but itself blindly endorses itself. We know that we know. Full stop.

The Emergence of the Positive Form

Joined practice is the warrant for the shared belief that is a social fact.[25] To ascertain more clearly what folks, as a collective unit, really believe in matters legal one cannot but stick to this warrant that is practice.

Owing to its outward manifestation, custom lends itself to recognition. From the perspective of recognition, it takes on the form of customary *law*. It is possible to attribute to it the basic relation between a rule, which is inferred by abduction,[26] and its endorsement. *This* is what they practice. *This* is the warrant for what they believe to be law, and their belief is manifest in the voluntary endorsement of practice. It does not take much to cast this warrant as an object of belief. The Iranians practice x. It demonstrates that they believe x to be law. Practice is all we have to determine the belief's substance.

Customary law, thus, comes in this dual form of *usus*, on the one hand, and *opinio juris*, on the other. *Usus* is the object, *opinio juris* the belief that can be read as the acceptance of what is practiced. The law begins to exist in this object form. It simply has put itself outside of itself by bracketing its subjectivity.

The Return of the Necessary Form

With the emergence of this first full-fledged positive form of recognition, the necessary form can rescind its own negation (see pp. 93–94). It can emancipate itself from the positive form and recover from its kenosis.

25 Much of what follows below has benefited from Puchta's monumental work on customary law. See Georg Friedrich Puchta, *Das Gewohnheitsrecht*, vols. 1 and 2 (Erlangen: Palm, 1828 and 1837).

26 On abduction, see Charles Sanders Peirce, *Reasoning and the Logic of Things* (ed. K.L. Ketner, Cambridge, Mass.: Harvard University Press, 1993) at 139–142.

Once *usus* and *opinio iuris* are fused into an object that is composed of a rule and its endorsement ("acceptance"), it is possible to demand that the validation of the legal knowledge claim concerning the endorsed rule be conditioned by the social endorsement of that rule. The social validation of *usus* – the fact that *usus* is taken to be by the social participants as a warrant of what they endorse – can be taken to be a condition for the existence of the rule. Whether or not the rule and its source – custom – have been recognized correctly becomes a matter that is of relevance to the necessary form of recognition ("Have we seen enough instances of practice?" "Is it consistent?"). The necessary form retrieves itself after having given birth to positive law, namely, customary law.

Knowledge and Endorsement

The necessary form recognizes the endorsement inherent in the positive form. Yet, no endorsement is without an element of knowing, and no knowing would be complete without endorsement. If reasonable, endorsements are given for the reasons underpinning the endorsement.

This explains why any positive form is an abstraction. It insulates the endorsement vis-à-vis the considerations concerning its soundness. This abstraction is necessary, however, to move toward law as a whole. The law needs to be fixed. This is part of the teleology of legal knowledge. In a like manner, knowledge involves an element of choice. Otherwise, deliberations could scarcely ever come to an end.

The Ontological Transformation

Customary law is an embodiment of knowledge: "We know that it is the law that . . . " It is knowledge, however, that does not take responsibility for what it claims. All it says is that we know what we know. The knowledge renders itself as a social fact. It thereby brackets its substantive claim to validity. It presents itself as a mere choice that has to be reckoned with.

From Custom to Legislation

It is a truism that custom is a particularly unreliable source of law. From the perspective of the law as a whole, customary law is plainly defective. Not only is it not clear how many and which instances of practice we must have seen to observe consistency, it is also notoriously unclear how many and which members of the community are required to establish a collective endorsement. These deficiencies are overcome by *legislation*. The proposal of a bill introduces written rules. Voting rules clarify whose (or how many) endorsements count.

Against this background, legislation can be perceived as a source that allows customary law to arrive at a clearer picture of itself. What must remain inchoate at the customary level attains greater clarity once a legislature has laid it down.

Legislating

Of course, such an understanding of legislation actually regards legislating as an act of *jurisdiction* or, more precisely, as a clarification of the law. It is an endorsement of the law based upon knowing some law. This understanding seems to be hard to square with our modern and more dynamic conception of legislation that conceives of laws as active and future-oriented interventions into social life. But, indeed, they are not incompatible. Already in its backward-looking function is legislation based upon a decision that is more disentangled from knowing than the inchoate belief underlying customary endorsement.

A decision does not simply possess authority because it reflects some undefeated belief. Rather, a decision severs practical knowledge from a potential tie between competing claims. It allows one to overcome the paralyzing effect that insufficient reasons have on action. Decisions are a ways of "making up one's mind," that is, of knowing what to do. They are sources of knowledge that sustain practical knowledge in a form in which it is not burdened with having to defend its claims. The legislature decided that we no longer build any bridges. For its validation, the claim that it is sound to abstain from building bridges no longer has to be supported by arguments. With the emerging distinction between endorsement by means of decision and legal knowledge, the difference between the positive and the necessary form also becomes quite pronounced.

Legal Scholarship

Legislation, however, has a defect of its own. Typically, it just creates a bundle of rules. But rules do not apply themselves to situations. For law to stay true to itself, another source has to intervene. This source has to overcome the deficiency of legislation to be systematically vulnerable to arbitrariness in its application. The relevant repair task has to be accomplished by the necessary form, for the latter is all about assisting the law in making itself known.

As pointed out earlier, legal scholarship uses various conceptual classifications and interpretive constructs to determine which rule is to be applied in which case. It thereby attempts to prevent arbitrariness by facilitating the like treatment of like cases. Moreover, it also produces a representation of law that is congenial to law as a whole, namely, the situation in which the legal significance of every social fact is clear or at least amenable to clarification. Law that is accessible to intellectual apprehension is at least by design not arbitrary in its application. Thinking means positing something as general.

It thus turns out that to realize its ambition to regulate, legislation has to transcend its aggregate appearance, in which it is merely a bundle of norms and take on a new shape. It is in the medium of systematic legal knowledge that the law can grow into legislation in systematized form.[27] Of course, these observations suggest that the lintels of the doorpost of law do not bear the inscription of whim.[28]

Knowing and Legislating

Legislation lays down rules. Their application is supposed to be non-arbitrary. Otherwise laying down rules would be quite pointless. But legal science is necessary to help legislation realize what it cannot achieve of its own. Knowledge of norms is necessary for norms to be what they are. It is essential to the law not only to be endorsed but also to be known in the systematic manner epitomized by scholarship.

The same matter can be viewed also from a slightly different angle, which develops the moral implication of knowing the law. The consistent application of rules avoids arbitrariness. Rules themselves are supposed to meet the test of universalization. Legal scholarship applies the principle of universalization across a whole set of rules. The application of rules to situations is to be guided by considerations concerning the appropriateness of selecting the relevant rule. What mediates this second form of universalization is the concepts developed by the science of law.

The Sequence of Sources

It appears, therefore, that these three sources can be arranged in a sequence[29] in which the law as an object becomes more clearly to apprehend because the law itself is more clearly rendered in subjective form. All sources embody

27 See G.W.F. Hegel, *Elements of the Philosophy of Right* (trans. H.B. Nisbet, Cambridge: Cambridge University Press 1991) § 211.

28 See Ralph Waldo Emerson, *Essays: First and Second Series* (New York: Vintage Books, 1990) at 32.

29 The idea of such a sequence is old. See Carl Friedrich von Savigny, *Of the Vocation of Our Age for Legislation and Jurisprudence* (New York: Arno Press, 1975).

subjectivity. The subjective element is the endorsement that bases itself on what it takes to be legal knowledge. Each source in the sequence lends the law a different appearance because of the distinct subjectivity of the endorser/knower involved. Custom is law for the ordinary member of a community speaking in the first person plural ("We find that . . ."). Legislation is law for people occupying some commanding heights ("We order that . . ."). Finally, legal scholarship is law not only for the bigwigs sitting on adjudicating bodies ("It is the law that . . ."), but also decidedly for all those who are involved in a legal relationship. A relationship of this type is not based upon caprice and "domination."

The later source in the sequence elaborates what the prior source should have said but was unable to articulate itself. The sequence of sources is a process of *Verstehen* (understanding).[30] While knowing and endorsement are fully intermingled in the case of custom, they are more neatly separated in the case of legislation and legal scholarship. Nevertheless, it would be an error to suppose that volition is absent. Legal scholarship – the agent of the necessary form – wants the law to be whole. On every stage of knowledge, reasons of *jurigenesis* fall by the wayside and are replaced with intrasystemic considerations.

Rationalization

Legal science invariably has a tendency to rationalize the law. This is a by-product of avoiding arbitrariness of application. Any rationally intelligible and fair application of rules depends on assembling principles into coherent schemes.[31] In this context, it is essential to make the best possible sense of these principles: "This is a case for rule A, that for rule B. Why? Because of principle C." The reasons that legal science adduces to determine the applicable norm indirectly invest these norms with an aura of reasonableness. While their validity cannot be put into question, a rational determination of their scope of application will have to suppose that they are themselves an expression of practical reason. Assuming that a law-applying official is confronted with the question of having to choose among different "interrogation methods" in the context of the implementation of anti-terrorism policies, this official will have to draw out the relative merits of, say, either water boarding or electroshocks. In the course of a determination of the types of case where

30 See Jürgen Habermas, *Zur Logik der Sozialwissenschaften* (5th ed. Frankfurt aM: Suhrkamp, 1982) at 337–338.

31 See Dworkin, note 4 at 116.

the former rather than the latter ought to be used, the practice of torture will appear to be normal and, even worse, as based upon principles of rational conduct.

Objectification

We have observed that the necessary form has to go under in order to turn into its own object (see p. 93). The first positive source of law is knowledge that is merely socially shared and therefore not knowledge proper. It is neither true nor false. However, this primordial source, custom, must intuitively *presuppose* what will be articulate d by the necessary form, namely, that the law is (a) whole, for it must posit the non-arbitrariness of its application. Put differently, the belief in law with which the law begins before it even begins must be vindicated by the elaboration of the legal system.

Conversely, the last source is the sibling of the first. It is objective. It is socially shared and often largely conventional. Scholars do what they do inasmuch as they belong to a group. They say: "This is what we do." Scholars also often go with the crowd to share a language and a sense of relevance that allows them to be heard. They say: "I do as all others do." The historicity of custom is thus preserved in the historicity of scholarly constructions. Much legal knowledge rests upon endorsing elements of the necessary form qua historical artifacts.

THE COMMON LAW

Legal Concepts

The task of knowing the law is completed if the law takes on, as Jhering memorably put it, a different aggregate state.[32] From an assemblage of rules it is turned into the capacity to classify and elaborate the normative significance of facts and events. The terms of classification are provided by a series of concepts – such as "interference," "rationality," "delegated act" – that construe the normative import of rules in a manner that allows for their combined and coherent application. The very notion of "interference" contains a certain interpretation of the role of fundamental rights and of the task of governments. The law comes to recognize itself in these concepts. They represent the contribution made by legal scholarship on behalf of law as a whole.

[32] See Rudolph von Jhering, *Geist des römischen Rechts auf den verschiedenen Stufen seiner Entwicklung* (6th ed. Leipzig: Breitkopf & Härtel 1907) vol. 1 at 37.

In this state, the law is an object only from Hart's external perspective. Internally, it is thoroughly subjective, that is, the power to reason and to reach conclusions on the basis of relevant premises. This subjectivity is nonetheless a social reality. This is why it is called a "practice." It would not be inaccurate, either, to characterize it as "objective spirit."[33]

Evidently, the degree of guidance that one believes to obtain from substantive concepts within this practice depends often on the confidence that one has in the capacity of practical reason to absorb any apparent indeterminacy. But even if the level of confidence is low, legal science can still embrace a dynamic approach and state that the law is what judge So-and-so will say it is. The one available substantive answer will then be the substantive answer given by So-and-so.

Forgetting and Remembering Cases

The development of a conceptual structure depends very much on the challenge posed by cases. The magnitude of the challenge is not least indicated by the embarrassing recurrence of awkward "quasi"-concepts, ranging from the ancient "quasi-contract" all the way up to the modern "quasi-state." At the same time, cases are food for legal thought. They are necessary, as it were, to build its body.

Once they have given rise to a new classification, they may be legitimately forgotten. Or, in other words, legal science remembers cases by means of recalibrating distinctions and classificatory schemes. The case itself – the facts, in particular – can be ignored. The general ideas or nuances to which the case has given rise can be explained without any reference to it. They can equally well be demonstrated by using a hypothetical case. The particular case is inessential.

Given that legal science absorbs the challenge posed by cases into modified doctrines, it is fair to say that it remembers cases *in legislative form*. After all, knowing the law conceives of itself as nothing short of the realization of legislation.

This is not to say that cases are as good as laws. On the contrary, legal science remembers cases, if at all, via recalibrating doctrines. Whether or not the idea expressed in a judicial opinion is of lasting normative significance is determined by revisiting systematic elaborations of the law. If it turns out that in light of this or that case classifications need to become more fine grained or

33 See Robert B. Pippin, *Hegel's Practical Philosophy: Rational Agency as Ethical Life* (Cambridge: Cambridge University Press, 2008) at 242.

consequences adjusted, the case is remembered in virtue of a modification. In contrast to a validly adopted law, the case has no authority of its own. It merely triggers growth of legislative proportion. Prior cases matter, of course, in the context of adjudication. But they matter only inasmuch as they mediate adjudicatory consistency in the application of rules.

We have seen enough to perceive the difference to the common law. Legal science remembers cases by adjusting classifications. The common law, by contrast, remembers cases by revisiting the significance of facts.

False Common Law

It may be objected that the common law also recognizes doctrine and not least also remembers cases by modifying the law. Yet, once cases are merely treated as "specimens" of concepts and doctrines, we are confronted with a common law that is legal science in disguise.[34] This is false common law. Its historical occurrence should not surprise us – as in the case of Langdell[35] – nor should it amaze us to see it recur (*e.g.*, in the work of Charles Fried).[36]

What is at issue, evidently, is a form of the common law that is decidedly different from legal science. Elaborating the difference between false and genuine common law will in and of itself reveal why the latter poses a problem. Unfortunately, however, the existence of false common law creates a cognitive problem of its own. It obscures our perspective on genuine common law. This does not happen by accident. The incidence and, indeed, prevalence of false common law is a consequence of the fact that genuine common law is not legal knowledge at all.

Genuine Common Law

From the perspective of legal science, a substantively wrong decision can only attain finality. If this condition is met, it is valid as between the parties. It does not introduce a new general rule. The wrong decision is sustained because of a law demanding that litigation come to an end. But the decision does not alter the substantive rules on which it is based.

[34] For one of the few accounts, see Thomas C. Grey, "Langdell's Orthodoxy" (1983) 45 *University of Pittsburgh Law Review* 1–45.

[35] See Christopher Columbus Langdell, *Selection of Cases on the Law of Contracts* (Boston: Little Brown, 1871) at vi.

[36] See Charles Fried, *Saying What the Law Is: The Constitution in the Supreme Court* (Cambridge, Mass.: Harvard University Press, 2004) at 1–13.

Genuine common law, by contrast, embraces *stare decisis*.[37] New cases have to be decided in accordance with prior cases. By implication all cases are equal. *Stare decisis*, if taken seriously, means that no case has more weight than any other case. This explains why common law reasoning must at its core be engaged in the medieval task of perceiving concordance among the potential discord of cases (*concordantia discordantium casuum*, to paraphrase Gratianus).[38]

The equal weight of cases, however, extends also to their pedigree. Since all cases are equal, even a new case that is not substantively derivative of prior cases immediately joins the rank of prior cases ("precedents"). It is *aequus inter pares*. Subsequent cases have to elaborate whether the new case is closer to the center or the margins of a pertinent field. It is also the prerogative of the subsequent cases to follow the new case or to dismiss it as a one-time aberration. It would not make sense, however, to find that the new case is void and hence inexistent. It exists and has therefore already somehow altered the law.

Genuine common law is, in this respect, of a piece with British parliamentary sovereignty. A highest authority can alter the law as it sees fit without being able to strip any future highest authority from exercising the same discretionary power. *Stare decisis* means to stick to "law as it is." But it does not preclude the creation of new law that gives rise to new "law as it is."

Genuine common law posits, therefore, that each case has the power to introduce a new general rule regardless of the prior state of law as a whole. New law can spring up in each new case. Overruling – the overturning of old and the creation of new precedent – is not in conflict with *stare decisis;* it is its consequence. It is a consequence of the fact that the new case has the power to determine the law (at least until it will have become old).

Genuine common law operates very much in the manner in which social system's theory imagines autopoiesis to work.[39] The later reproductive act of legal system draws on prior acts from within its very own perspective. The whole legal system is regenerated in each and every case.

The Obliteration of Legal Knowledge

On its face, *stare decisis* does not seem to be a terribly momentous idea. Once it is perceived in the context of genuine common law, however, its significance

[37] According to Gardner, note 23 at 85, the common law is a combination of case law and the customary acceptance of *stare decisis*.

[38] See *Corpus Iuris Canonici*, vol 1: *Decretum Magistri Gratiani* (ed. A. Friedberg, Leipzig: 1879).

[39] See, generally, Niklas Luhmann, *Law as a Social System* (trans. R. Nobles and K. Ziegert, Oxford: Oxford University Press, 2004).

is fully revealed. *Stare decisis* is the nemesis of legal science. If a court is in a position to alter the law in spite of existing legal knowledge, there can be no systematic elaboration – no "whole" – from the perspective of which it can be determined that cases have been decided correctly or incorrectly. At any rate, an elaboration would have no authority. The new, purportedly wrongly decided case alters the legal situation. Its existence, however, preempts the finding that the decision is incorrect.

It may seem that the whole would merely have to be reconstructed in light of the new situation. Yet, reinventing the whole must indeed appear to be quite pointless. Why construe something that cannot have any epistemic authority? Without such a whole, however, there is no role for the necessary form of recognition. It simply goes under.

In other words, in the new case the necessary form of recognition is turned into an object. The new case represents the social dimension of knowing the law, for it is generally recognized to be law. But what is known, as law, in the new case may not be knowledge at all for want of an appropriate pedigree.

Genuine common law is not a system of legal knowledge. It is a system of endorsements. In fact, it is law in the state before we encounter the first positive form. It resembles custom in its plain and legally primordial form (see p. 94). It is knowledge that does not really know. Whereas in the case of custom, the participants say "This is what we have done before"; in the case of the common law, it is said that this is what has been laid down by a court of law.

Holdings, Not Laws

In a genuine common law context, legal rules are not systematized. They are just differentiated from one another. While in the intellectual universe of legal science legislation is supposed to be non-arbitrary due to the intervention of systematic determinations, the common law entrusts the guarantee of equality of application to the skillful differentiation of rules in their context.

More precisely, law that is genuine common law is composed of "holdings." A holding is that which, normatively considered, is decisive for the outcome of the case. It can be a rule as relevant to its application. The relevance depends on the facts. This is why the common law has to remember facts. The differentiation of case-specific rules is informed by the comparison of underlying facts.

In contrast to laws, holdings are not clearly written out in an authoritative text. It is much more difficult to recognize a holding than it is to identify a provision in a statute. The determination of a holding is a "skill" that is imparted to students in the course of legal research and writing instruction.

Genuine common law sheds light on cases in other cases. A great number of important cases contain statements in which courts reconstruct bits of doctrine. Hence, cases may present themselves as little specimens of legal science. We cannot tell whether these reconstructions are to be classified as either holdings or dicta. But it would not make a difference either way. If they are dicta, they are irrelevant in any case. But even if we deem these elaborations of doctrine to be holdings, they are liable to suffer destruction and perturbation in subsequent cases. The knowledge articulated in one case can be undone in the next.

Primordial Cases

It may be objected that a system that inductively develops doctrines from case to case is capable of identifying mistaken precedents without thereby having to embrace legal science. A precedent can be identified as mistaken on the basis of prior law that is itself composed of cases. As long as these prior cases avail of impeccable pedigree, their authority is fully vindicated. The chain of cases can be followed until one arrives at the time immemorial when primordial cases were decided, possibly by demigods. The primordial cases are neither right nor wrong. They are just the outgrowth of an original power to articulate the law.

Interestingly, the *stare decisis* principle implicitly ascribes this very same power to every case once it has been laid down. All cases are equal. The skillfully crafted edifices of legal science developed in cases are bound to collapse.

Why Genuine Common Law Is Rare

Understandably, ordinary common law embraces the development of doctrine. Intriguingly, it does so either as a matter of sound policy or on the basis of a self-critique. In the first case, the relevance of some legal knowledge is recognized as a matter of prudence. The expectations of interested parties would be frustrated by too much judicial caprice. In the second case, the common law embraces legal science. It does so in the minimal form of doctrines concerning overruling. They are supposed to curb the scope of *stare decisis*.

The first strategy often gives rise to all kinds of pragmatic reconstructions of the legal system from the perspective of other disciplines. The operation of law is then subject to exposition in economic or moral terms. Legal knowledge is not accepted as genuine knowledge but as a useful tool to attain extralegal ends, such as greater economic efficiency.

The second strategy forces the common law to embrace legal science and to say that under such-and-such conditions a new case must not benefit from *stare decisis*. The position transcends, in principle, the intellectual horizon of the common law, for it accepts an authority over and above the cases, namely, the authority of legal science, the task of which is to finish the making of general rules.

False common law, however, does not wholeheartedly embrace this conclusion. It juxtaposes *stare decisis* with the authority of legal science and leaves it open how a conflict between them could ever be resolved. In particular, it remembers cases in terms of both systematization and sheer facts. It thereby sustains the possibility to challenge doctrine by rereading cases in their factual context. The disintegration of doctrine remains a life possibility.

Does Legal Science Fare Any Better?

It may be objected that legal science does not fare any better than the common law. While in the context of the common law, cases are able to shatter doctrinal edifices, legislation is able to upset legal knowledge in the same way. New legislation can doom centuries of legal science to irrelevance.

While the observation concerning the susceptibility of legal science to changes of the law is in principle correct, it overlooks a basic asymmetry between legislation and cases. Changes of legislation are not a manifestation of the futility of doctrine. They merely change its premises. They do not, however, give rise to a situation in which the application of the norm is neither true nor false but only new. The common law is like a system of knowledge that accords to false statements the status of new facts.

It cannot be denied, however, that at the end of the day Kirchmann's legendary observation is entirely correct.[40] Legislatures have the power to consign whole libraries of scholarly elaborations of law to the rank of scrap paper. All legal knowledge is like art. It is quite useless.[41]

CONCLUSION

This chapter tried to explain what it means to know the law objectively. Such objectivity is achieved if the law as a whole endorses the law that is known as an

40 See Julius Hermann von Kirchmann, *Die Werthlosigkeit der Jurisprudenz als Wissenschaft* (Berlin: Julius Springer, 1848).

41 See Oscar Wilde, *The Picture of Dorian Gray* (1891).

object. Sources are modes of actualizing the subjectivity of law. Legal science objectively recognizes legislation by systematically elaborating its meaning. Legislation determines what mere use and experimentation cannot pin down. Custom implicitly anticipates law as a whole.

This elaboration of the dynamic of sources has so far only presupposed that if there is to be law, it has to be known. It has not yet integrated the process of legal knowledge into an appreciation of law as a mode of relating to one another. This is the task of the next chapter.

4

The Legal Relation

The law permits doing either good or evil. Taking this apparent puzzle as its point of departure, this chapter develops the relation between law and morality on the basis of distinguishing between a basic and a reflective level of moral universalization. While the legal relation represents morality growing beyond itself, law nonetheless has to resort to morality to determine legal rights and obligations. The mood of morality changes, however, once it becomes relevant for the legal relation. The pursuit of legal arguments infuses moral thinking with serene irony.

PUCHTA'S PUZZLE

In his *Course of Institutions* – a treatise on Roman law – the nineteenth-century German scholar Georg Friedrich Puchta famously characterized the relation between law and morality by saying that legal rights constitute the possibility (*Potenz*) of choosing either good or evil. Morality would never present us with such a choice, for it urges us to do good.[1] The basic principle of law, by contrast, is freedom of choice, and legally free are the sinners as well as the righteous.[2] An act is not legal for the reason of being moral and, conversely, it is not illegal for the reason of being immoral.[3]

While there can be little doubt that Puchta hinted with his words at Schelling's rather enigmatic theory of freedom,[4] the complicated relation to Schelling's later philosophy should not concern us here.[5] What is, at any rate, of lasting significance is how Puchta highlights a general feature of legal rights

[1] See Georg Friedrich Puchta, *Cursus der Institutionen*, vol. 1 (Leipzig: Breitkopf & Härtel, 1841) at 9.

[2] See Puchta, note 1 at 10. [3] See Puchta, note 1 at 11.

[4] See F.W.J. Schelling, *Philosophical Investigations into the Essence of Human Freedom* (Albany: State University of New York Press, 2006).

[5] See Alexander Hollerbach, *Der Rechtsgedanke bei Schelling: Quellenstudien zu seiner Rechts- und Staatsphilosophie* (Frankfurt aM: Klostermann, 1958) at 331–335; Hans-Peter Haferkamp,

that is as straightforward as it is puzzling. People wear fur coats, eat meat, and drive fuel-inefficient cars. They abort fetuses and extract high rents from poverty-stricken tenants. Some or all of this may strike some or all of us as immoral. But if we confronted these people and pointed out to them that what they do is wrong, they might well reply that they do not care how we judge them, for they do what they do.

What Puchta suggests by saying that even the sinner is entitled to his or her legal freedom is that the law permits conduct even if it is objectively morally wrong. While, according to Puchta, moral freedom is freedom from being given to sin, legal freedom constitutes and recognizes the possibility of choice.[6]

This is the puzzle identified by Puchta: why should anyone accept morally repugnant acts simply because they originate from a legally permitted choice? Why should "servitude to sin" command our respect?[7]

THREE WAYS OUT

There are at least three ways of addressing these questions. The first recognizes conflicts between positive law and morality without perceiving any reconciliation from an overarching perspective. The second also admits of real conflicts and demands that individual moral judgment cede ground to legally permissible choices. It appeals to an overarching perspective that reflects the normativity inherent in human nature. The third way actually claims that the conflict between law and morality is spurious. It suggests, rather, that if there is any conflict at all, it must be a conflict within morality.

The first way of addressing the problem is familiar from the discussion of "statutory lawlessness."[8] Even though the focus of this discussion rests on particularly wicked laws ("Nazi law"), it is nonetheless also relevant to Puchta's puzzle.[9] H.L.A. Hart famously argued against Gustav Radbruch that drawing a sharp line between positive law "as it is" and law "as it ought to be" has greater intellectual purchase and moral candor than imagining any

Georg Friedrich Puchta und die "Begriffsjurisprudenz" (Frankfurt aM: Klostermann, 2004) at 315–345.

6 See Puchta, note 1 at 10.

7 Ibid. This raises, as Puchta suggests, the further question of how an immoral choice can ever pass as free.

8 See Gustav Radbruch, "Statutory Lawlessness and Supra-Statutory Law (1946)" (2006) 26 *Oxford Journal of Legal Studies* 1–11 (trans. Bonnie Litschewski Paulson & Stanley L. Paulson).

9 On the following, see H.L.A. Hart, "Positivism and the Separation of Law and Morals" (1958) 71 *Harvard Law Review* 593–621.

legal limits that are purportedly a priori drawn to immoral laws. It is of greater clarity to arrive, in certain instances, at the conclusion that while some act or norm is of impeccable legal pedigree, it is still too evil to be observed or to be respected. The line between law and morality is thereby sustained. Practically, however, morality has to have the last word for the simple reason that individuals will determine on moral grounds whether or not a law has to be respected. Hart did not really provide an account of this priority.[10]

It was left to Joseph Raz to explain what lends unity to such a conflict. In his view, the law provides reasons for action only if its existence amends or alters our moral obligations.[11] This is the case if the law possesses practical authority.[12] Under this condition, following legal directives rather than judging ourselves or acting alone assists us in maximizing conformity with the underlying reasons that apply to us.[13] Practical authority involves abstention from acting on the balance of reasons and surrendering one's own judgment to the judgment of another – in this case, legal institutions. The existence of practical authority is therefore expressed in an exclusionary reason for action. This means, in the case of law, that one has reason to do what the law says to the exclusion of acting on the balance of reasons that one would arrive at if it were not for the existence of a legal rule.

The authority that is expressed in exclusionary reasons provides an excellent explanation for the existence of Puchta's puzzle. Indeed, according to Raz, the model case for the existence of an exclusionary reason is a case in which a substantively overriding reason is excluded and a reason that would have been ordinarily overridden prevails.[14] The U.S. soldier who is ordered to use water boarding as an interrogation technique surrenders to the authority of American law and conforms to a substantively defeated reason that offends human dignity.[15] In this vein, Gardner points out, quite lucidly, that the

10 Gardner recently did by saying that while the reason-responsiveness epitomized by morality is "natural," the reasons created by the practical authority of law are not. See John Gardner, *Law as a Leap of Faith: Essays on Law in General* (Oxford: Oxford University Press, 2013) at 175. The naturalness explains a priority according to which law is answerable to morality and law binds only "by the grace of morality."

11 See Joseph Raz, *Ethics in the Public Domain: Essays in the Morality of Law and Politics* (2d ed., Oxford: Clarendon Press, 1996) at 343–344.

12 On the difference between theoretical (concerning beliefs) and practical (concerning actions) authority, see ibid. at 211.

13 This is the gist of the "normal justification thesis" of authority. See Joseph Raz, *The Morality of Freedom* (Oxford: Oxford University Press, 1986) at 53, 61, 71, 78, 80.

14 See Joseph Raz, *Practical Reason and Norms* (2d ed., Princeton: Princeton University Press, 1990) at 41.

15 Raz, ibid. at 45, suggests that we are less inclined to condemn the act of a person that complies with the exclusionary reason and conforms to the overridden reason than an act by a person

nature of this conflict – Puchta's puzzle – demonstrates that the law does not claim moral correctness but only to be based upon practical (moral) authority.[16] While, in his view, the acceptance of the authority of law is amenable to various considerations, it also involves establishing some allegiance to the overall better judgment of legislative or adjudicative institutions, which makes the believer tolerate at least a modicum of immoral laws.[17]

The second way of addressing the puzzle is reflected in the work of Thomas Hobbes.[18] He claims that the diversity of moral opinion is prone to give rise to conflict and strife. The resolution of moral questions with a public dimension requires an authoritative decision. It means that the sovereign has to announce what is to be regarded as right or wrong.[19] The importance of this move can barely be overstated because it suggests that the only way for moral ("natural") reason to be fully reasonable and to fulfil its role of peaceful conflict resolution is to have the sovereign tell everyone what is required by morality. The medium thereto is law.[20] In a shrouded way, positive law is right reason and morally fully vindicated: "[. . .] [N]o Law can be Unjust. The Law is made by the Soveraign Power, and all that is done by such Power, is warranted, and owned by every one of the people; and that which every man will have so, no man can say is unjust."[21]

Hobbes does not, however, suggest that we do not remain entitled to our moral views *intra muros* and *privatim*. Hence, this view recognizes a true conflict, which can be resolved, however, on the basis of natural reason and human nature. To enjoy public tranquillity, we have a content-independent reason to regard what the sovereign says as morally right.

The third way, which is most clearly articulated in Dworkin's legal theory,[22] does not perceive any real conflict. Legal rights obtain their authority from within a political theory that is an element of a larger moral theory. The political theory reflects the effort to arrive at the best possible interpretation of

that strikes the wrong balance of reasons. Hence, we find a soldier who follows orders and violates human dignity less morally at fault than a soldier believing that human dignity may legitimately be trampeled upon if there is a remote possibility that this would help national security. I am not so sure that Raz is right about this.

16 See Gardner, note 10 at 141–142. 17 See ibid. at 12, 15.

18 For very helpful commentaries, see Gerald J. Postema, *Bentham and the Common Law Tradition* (Oxford: Clarendon Press, 1986) at 54–60.

19 See Thomas Hobbes, *Leviathan* (ed. I. Shapiro, New Haven: Yale University Press, 2010) chap. 17 at p. 105.

20 See Hobbes, note 19, chap. 29 at p. 194, chap. 30 at p. 208; Postema, note 18 at 59.

21 Hobbes, note 19, chap. 37 at pp. 266–267.

22 This has been consistently his position since the publication of *Taking Rights Seriously* (2d ed., Cambridge, Mass: Harvard University Press, 1978).

the legal materials seen against the background of community morality. Apparent conflicts between, on the one hand, the rights that people are perceived to have as a result of a coherent and morally most appealing interpretation of the legal materials and what, on the other, may seem to be morally correct independent of these rights are conflicts between different departments of moral theory. Plainly speaking, they are conflicts between an interpretation of law that claims to take the position of a particular community and opinions on moral matters that detach themselves from community history and community understandings. At its core, this is a collision of competing moral arguments. While one is informed by an elaborate political theory, the other reflects moral convictions more generally. Undeniably, any moral theory that makes room for a political theory that elaborates values such as democracy and freedom of choice will most likely see interpretations of legal rights prevail over more detached views on moral issues. At the end of the day, however, there is no conflict between law and morality. That people get away with chanting racial insults because doing so counts as exercising the right to freedom of expression is the right answer to the question of what is morally best, all things considered. As in the case of Hobbes, an overarching perspective supposedly resolves the conflict. In contrast to Hobbes, however, one finds only an internal collision among different parts of a person's moral theory and no conflict between public and private morality. While, according to Hobbes, the views of the legal order merely have to be *regarded* as morally correct, they are *truly* correct if they are correct, according to Dworkin.

THE UNASKED QUESTION

Even though the three views differ as to how they perceive conflict and how they arrive, if at all, at a resolution, they are also similar in one respect. They take it for granted that there is a default relation between and among people. Or, putting it differently, all three views presuppose that when we are confronted with Puchta's puzzle, we have to step outside the law and talk about it from within a relation in which we expect us and others to provide reasons for action.[23] It is with this normative expectation that we relate to others morally. We attempt justifications; if these appear to be out of reach, we still attempt to arrive at explications that show that our conduct is, even if it is not defensible, in one way or the other intelligible, that is, reason based, even if, for example, based on the wrong balance of reasons:

[23] On the justifiability of action, see T.M. Scanlon, *What We Owe to Each Other* (Cambridge, Mass.: Harvard University Press, 1998) at 168–169.

"Why did you kill the white police officer?"
"His racism enraged me."

There is, of course, more to morality than giving reasons for what we do. But at its core it is about proving to others one's reason-responsiveness, not least because if and as long as one has it, one rises above mere nature. It accounts for agency and allows one to pass as the author of what one does. We demonstrate reason-responsiveness by justifying or at least explaining action in terms establishing a connection to reasons. This is why we say things such as

"Someone was pushing me."
"I was beside myself."

But also

"I took the loaf of bread because I was hungry."
"I am cool with it."

In the case of justifications, the reasons that we give to pass as responsible agents are supposed to be universal, for we would fail at justifying our actions when we said that we do what we do because we are who we are.[24] Others would have to be us, and nobody else, to be able to agree with us.[25] Reasons that cannot be shared with others do not amount to moral reasons:[26]

"Nobody who is so hungry should be reprimanded for taking the loaf of bread."
"This is a matter of personal preference and if people are cool with it that's fine."

The moral relation is, as Puchta perceptively observed, the relation where nothing is decided and everything is supposed to be based upon thinking it through. Of course, Puchta would not have denied that morality recognizes choices. Morally understood, however, the point of recognizing choices is that if something is left to decision, then it is for the reason that letting someone

24 It is an old question of practical philosophy whether we can be responsible for unreasonable actions given that we are only free and can, hence, only count as the authors of our action if we behave reasonably. Reason is universal. *Freely* not living up to universality implies the outright revolt against it. Bad action, hence, is a deliberate rejection of reason. Choosing evil involves the embrace of particularity in an act of choice that precedes the moral relation; in fact, it even precedes reason itself. See F.W.J. Schelling, *Über das Wesen der menschlichen Freiheit* (ed. W. Schulz, Frankfurt aM: Suhrkamp, 1975) at 59. The choice for or against good or evil is a pre-moral choice. See Michelle Kosch, *Freedom and Reason in Kant, Schelling, and Kierkegaard* (Oxford: Clarendon Press, 2006) at 62.

25 On the intelligibility condition, see J. David Velleman, *How We Get Along* (Cambridge: Cambridge University Press, 2009) at 13, 17–18.

26 See Christine M. Korsgaard, *The Sources of Normativity* (Cambridge: Cambridge University Press, 1996) at 137–138. It is a different matter, of course, that having an experience that cannot be shared can be shared as a reason.

choose is the right thing to do. For example, it makes much sense to give folks space to express their preferences where it is morally appropriate to let preferences be the determining factor. Allowing people the choice of their food is morally right. The resolution of many practical questions does not admit of mathematical precision. If it is necessary that judgment be exercised by some experienced and qualified decider, then giving such a person a choice serves a morally legitimate purpose. Granting the right to choose is then part of the morally right answer.

We have not looked deeply enough into Puchta's puzzle, however, until we recognize that to resolve it, we automatically return to morality. We barely notice that we do and that we are thereby leaving the legal relation. If we stayed inside this relation, we would perceive "mere volition,"[27] which is indifferent to whether what is at stake in a choice is of moral significance. Puchta observes that just like morality ignores the will qua power of free choice (*Potenz*), the law pays no heed to whether the choice is about either good or evil.[28] It is part of Puchta's puzzle that this distinction does not show up within the legal relation.

This raises the question of how it is morally possible that people relate to one another legally in the first place. In the cases of the second and the third view sketched earlier, the explanation for the existence of the legal relation is given in terms of either rationality or morality. We are in a legal relation when we obey orders that are backed up with coercive threats. We are telling ourselves that we obey because obedience is in our own self-interest, or we are telling ourselves that we are in a legal relation in order to avoid exposure to immoral coercive acts. The legal relation is morally good because it facilitates external freedom.

What the usual accounts overlook, however, is that the legal relation is not merely of instrumental value. It does not merely serve some valuable purpose. Rather, it is the consequence of solving an antinomy inherent in morality. This is what makes Puchta's puzzle all the more puzzling, for moral revulsion of legally permissible choices reintroduces this antinomy. From this follows that stepping outside the legal relation to address Puchta's puzzle ignores that something happens to the moral relation once it becomes legal. This, at any rate, is what the following observations attempt to demonstrate.

HEGEL'S PUZZLE

Claims as to what is morally right or wrong have to observe the principle of universalization. You universalize if you regard a rule as binding for all after

[27] See Puchta, note 1 at 10. [28] See Puchta, note 1 at 14.

putting yourself into the shoes of affected others, finding that the rule is acceptable also from their point of view. This formulation, which actually borrows from Hare,[29] captures what Mackie describes as a second stage of universalization.[30] The first stage, by contrast, extends only to ruling out that the mere difference between you and me is of any relevance to moral judgment.[31] It precludes, for example, claiming exemptions from moral demands on the ground that I am I (because I am special). It does not preempt, however, the endorsement of any factor invoked in favor of differential treatment. At the first stage of universalization, it can be validly claimed that I am not subject to a rule because I am white, at least as long as I am applying this criterion consistently to all white persons. Evidently, however, the criterion needs to be dismissed at the second stage because nonwhites have no reason to accept unwarranted white privilege. Putting yourself into the shoes of nonwhites, you see no reason to accept white privilege because there is nothing that could be claimed in its defense. It is the extension of giving unwarranted preference to oneself by using a factor that is as arbitrary as the fact that I am I.

Universalization involves a certain puzzle, which was famously identified by Hegel.[32] Universalization makes room for particularity without thereby losing its form. For reasons that are external to the principle of universalization, two or more persons may reach different conclusions without violating this principle. The explanation lies in the different *evaluative outlook* from within which people appraise how actions may legitimately affect others.[33] While the form of universalization detaches judgments from concrete contexts, the evaluative outlook indicates the relevance of an imagined form of life. The latter comes to the fore in how moral judgment tacitly draws on holistic visions of how people have to live in order to live rightly. Such visions mediate

29 See R.M. Hare, *Moral Thinking: Its Levels, Method, and Point* (Oxford: Oxford University Press, 1981) at 108.

30 See J.L. Mackie, *Ethics: Inventing Right and Wrong* (Harmondsworth: Penguin Books, 1977) at 90.

31 See ibid. at 83, 87, 88.

32 See G.W.F. Hegel, *Elements of the Philosophy of Right* (trans. H.B. Nisbeth, Cambridge: Cambridge University Press, 1991) § 135 at p. 162; G.W.F. Hegel, *Philosophie des Rechts: Die Vorlesung von 1819/20 in einer Nachschrift* (ed. D. Henrich, Frankfurt aM: Suhrkamp, 1983) at 105. For an introduction, see Sally S. Sedwick, "Hegel's Critique of the Subjective Idealism of Kant's Ethics" (1988) 26 *Journal of the History of Philosophy* 89–105 at 97. In all fairness, it needs to be said that a similar observation had been made by Hegel's fierce and stalwart opponent Arthur Schopenhauer. See Arthur Schopenhauer, "Preisschrift über die Grundlage der Moral" in *Werke in fünf Bänden*, vol. 3 (ed. L. Lütkehaus, Zurich: Artemis, 1988) at 512–514.

33 Within Mackie's analytical framework, the problem comes to the fore at the third stage of universalization. See Mackie, note 30 at 89. It emerges, then, that people come to the table of universalization invested with different tastes, values, and ideas.

the trade-off of values. They are holistic in that they cannot be broken down into discrete unrelated ideas. They would disintegrate – lose their force – if they were explicitly stated in analytical fashion.[34]

Teenagers turn their speakers up because they would not mind if their neighbors did, at least occasionally. Aging legal philosophers do very much mind being disturbed by lousy background beats. Teenagers expect philosophers to recognize that bustling fun is of greater value than tranquil serenity. Aging legal philosophers expect the reverse. Their respective attitudes are expressed in valuing something more highly than something else (fun and tranquillity, respectively). This is intrinsic to their form of life.[35]

Both teenagers and aging legal philosophers are guided in their judgment by certain images of what living well is all about. However, what they take to be a good life would be only incompletely stated in the form of objectives or goals. The power of guiding ideas stems from the emotional pull of fragmentary imageries derived from cultural sources. We encounter an idealized form of life in movies, soaps, or the *Belle Lettres*. Forms of life are reflected aesthetically, not philosophically.[36] The reflection reveals what "feels right" to us, while that which feels right to us remains conceptually indeterminate. This should not come as a surprise. Happiness is, if it is anything, the feeling of feeling good about one's life.[37]

[34] On the concept of the life world, in this vein, see Jürgen Habermas, *Theorie des kommunikativen Handelns*, vol. 2: *Zur Kritik der funktionalistischen Vernunft* (Frankfurt aM: Suhrkamp, 1981b) at 188–189.

[35] There can be no doubt that being an aging legal philosopher is a form of life. It is, in fact, a perfect way of having a fully human form of life.

[36] On the difference between philosophical and aesthetic reflection, see Christoph Menke, *Kraft: Ein Grundbegriff ästhetischer Anthropologie* (Frankfurt aM: Suhrkamp, 2008) at 77, 89, 103.

[37] This indicates, incidentally, that universalization is necessarily mediated by a teleological element. This can be seen by examining more closely how Kant sought to determine the conditions under which maxims are not universalizable. According to Kant, a maxim cannot pass the "test" of the categorical imperative if it can neither be *concieved of as* nor *willed to be* a universal law. See Immanuel Kant, "Grundlegung der Metaphysik der Sitten." In *Kants gesammelte Schriften* (Royal Prussian Academy edition, reprint, Berlin: de Gruyter 1963) vol. 4, 385–463 at 423. On the distinction between the contradiction in conception and the contradiction in will, see Onora O'Neil, *Acting on Principle: An Essay in Kantian Ethics* (2d ed., Cambridge: Cambridge University Press, 2013) at 26–27, 136–142. One is confronted with a contradiction in conception if the action would be impossible were the underlying maxim a generally recognized law. There would be no practice of lending money if lenders knew that borrowers never repaid their loans. By contrast, one is confronted with a contradiction in will – very roughly speaking – if one does not treat others as an end in the same manner in which one regards one as an end oneself. J. David Velleman, "Reading Kant's Groundwork" http://ssrn.com/abstract=2088330 offers a sophisticated analysis of Kant's distinction. This analysis reveals that role taking and the reversibility of perspectives are an element of the categorical

The sentimental reflection of what mediates trade-offs of values must not be mistaken for the relativity of moral values. Both teenagers and aging legal philosophers may well attribute value to fun and serenity. What they disagree about is their relative weight in concrete cases. What accounts for disagreement is how overall goodness is articulated in aesthetic form. Some find themselves moved by different imageries than others. This dynamism gives life to morality. The determining role of the imagination implies *conceptual indeterminacy*; but it does not in and of itself imply the relativity of values.

Nevertheless, the simple example suggests that, borrowing Korsgaard's parlance, different people "pull themselves together" differently. The reasons that they use have different weight. This weight indicates holistically posited forms of life. Since reasons function as reasons only as a result of their weight, this implies that in the practice of moral judgment we encounter practical reason in dispersed form. Reason tracks, as it were, different centers of gravity. The force of reasons appears to be tainted with contingent factors. In this case, it depends on how old you are, how you feel, or what you view to give sweetness to life.

imperative, too. One cannot "think" to act on a maxim if it contains a contradiction of conception (ibid., 10). If everyone knew that you do not return deposits, no one would ever give you one. Actions suffer from a contradiction of conception if their goal cannot be attained. Unless people misunderstood the meaning of what a deposit is, they would know that you are the worst person to give one to (ibid., 14). By contrast, there is a contradiction of the will if you would want to be affected by an action even though it does not suffer from a contradiction of conception. Withholding money from needy persons in the interest of saving money is not on its face as self-defeating as would be giving a deposit to someone who does not return it. Yet, the rule cannot be universalized if you cannot want to suffer, as a needy person, from the avarice of others. Interestingly, Kant goes to some lengths to point out that the part of the categorical imperative that enjoins one from acting on pain of a contradiction in will is different from the golden rule that proscribes doing unto others as one would not want to have done unto oneself. The reason why Kant wishes to draw a line vis- à -vis the golden rule is that the latter anchors universalization in a contingent want and thereby assimilates it to a reciprocal contractual arrangement. For an illuminating commentary, see Christoph Horn, Corrina Mieth & Nico Scarano, *Immanuel Kant: Grundlegung zur Metaphysik der Sitten* (Frankfurt aM: Suhrkamp, 2007) at 253–254. Such a line-drawing exercise can only be successful, even within Kant's deontological framework, if the having of certain ends, such as seeking one's own perfection or fostering the well-being of others, is morally categorically required. Kant's moral theory, therefore, posits that the adequate development of beings that are capable of pursing ends is an end in itself. See ibid. at 245–246, 252. Kant's contradiction-in-will test is different from the application of the golden rule only if there are necessary ends that follow from the premise that human beings are ends in themselves. Perhaps promoting the happiness and well-being of others is such an end. The *teloi* mediating universalization are either contingent (golden rule) or allegedly necessary (categorical imperative), but they are required to conduct the test concerning a contradiction in will.

Consequently, an antinomy arises, which is usually trivialized by calling it "reasonable disagreement."[38] Undoubtedly, neither the aging legal philosopher nor the teenager judge unreasonably. Both abide by the principle of universalization. At the same time, from neither perspective is it substantively reasonable that the other does not universalize in the manner in which they do themselves. This is not to say, however, that it is not socially adequate to pay respect to the other.

THE BASIC AND THE REFLECTIVE LEVEL

It would be wrong to conclude, however, that the end of the story is relativism with regard to practical reason. Rather, the relativity of moral universalization is only the beginning. The Hegelian observation suggests that moral judgment is possible only if the judging person rightfully demands that everyone else share his or her evaluative outlook.[39] As a demand of universalization, this is subject to strictly impersonal reciprocity. Hence, not only are you to put yourself into the position of others affected – for example, by imagining exposure to unwanted sonorities from the neighboring apartment – you are also to put yourself into the shoes of others by wearing the shoes of another universalizer. The aging legal philosopher is supposed to appear in the evaluative guise of the teenager. As Mackie correctly indicated, he has to lose himself by taking the position of another person.[40] Consequently, these "double-shoes" of *reflective universalization* lead to a situation of double contingency.[41] You are only willing to

[38] The talk of "reasonable disagreement" goes back to Rawls's *Political Liberalism* (New York: Columbia University Press, 1991) and has been introduced by Rawls with reference to the "burdens of judgment." The concept has attained particular prominence in the legal philosophy of Jeremy Waldron and his disciples. See Jeremy Waldron, *Law and Disagreement* (Oxford: Oxford University Press, 1999); Samantha Besson, *The Morality of Conflict: Reasonable Disagreement and the Law* (Oxford: Hart Publishing, 2006). The concept masks the fact that we are confronted with disagreement where we should not have it and where nobody can be blamed for being unreasonable. Rawls's explanation of disagreement by pointing to the burdens of judgment suggests that moral disagreement is the consequence of some imperfection of reason. This view is unpersuasive not least because it must see moral belief mediated by imperfect insight. Moral cognitivism is not well served by this idea.

[39] Mackie, note 30 at 94, has hinted at the fact that the idea of giving equal weight to different evaluative outlooks, albeit practically a nonstarter, would also reflect a particular outlook, namely, the outlook of liberalism. He thereby correctly identified the problem that the first-order outlook carries over into the second-order outlook that is supposed to mediate the clash of first-order outlooks. Evidently, the only principle capable of pointing the way forward is the formal principle of reciprocity: I yield to your outlook if you yield to mine.

[40] See Mackie, note 30 at 93.

[41] See Niklas Luhmann, *Social Systems* (trans. J. Bednarz Jr. and D. Baecker, Stanford: Stanford University Press, 1996).

surrender your evaluative outlook to others provided that they surrender their own to you. There seems to be no way out of this predicament.

This seeming impossibility masks a possibility that is already latent in this situation. On the basic level of universalization, the teenager has to put herself into the shoes of the aging legal philosopher by looking at the matter from the perspective of the philosopher's preference for tranquillity. This preference, however, invariably loses out in the course of the trade-off of values that is intrinsic to the teenager's evaluative outlook. On the level of reflective universalization, however, the teenager has to put herself into the shoes of the legal philosopher invested with his emotional outlook, which accounts for ascribing greater weight to tranquillity than to fun. Wearing these double-shoes, she yields to how the aging legal philosopher would put himself into his own shoes. Necessarily, universalization becomes particularistic. What is more, the teenager becomes self-effacing. For the reason of reciprocity, the same applies to the legal philosopher.

Reciprocity with regard to self-effacing behavior ("I am you if you are I") loses its paradoxical air if the negation of the own evaluative outlook becomes universalized. What disappears, consequently, from the horizon of judgment are the particular evaluative outlooks themselves. What remains of them is "the having of" an outlook that is swayed aesthetically. This marks the moment at which moral judgment reaches out beyond itself and begins to address its own operation.

The focus of universalization shifts, consequently, from assessing the acceptability of particular rules or principles to dealing with the particularity of rules and principles that are intended to be universal. The existence of particular instances of universalization (the "having of an evaluative outlook") has to be universalized. Consequently, the aging legal philosopher and the teenager can establish reciprocity by conditionally yielding to the particular universalization of others. They can thereby lend universalization existence within limited spheres.

THE TRANSMUTATION OF REASONS INTO CHOICES

When we concede to each other our evaluative outlooks within limited spheres, something happens to what we take to be the reasons of others (and *a fortiori* the reasons we happen to have ourselves). While each of us may still experience the pull of our own reasons, the reasons of others lack gravity for us. When we examine the reasons of others, they are severed from the fictive center of the evaluative outlook of the other person.[42] More precisely, they cannot even count as reasons for us.[43] They have the status similar to Raz's excluded reasons,[44] namely, of reasons that we principally must not engage with. If, therefore, we recognize the determinations of others, we recognize something – give it even authority over us – that is different from what we take to be practical reasons. This is the case even if claims by others are cast in universal form. For example, if we recognize that Søren believes it necessary go to church on Sunday, we may not share Søren's reason. We only understand the fact that people like him have reason to do what they do on a Sunday. We recognize the having of a reason, but not the reason itself. We treat having some reason as a factual occurrence to which we attribute normative significance. The claim of the reason itself is disclaimed. The having of a reason for action is taken by us to be a universally valid reason for making room for that action.[45] If Søren thinks that he has reason to go to church on Sunday, he is, from our second-personal perspective, entitled to go to church. This is how universality within limited spheres results in the recognition of freedom of action in the external sphere.

We are thereby establishing a new type of relation with Søren. Its ground is the universalization of the having of evaluative outlooks. The latter keep us going as moral beings. They allow us to have views and to be opinionated. We mutually recognize that outlooks make it possible for us to fixate moral beliefs. They make us settle on something.

42 The formulations hint at Vellemanian ideas. See J. David Velleman, *Foundations for Moral Relativism* (Open Book, 2013) at 52–53.

43 See Korsgaard, note 26 at 140.

44 Strictly construed, Raz's excluded reasons are reasons that one must not comply with. See Joseph Raz, *Practical Reason and Norms* (2d ed., Princeton: Princeton University Press, 1990) at 194, 190, where exclusionary reasons are characterized as excluding considerations of excluded reasons regardless of their weight.

45 A reader of this chapter raised the probing question whether it is indeed possible to understand a reason that others have while remaining unswayed or unaffected by its normative force. Claiming this to be possible seems to commit one to the view that we are like normatively closed systems that merely process information. Answering this questing fully would require delving deeply into hermeneutics. This cannot be done here. It can be pointed out, however, that Brandom defended the possibility of viewpoint-relative *de dicto* interpretations of beliefs and distinguishes those from *de rei* interpretations that engage with beliefs substantively. Suffice it say, hence, that accepting that Søren thinks to have a reason is equivalent to a *de dicto* interpretation of his belief. We understand the significance of the belief *for* a religious believer, but we do not share it. See Robert B. Brandom, *Tales of the Mighty Dead: Historical Essays in the Metaphysics of Intentionality* (Cambridge, Mass.: Harvard University Press, 2002) at 94–102; for a critical analysis of Brandom's claim, see Cristina Lafont, "Meaning and Interpretation: Can Brandomian Scorekeepers be Gadamerian Hermeneuts?" (2008) 3 *Philosophy Compass* 17–29.

At the same time, the reasons of Alter may not at all count as reasons from within Ego's outlook. Indeed, Ego would fail to give sufficient room to Alter's very own reason-responsiveness if she did not respect Alter's own determination of what counts as a reason for him. Surprisingly, then, since the force of reasons is irrelevant for respecting Alter's wants from a second-personal view, it follows that what is decisive is *that* he wants something, no matter whether Alter "really" wants it, purports to want it, wants it for a reason or no reason at all. For if the reasoning leading up to having a reason must be largely irrelevant from a second-personal perspective, then having a reason condenses into an act in which someone determines what he or she wants to do.

Consequently, moral judgments that are intended to be universalizable become socially significant – translate into permissible action – only by viewing them as *choices*. Most intriguingly, fitting a smaller box – acting on moral judgments – into the social world gives rise to a larger box – acting on mere choices – that encompasses action without regard to the moral quality of reasons. The element of universality attaches itself to mere choices after traveling from the first-personal moral judgment to the second-personal having of reasons.

THE EMERGENCE OF THE LEGAL RELATION

This explains how the legal relation emerges from the moral relation. It emerges by necessity on moral grounds. What has begun with meeting the expectation to justify or to explain actions becomes thereby condensed into "because I want it."[46]

The legal relation is much broader than what may be recognized as law by any official system of positive primary and secondary rules. It is a way of relating to others that is possible, however likely not sustainable, without police officers or courts. It is manifest in every act in which we lift from one another the burdens of justifying acts other than by saying "I have a right to."[47] On a level that precedes action, it is manifest, for example, in politely enduring the wrong-headed political statements of your relatives. You resign yourself to considering them entitled to their opinions. But it also comes to the fore in

[46] For a brief analysis of "claims," see Stephen Darwall, "Because I Want It" in his *Morality, Authority, and Law: Essays in Second-Personal Ethics* I (Oxford: Oxford University Press, 2013a) 93–113 at 108.

[47] Importantly, saying that I have a right to something in a manner that attains the desired morality-shedding effect presupposes some source that is itself not the "non-coercive force of better arguments." Rights, in order to work as rights, have to have a social source or to originate from some divine ordinance.

the demeanor of students who disclaim intellectual responsibility for voicing their views by pointing out that what they say is merely their view. Wherever we yield to the perplexing fact that practical reason comes in various shades of gray, we encounter the prototype of law, which grows into law when we enter external actions.

Law is the morally legitimate way of shedding morality's onerous burden.[48] There are two sides to this. While the first is facilitating, the other is emancipating. Once we mutually grant to one another our moral beliefs, such believing becomes a real practical possibility. Moral beliefs can be acted out even if one may occasionally befall doubts regarding their accuracy when others do not share them. Not by accident, insufficient reasons are the social sibling of the inscrutable inner voice.[49] There is a certain irony to this. After all, it is the right to believe morally, and not universally shared insight, that mediates the practice of moral belief.

But the law also accomplishes the reverse. The reciprocity inherent in the legal relation invites Ego to conceive of herself as another Alter, namely, as a chooser whose reasons for choice may well remain inscrutable.[50] As soon as Ego internalizes the legal relation – that is, enters into a legal relation with herself – she can escape the strictures of moral conscience, about which one may have misgivings anyway. Such emancipation from the inner voice is mediated by the recognition that one encounters otherness within the legal relation. This is how we are made, through the encounter with another, into others for ourselves.[51] Each can recognize himself as another. The law offers, therefore, a path toward self-transcendence. By virtue of law, people are not just secure in their autonomy. They are freer than they would be without it, for they would hardly dare escaping from the dictates of morality if rights did not enable them to be free choosers.

More remarkably, only from within the legal relation can it occur to a person that she can "choose" to be moral. Morality itself would categorically exclude such a choice,[52] not least because guidance of such a choice presupposes, from a moral perspective, the reason-responsiveness that is intrinsic

48 See also Jürgen Habermas, *Faktizität und Geltung: Studien zur Diskurstheorie des Rechts und des demokratischen Rechtsstaats* (Frankfurt aM: Suhrkamp, 1992) at 151.

49 Concededly, this is a very Hegelian point.

50 There is, generally, something enigmatically second-personal about volition in general. This explains why it is so difficult to get oneself to want something. Our best experiences of our wanting something are experiences of being taken over by oneself as if one were conquered by another person.

51 On *Veranderung*, see Michael Theunissen, *Der Andere: Studien zur Sozialontologie der Gegenwart* (2d ed., Berlin: De Gryuter, 1977) at 84.

52 See Gardner, note 10 at 152–153.

to morality. If morality is rendered, within the legal relation, as something that is potentially chosen, it thereby alters its mood. While, as morality, it has to remain categorical, it is also held at a distance.

The transcendence vis-à-vis morality is symbolized in the abstractness with which legal persons encounter one another on the level of the legal relation.[53] Persons are perceived as choosing regardless of whether or not they are striking some balance of reasons. They are cast as being capable of pure choice. The evaluative outlook drops out of the picture. The *persona in abstracto* has no biography. She exists, as it were, in the moment of choice and for the moment of choice. She is free even if her exercise of freedom would from a moral perspective be discounted as wantonness. She is for others, and for herself, not what she is individually.[54]

AUTHORITY

The facilitation of and the emancipation from morality represent the liberating dimension of the legal relation. Its authoritative dimension, by contrast, comes to the fore when we examine more closely how reflective universalization affects reasons for action.[55]

The reasons that Alter yields to when Alter yields to Ego's legal claims are person-relative. It is irrelevant, indeed, whether what Ego may believe to have reason to want would count as a reason for Alter. As many people who delight in listening to classical music know, concerts are often attended by people whose lack of interest in the performance is manifest in audible skimming through the program notes or, even worse, intermittent chatting with their companions. True insiders cannot but wonder what it is that drives such outsiders to prepare for themselves such costly boredom. Morally speaking, insiders would have all the right to confront the outsiders during the intermission and to exhort them to leave, for their conduct constitutes an annoyance

[53] This is an old staple of nineteenth-century German legal theory. See Puchta, note 1 at 18–19; Hegel, *Elements*, note 32 at § 35 at 68.

[54] It bears mentioning, at this point, that one of the few writers who emphasized the relational character of law was the British philosopher Michael Oakeshott. He did so on the basis of distinguishing types of relationships and by identifying the type of persona that we create within them. See "The Rule of Law" In Michael Oakeshott, *On History and Other Essays* (Indianapolis: Liberty Fund, 1999) 129–179.

[55] It is essential, in this context, to stay within the bounds of the legal relation. Dworkin, for example, correctly perceives an intrinsic connection between law and the justification of coercion. Ronald Dworkin, *Law's Empire* (Cambridge, Mass: Harvard University Press, 1986) at 139. However, the justification is supposed to take place from within the moral relation. Dworkin ignored how coercion is written into the very form of the legal relation.

for others; in any event, they are wasting their time (don't you agree, reader?). Evidently, the legal relation prevents such a confrontation. This does not mean that insiders would violate a code of law if they undertook to lecture outsiders during the intermission about their having no business being here; what it means, however, is that such a claim can be simply dismissed by saying that, like it or not, the impugned outsiders have a right to attend. Whatever may motivate them to enter a concert hall, the law counts the outsiders' presence as a reason for the insiders to respect their presence even if insiders would never attend a performance to skim languidly through the program notes let alone chat with their neighbors.

Generally speaking, this means that Alter would not have a reason for action if it were not for Ego's claim. Not only would Alter never do what Ego does if he were in her shoes and merely concerned about himself, he would see Ego's reasons for action overridden by the interests of affected others. If the world were composed of Alters alone, Ego would never show up in a concert hall. In the world that is composed of both Alters and Egos, Ego's action gives rise to new and separate reasons for Alter.

Ego's act changes Alter's reasons for action. This means, borrowing Raz's parlance, that Ego has authority over Alter. The fact that Ego has decided to attend the performance provides Alter with a reason to respect her behavior. The reasons upon which her choice depends – Raz's "dependent reasons"[56] – do not and must not matter.

TECHNOCRACY OR POLITY

The contrast to Raz's service conception of authority is stark, nonetheless. According to the service conception, authority exists to make an agent indirectly better conform to reasons that apply to him by not allowing him to comply directly but by substituting his judgment with that of another person.[57] In at least three respects, the conception of the authority of legal claims developed here is different.

First, the point of Ego's activity is not to identify the reasons that apply to Alter regardless of Ego's action.[58] Rather, her acts constitute such reasons. Second, the authority sweeps broadly and encompasses not only relations in which Ego tells Alter what he ought to do but also the whole array of situations

[56] See Raz, note 13 at 41. [57] See Raz, note 14 at 193.

[58] See Joseph Raz, *Between Authority and Interpretation: On the Theory of Law and Practical Reason* (Oxford: Oxford University Press, 2008) at 140, where the point of authority is explained as enabling subjects better to conform to reasons.

in which Ego's action lead to a change in Alter's reasons.[59] Third, Ego's authority does not maximize reason-responsiveness in the sense envisaged by Raz. This point requires further elaboration.

The realm of reasons is vast and complex. In various cases, self-abdication appears to be the best way of being reasonable. It is left to those who are subject to authority to judge under which circumstances a surrender of judgment is reasonably warranted. Owing to better insight or greater organizational capacity authority maximizes their reason-responsiveness. Thus understood, it is inherently technocratic.

By contrast, the authority of law that emerges from the legal relation is an authority of rights. It is not technocratic; rather, it is political in the sense that it addresses the ineradicable plurality of human beings. Nobody has ever stated this point more beautifully than Hannah Arendt: "Only where things can be seen by many in a variety of aspects without changing their identity, so that those who are gathered around them know they see sameness in utter diversity, can worldly reality truly appear."[60]

Ego and Alter have different views of concert performances. They share the relevant cultural space together politically inasmuch as they are aware of this difference. If Alter's private world were extended into the public realm, a special police squad would apprehend, handcuff, and expel all chatters and program note browsers. Alter's disgust of these people would have its way, and the service conception would underwrite the authority that aids him.

The political authority that emerges from the legal relation is different. Reflective universalization makes one yield to practical reasons that may appear hermeneutically explicable, but not persuasive. Viewed from Alter's perspective, Ego's doings are silly, but understandable, for they seem like the behavior of someone who is mindlessly following bourgeois conventions. Apparently, however, the reasons are good enough for Ego. What Alter encounters, therefore, in Ego is practical reason in a state in which it is different from his own. Since reason can be reason only if it is the same for all, he encounters practical reason as *different from itself*.[61]

Distinguishing between the technocratic and the political account of authority also reveals an intriguing similarity. In both cases, authority requires yielding to another's reason even though the reason remains opaque. This similarity casts an even clearer light on how differently the realm of practical

59 It should be noted, however, that the resolution of prisoner-dilemma type situations also works through creating a situation that alters reasons for action. See Raz, note 14 at 198.

60 Hannah Arendt, *The Human Condition* (Chicago: University of Chicago Press, 1958) at 57.

61 See Theunissen, note 51.

reason is conceived in these accounts. According to the service conception, practical reason is always universal and one. Authority is supposed to assist individuals in identifying the universally valid answer in particular cases. Its service is delivered if it helps people conform to reason. It removes obstacles that arise either from the perceived inability to identify the right reasons or from adverse conditions for the attainment of moral objectives. What the service conception does not reflect, even though it depends on it, is that the particular realizing the universal also involves the negation of the latter. The service conception claims that the particular – the determination by authority – may preempt the truly universal. But, as we have seen in the first chapter, it cannot account for the reasons why individuals should do as authority tells them to do if they know that what authority orders them to do is wrong. Rather, from the vantage point of the service conception, a clear mistake by authority must count as evidence that in fact it is none. The service conception cannot sustain the split into different levels of reasoning.

According to the alternative construction offered earlier, authority arises from reflective universalization. The problem addressed by reflective universalization is that universalization is possible only by virtue of a particularization that negates universality. In the context of the service conception that would be tantamount to recognizing that there are cases in which authority is substantively wrong. It is possible to sustain universality only by revoking authority. Reason is still one. This one reason, however, is the reason of each individual.

According to the account offered here, universality is sustained by creating the second-personal authority to have wants respected.[62] Just as in the case of the service conception, this creates room for the operation of underlying reasons and for the recognition of their impact on Alter. The mark of this authority is *legality*. Alter makes room for Ego's wants without regard for the reasons underpinning these wants. Remarkably, however, by virtue of the legal recognition of wants, one conforms, to a certain extent, to the reasons of others. One is, in a certain respect, made into an extension of their world and becomes part of its realization.[63] Through standing in a legal relation, our actions become the means for the realization of the ends of others.

62 On second-personal authority qua authority to make demands on others, see generally, Stephen Darwall, *The Second-Personal Standpoint: Morality, Respect, and Accountability* (Cambridge, Mass.: Harvard University Press, 2006) at 11. Darwall notes correctly "that the duly authorized claim creates a distinctive reason for compliance" (ibid.).

63 How the resulting patchwork of social worlds can be put together is the problem of social freedom to which we return in the final chapter.

Reflective universalization reconciles the universality of practical reason with its particularity. In contrast to the one practical reason that is individual in the case of the service conception, reason is intersubjective. Reflective universalization augments the scope of practical reason. It grows as the reasons of others are added. The one practical reason is internally pluralistic. Owing to the authority structure of law, one always encounters reason in the state of *Veranderung*. I would not encounter this reason if the world were constituted by the likes of me. Owing to the legal relation, reason is intersubjective. The practical reason of law indirectly endorses what is for us perhaps explicable, but not persuasive. It makes us respond to something that we would otherwise not even recognize as a reason.

A RELATION BEARING THE FORM OF COERCION

The last sentence reveals that within the legal relation we only unwillingly will what others want. You make yourself into an instrument for the realization of the wants of others not because of a substantive reason to oblige, but for the reason that you have to make room for others to be given room by them in return. You choose the lesser evil, for the alternative would be to drop out of the structure of reciprocity that allows you to pass as an agent.[64] It is this very reciprocity that leads, at the point of the resolution of the antinomy, to the recognition of choices.

Having to choose between two disagreeable alternatives means choosing under duress.[65] The legal obligation is inherently coercive. The threat of sanctions merely spells this out. The commitment to yourself as an agent that sustains reciprocal relations with others makes you choose the lesser evil. In yielding to what others apparently have reasons to do, you comply externally.

64 You realize that others would have reason to rescind their recognition of your standing as a chooser. You want to count as entertaining views and authoring actions. If that were not the case, you would be nil in our social world. This explains why Fichte called the necessity of law as something that is derivative of theoretical reason, a *Denkgesetz*. See Johann Gottlieb Fichte, *Grundlage des Naturrechts nach Prinzipien der Wissenschaftslehre* (ed. F. Medicus, Hamburg: Meiner, 1979) at 89.

65 A coercive threat makes a person do what that person would have never reason to do were it not for the threat. Someone tells you that y will happen unless you do x. Owing to z, doing x counts as a lesser evil for you than allowing y to happen. Choosing a worn-out example, the abductor tells you that your child will die unless you pay ransom. Paying ransom is a lesser evil for you than the death of your child. But, of course, it would have never occurred to you to give money to the abductor had it not been for the threat.

Two clarifications are in order. First, since coercion originates only by virtue of the relation created by reflective universalization, it is *legitimate*. Law is a legitimate form of coercion. It is not, however, as it is often suggested, for the reason that coercion is put to a good end. Law is a legitimate form of coercion for the entirely different reason that by virtue of the coerciveness at the heart of our social existence, the legal relation gives rise to reasons for action.

Second, the greater evil that gives rise to a threat is, quite paradoxically, both merely remote and unduly harsh. It is remote since it is unlikely that anyone would immediately lose moral standing among others for a breach of law, in particular if offenders were not likely to be found out. On the other side, however, expulsion from the sphere of morality must appear unduly harsh. It is for this very reason that Fichte suggested that legal sanctions be based upon a hypothetical agreement in which all, in order to stay within the moral domain, mutually promise one another repentance (*Abbüßung*).[66] Yet, such a hypothetical agreement does not alter the fact that actual sanctions merely implement the coerciveness that is inherent in the legal relation. The law does not back up good things with force. It is the force reflecting our drive to pass as a responsible human being.

SERENE IRONY

Puchta's puzzle was that the law might present something as a matter of right even though it is objectively morally wrong. We are now in a better position to specify what this means. What is permitted at the reflective level of universalization may look immoral when perceived from its basic level. Since the law facilitates the full expression and realization of morality, it must systematically give rise to conflicts between these levels. Puchta's puzzle would be misunderstood, hence, if it were taken to raise the question where morality must draw the substantive limit to law. Rather, the puzzle serves as a *signifier* of the legal relation. Wherever there is law, it can be challenged to be morally wrong. The observation is true also of the reverse. Wherever a claim can be made that something is legal, but immoral, there is law.

This is not the end of the story. Rather, it is the beginning of an intriguing change in the mood of moral reasoning. Recognizing rights at the reflective level of universalization does not entail that rights are absolute or exclusively to be determined by means of reciprocal concessions. The principle of universalization entails the equal enjoyment of rights. The latter is the categorical

[66] See Fichte note 64 at 254–255.

imperative in the form in which it is relevant for the legal system. What the principle of equality demands cannot be drawn out, particularly not in concrete cases, without resort to morality, not least because equality is a moral principle. While the legal relation stands for morality rising above itself, one needs to draw on morality from within it to determine the scope of rights. There can be no strict separation of law and morality.

One may be inclined to conclude, at this point, that this shows that the moral relation wins out and that, as soon as matters become delicate, one needs to step outside of the law and back into morality. This conclusion would reconfirm the view sketched earlier according to which freedom of choice facilitated by law is but a strategy for the attainment of moral objectives. Consumers have to have choices because this is good for consumer welfare. People have to have some "ownership" of their life because it makes them happy. They need choices, and possibly even "options."

But this view is mistaken. Moral reasoning is a component of the legal relation because law is about right or wrong. But the fact that moral reasoning is taken up within a legal context does not leave this reasoning unaffected.

First, the moral reasons used in the legal context are in principle – and often in fact – the reasons of others (*e.g.*, courts) and sometimes opaque or even inscrutable (courts, again). Reasoning from the perspective of the legal system, one abides by the semantics and syntax of conventional discourses. They abound in inventions that are tailored to fit abstract personhood in more specific legal relations: the "ordinary person" qua tortfeasor, the "circumspect consumer," the "diligent mother." Legal discourse reasons about individual conduct by taking individuals as tokens of general types. A story about an accident is narrated differently when told either in a court of law or among friends. The broader moral context would admit to the story many elements that the type-oriented legal discourse would consider to be irrelevant. Morality can only do justice to individuals by sustaining this openness. The law can only do justice to persons by insisting on closure.

Second, the discursive semantics and syntax of legal reasoning can be used with the same irony that is inherent in the attitude with which academic philosophers go about expounding the work of some master thinker (Kant and Wittgenstein are among the most notorious suspects). Successful scholars cast the work of important thinkers in a light that elucidates some of the darkness at the heart of their texts. Frequently, the thinker's thoughts are translated into an idiom that is more hospitable to the present-day reader. Most importantly, the scholars expounding the work of great thinkers often make an effort to defend it against subsequent or contemporary critique. Nonetheless, to be successful such hermeneutical efforts never have to commit themselves fully to the views of the master thinker.[67] The scholars may limit their role to that of virtual participants in substantive debates.[68] When all is said and done, the interpreters could disavow any allegiance to the thoughts of the thinker and debunk everything that the master said as nonsense because of this or that false premise. Even though the latter is unlikely to happen, it would be consistent with the hermeneutic maxim to cast a work in the best possible light with respect to the genre to which it claims to belong.[69] The otherness of the reasoning can be preserved throughout.

The simultaneous pursuit of perfection and detachment is not merely a specific difference that sets interpretation off against general reasoning. Serene irony alters the quality of reason. Reason is transmuted into a mask that conceals whether what the mask represents is worn with an attitude of admiration or contempt. Those who expound a philosophical approach step into the reasoning of the master to restate it with greater clarity; at the same time, the mere fact that the work requires commentary and exposition to be understood indicates that it is too weak to speak for itself. Lending the master one's own voice involves the basic ironic gesture of rising above from below (see p. 74). Scholarly commentary that articulates a work better than the author could have done herself rises above the work by virtue of its ostensible humility. What is more, admiration is paired with a symbolic emancipation from the spell of the master since the interpretive elaboration of reasoning is free to leave open whether that reasoning makes any sense at all. Reasoning is turned into a mask by virtue of which reason ends up being itself up for grabs. The serious engagement with a thinker is free to play at thinking.[70] Reason may legitimately grow entirely uncommitted to itself. It can end up having a good laugh about itself.

Elaborating a body of law from within the relevant legal discourse is very much like expounding the work of a master. The irony that is manifest both in the scholarly elaboration of a work and in making the best of a received body of legal thinking – such as the discourse of civil law – is clearly serene. It is the irony inherent in absorbing a genre or style of discourse while leaving open whether it makes any sense. It is uncommitted without being bitter. Such irony is particularly healthy when scholarship is under the impression of

67 This claim is, admittedly, debatable. See Lafont, note 45.

68 See Jürgen Habermas, *Theorie des kommunikativen Handelns*, vol. 1: *Handlungsrationalität und gesellschaftliche Rationalisierung* (Frankfurt aM: Suhrkamp, 1981a) at 168.

69 See Dworkin, note 55 at 52.

70 Wasn't this exactly what Socrates taught us? See Ernst Behler, *Klassische Ironie – Romantische Ironie – Tragische Ironie: Zum Ursprung dieser Begriffe* (Darmstadt: Wissenschaftliche Buchgesellschaft, 1972) at 17–18.

"postness," that is, when it is assumed that the grand disputes of the discipline are over and that nobody really cares about having lost his or her moral compass.[71] Under this condition, the skilful practice of the discourse on rights is similar to composing music in the classical style for the twenty-first century. Why should one not just do it as long as it is paying one's bills?

Third, this serene irony is consistent with having moral reasoning, within the legal relation, take place in the shadow of an impending choice. Unless one resorts to some form of informal dispute settlement, one cannot simply exit the legal relation and shift back to morality. In a legal context, any morally significant argument has to reckon with a decider. This affects and alters its orientation. While moral argument is originally supposed to establish truth, in the legal context it has to persuade or assuage doubt. In the case of persuasion, the addressee of the argument is a court. To be persuasive, it has to mimic the intellectual demeanor of the adjudicating body and rely on its premises, no matter how questionable they may be. Courts, by contrast, speak to the vigilant profession and to scholars in order to prove that their reasoning is not camouflaging some hidden agenda. Most importantly, what accounts for the validity of the decision is not its substantive correctness but its jurisdictional accuracy. Even most outrageous moral mistakes have to be articulated as *ultra vires* challenges. That which grounds a decision is not the moral substance of reasoning but the right to make a choice. This explains also why decisions must appear to be intellectually impoverished and rather deficient in contrast to the erudition and nuance of the pros and cons that can be exchanged on the substantive issue. German philosophers of the romantic period, such as Friedrich Wilhelm Schlegel and Adam Müller, recognized that dialogue qua interchange of thought and "counter thought" realize irony, for they allow for an indefinite circle of creation and destruction.[72] An irony that is similar to the serene irony of the "indefinite conversation" obtains for the relation between legal reasoning and decision. The latter destroys the erudition of the former, which is nonetheless constantly rebuilt in anticipation of the next decision. The decision will again stop the intrinsically unstoppable. This fact provides additional encouragement to transform the argumentative exchange into some sort of play, the result of which may or may not really matter.

Granted, these observations fit more accurately the profession of the legal scholar than the mind-set of the practitioner. The irony of rising above that

71 See Richard Rorty, *Contingency, Irony, and Solidarity* (Cambridge: Cambridge University Press 1988) at 73–74.

72 See Behler, note 70 at 64, 95–96, 101.

which one cannot alter and of playing with what may not make much sense is serene only if one is in the position to add one or the other piece to an elaborate edifice. Matters look differently when one spends one's days churning out papers or consulting clients. Rising above that which one cannot alter may then express bitterness over compliance with conventions and give rise to gestures of detachment from all claims regarding the force of legal claims.[73]

[73] See Chapter 2.

5

Equality, Freedom, and Dignity

Rights are equal if the system of rights rules out discrimination. What is wrong with discrimination can be best understood by examining what a person would have to do to avoid being treated unequally. If such preemptive action involves self-denial – the hiding or repairing of who one is – a case of discrimination appears to be established. At the same time, any lively participant in a market society is legitimately expected to adjust his or her practical identity and life projects to what is feasible in light of overall demand. The virtues of agility and adaptability rule out that a case of discrimination can ever be fully established with reference to individual idiosyncrasies. It must appear, therefore, that what remains for the protection of discrimination is the focus on immutable characteristics that agile and adaptable individuals cannot alter. Hence, the protection from discrimination would have to be limited to discrimination on the ground of characteristics that individuals cannot change. Yet, what individuals, beyond physical inalterability, may legitimately regard as inalienable and unchangeable characteristics or beliefs is not subject to a prior determination but rather the subject of social struggles. The equality principle is in and of itself historical.

INTRODUCTION

Reflexive universalization demands that we mutually ascribe rights to each other. Rights allocate space for choices. The legal relation casts us as choosers. We are rendered explicable. Implicit in the legal relation are three fundamental ideas. As choosers we are regarded as free. As mutually respecting our rights we are equal. The legal guarantee of equal freedom is supposed to enable a life in dignity. The latter idea, however, is the most appealing conception of what it means to create presence by virtue of action.

Human beings want to be present in this world by virtue of their agency. Explicability is only the most elemental condition. As agents, we want to pass as being capable of pulling ourselves together and as not merely thrown around by circumstance or sudden impulses. We expect to be seen as our own sculptors, each as "*[. . .] [s]ui ipsius quasi arbitrarius honorariusque plastes et fictor*."[1]

These three ideas are internally linked and not easily disentangled. It is submitted, here, that focusing on the equality of rights provides the key to elucidating the meaning of them all. Once equality is understood as protection from discrimination, its internal link to freedom as self-determination comes to the fore. Freedom is determination of the self by the self. Discrimination is about depriving some, and not others, of the full realization of their selfhood.

Drawing out the ideas underlying the legal relation involves its self-reflection. This means that just as morality, in giving rise to the legal relation, reflects on its operation, the legal relation reflects on its own operation between and among people to make sense of what it is supposed to accomplish. Just as morality reaches out beyond itself to be successfully self-correcting, the law has to reach out beyond itself to live up to the ideas that compose it. What the law reaches out to is not some natural law. It is the sphere of political action. There is no natural law. The law is *intrinsically* historical. Legal philosophy can do no more than elucidate the significance of historical experience and to participate in its formation.

The discussion that follows begins with elementary intuitive ideas concerning equality qua prohibition of discrimination. It then turns to exploring how different meanings of discrimination are informed by different understandings of freedom. The analysis begins with how we appear within the legal relation and moves beyond this level. It will be seen that freedom of choice is essential to freedom understood as self-determination.

The latter is only adequately understood if the exercise of practical reason is tied to the construction and revision of practical identities. From this follows that whether or not people find certain demands made upon them to be reasonable depends on whom they take themselves to be. This connection between burdens and identity marks the bridge between the freedom to be who one is and equality. All that has to be done to cross this bridge is to conceptualize inequality from the perspective of what it takes to avoid unequal treatment. Young women cannot attend schools, while others can, if they are wearing headscarves. Taking the headscarves off would avoid inequality. Yet, some of the affected women will claim that publicly baring their hair demeans their self. They cannot appear toward others in the manner in which *they* would not compose themselves. It would detract from their dignity.

[1] Pico della Mirandola, *Oratio de hominis dignitate* (ed. A. Buck, Hamburg: Meiner, 1990) at 6.

But why should young women not be forced to change their views concerning pudency? The further question can be asked, therefore, whether it is not morally permissible to expect from people that they engage in self-repair – change their attitudes, for example – to avail themselves of equal opportunities. A line might have to be drawn to this expectation only when it concerns immutable characteristics. Protection from discrimination would at its core be limited to those.

But this can mean two very different things. First, immutable characteristics can be markers of social identity the wearing of which is next to impossible to avoid (*e.g.*, complexion, accent). This view of the point of protection from discrimination is usually aligned with an unflattering conception of the self that ignores the depth of individual self-determination and self-constitution. Hence, a second view is more plausible. It views immutable characteristics as internally related to exactly these activities. Whether or not, however, a certain characteristic becomes elevated to the level of a forbidden ground of discrimination is a matter of historical social struggles. The law is in and of itself historical.

WHAT IS WRONG WITH DISCRIMINATION?

What is wrong with unequal treatment? Instances of haphazard arbitrariness aside, there is, indeed, nothing wrong with it, unless, of course, inequality amounts to discrimination. Action is supposed to be rational, not least if it is taken by government. To behave rationally, actors had better make out what they occupy their minds with. Understanding a subject of regulation properly requires, necessarily, that distinctions be drawn for reasons of classificatory accuracy. If government believes that there are reasons to ban firearms to minimize what bureaucrats wryly call "preventable deaths," it would be false if a potential ban included toy revolvers (unless there was evidence showing that a straight line of causation leads from playing with guns in the sandbox to high school shooting sprees). The rational pursuit of good reasons for action gives rise to good reasons for drawing one or the other distinction. These reasons for unequal treatment remain good so long as acting upon them does not give rise to discrimination.

But what is wrong with discrimination? It is submitted, here, that discrimination is wrong because it denies people, without any fault of their own, the social presence that is mediated by enjoying social goods. Blacks are not allowed to sit with whites. Muslims are shunned and cannot find jobs. These are paradigmatic instances of discrimination. Spaces on public busses or jobs are social goods. Availing of them is not everything; but enjoying them is indispensable for *being* someone and *counting* as someone for others.[2] Excluding someone from these goods, or limiting access to them, signals that the person is of so little worth that "counting as someone" is not really an option for her. She is irrelevant. She is admitted to a social space only to be treated as if she were not there.[3]

Admittedly, the exclusion from the enjoyment of goods seems bad enough to make discrimination wrong; yet, its connection to not giving presence to others becomes obvious when one takes most elementary and crude rationalizations of unequal treatment into account. There ought to be freedom of religion. Sure, but no such liberty must be enjoyed by Catholics. They are dangerous and should not be in the position to proselytize.[4] Public housing should be available to those who are unable to rent a dwelling at market rates. But, of course, Austrians must not be included in this group. We do not want to have *them* in our midst.

The link between discrimination and disappearance is possibly ever more clearly revealed when one turns from the face of exclusionary acts to the efforts undertaken by victims to *pass* as members of the "in-group." What comes into focus, then, are strategies of "covering" or "ducking" and other forms of hiding one's self.[5] While the exclusion from the enjoyment of goods may thus be effectively averted, the disappearing of the person continues in subtler form. The discrimination against gays, for example, does not abate simply because gays choose to stay inside the closet. It shows, depressingly, that the victims enlist to the cause.

2 See, for a very apt characterization of what Rousseau called *amour-propre*, Frederick Neuhouser, *Rousseau's Theodicy of Self-Love: Evil, Rationality, and the Drive for Recognition* (Oxford: Oxford University Press, 2008) at 36, 73, 83. On the importance of "counting" in a social context, see also Axel Honneth, *Unsichtbarkeit: Stationen zu einer Theorie der Intersubjektivität* (Frankfurt aM: Suhrkamp, 2003) at 15.

3 Concededly, this characterization of discrimination must appear to be similar to Hellman's view of discrimination as "demeaning" unequal treatment. See Deborah Hellman, *When Is Discrimination Wrong?* (Cambridge, Mass.: Harvard University Press, 2008) at 31, 33, 35; at 57: "Demeaning actions are those that put the other down. To demean is to express that the other is less worthy of concern and respect and to do so in a manner that has power." In my view, this account is a bit too narrow, for it does not take the participation in social goods sufficiently into account. See my *Engineering Equality: An Essay on European Anti-Discrimination Law* (Oxford: Oxford University Press, 2011a) at 99–100. In addition, Hellman is not terribly subtle. Putting another person down is insulting. But it amounts to discrimination only if it is based on an inequality that eliminates someone from social space.

4 See John Locke, *A Letter Concerning Toleration* (ed. J. Tully, Indianapolis: Hackett, 1985).

5 For a pioneering study, in a legal context, see Kenji Yoshino, "The Assimilationist Bias in Equal Protection: The Visibility Presumption and the Case of 'Don't Ask, Don't Tell'" (1989) 108 *Yale Law Journal* 485–571.

HEGELIAN PERSONS

This view of discrimination must invite a serious objection. Linking discrimination to denying persons – in one way or another – social presence sweeps very broadly. We do not admit persons to our classes who are not enrolled as students. Are they discriminated against? This would strike one as odd. Hence, a conception of discrimination that focuses on "not counting" and "absence" requires a careful elaboration. In this context, that lack of opportunities to be who one is presupposes that the identity in question is not a matter of social station but determined by the person herself. Hence, a closer elaboration of discrimination needs to explore the relation between equality and freedom as self-determination.[6]

Beginning with the legal relation, the meaning of self-determination can only be developed step by step. The legal relation first casts us a person in a Hegelian sense.[7] A person of this type has freedom of choice. Indeed, such a person has a certain conception of what it takes to be a self-determining being. According to this conception, self-determination is manifest in the act of rising, through choices, above the desired options from among which one chooses. Even though the will of a person is clearly affected by desires, the fact that a person chooses demonstrates that it must be she who resolves on which desire to act.[8] Figuratively speaking, a person in the Hegelian sense is an "owner" of freedom of choice. This property is circumscribed. Any person living among others needs to accept restrictions on the range of her choices. However, whichever restriction the person may actually be confronted with, it does not affect a person's self-determination; it does not, that is, so long as there remains an opportunity to rise above desires and to pick and choose from among desired options. A person in a Hegelian sense is perfectly at ease with adapting. Her self-determination would not be affected if the consumption of cigarettes, alcohol, fast food, meat, and milk chocolate were prohibited for the ominous reasons of health and safety; her self-determination would remain intact so long as she were able to choose, for example, between low-fat yogurt and tofu. She would thereby remain self-determining and therefore "free" in the sense envisaged by Hegel for "persons." This explains why this form of freedom of choice is considered to be *formal*. It is indifferent to the substance of choices.

6 There is, to be sure, an entirely trivial relation, too. It concerns the fact, for example, that blacks who are not allowed to sit with whites are prevented from sitting with whites.

7 See G.W.F. Hegel, *Elements of the Philosophy of Right* (trans. H.B. Nisbet, Cambridge: Cambridge University Press, 1991) at para. 35 pp. 67–68.

8 For an illuminating commentary, see Frederick Neuhouser, *Foundations of Hegel's Social Theory: Actualizing Freedom* (Cambridge, Mass.: Harvard University Press, 2001) at 24.

HEGELIAN PERSONS IN A HAYEKIAN SETTING

Intriguingly, persons in the Hegelian sense are the denizens of Hayek's free society.[9] One remains free in the Hayekian sense if one is not forced by another to make choices *and* if the options available for choice do not themselves involve acts of coercion. In a culture where having a choice is all there is to freedom, this freedom would only come to an end, for example, when criminal suspects, before an interrogation begins, were given a choice between electroshocks and water boarding. Within Hayek's universe, however, a choice between either knitting rugs in a stuffy basement for 70 hours a week or suffering malnutrition is qualitatively the same as the choice between buying a Porsche Panamera or a Mercedes CLS 500. In Hayek's world, which is inhabited by persons in a Hegelian sense, options are never evaluated.[10] What matters is the spiritual moment in which the will rises above some needs or desires.

A conception of self-determination that views choice as the essential factor leaves the choosing agent in the dark. Freedom is supposed to be manifest, and exhausted, in the moment of rising above desires, no matter how such a rising might actually take place. A person counts as self-determining even if the choice between and among desires is occasioned by the relatively greater intensity of one particular urge. The transition from perceiving such intensity to an actual choosing does not have to reveal a "self" standing over and above her choices. This means that the person in the Hegelian sense does not have to be concerned about who she is aside from being a chooser. She may act wantonly.[11]

MERE IRRATIONALITY

The perspective of persons in a Hegelian sense is consistent with a concept of discrimination that views it as inherently *irrational*. Imagine that nationals stand a better chance of finding employment than non-nationals because of widespread prejudice against foreigners. Not employing foreigners is irrational if foreigners actually show comparatively more energy and application than citizens. Society is just in denial. The economic harm of discrimination

9 See Friedrich August von Hayek, *The Road to Serfdom* (London: Routledge, 1991; first edition 1944) at 76.

10 See, generally, Charles Taylor, "What's Wrong with Negative Liberty." In his *Philosophy and the Human Sciences* (Cambridge: Cambridge University Press, 1985) 211–229.

11 For the person in the Hegelian sense, the existence of a choice is sufficient to demonstrate that a rise above desires has taken place, regardless of whether it merely reflects the temporal ascendancy of one desire over another.

consists primarily, even though not exclusively, of the harm discriminators inflict upon themselves.[12] If, using a stereotypical example for a stereotype, African Americans are not employed owing to false beliefs about their alleged "in your face" attitude,[13] the net welfare of society is diminished. But none of this affects the self-determination of a person in the Hegelian sense.[14] There is no interference, that is, with freedom.

The question is, of course, whether a freedom that is never affected by limited options is of value for the self-determining subject. Put differently, the question is whether we would choose, if we could, to be beings for which self-determination amounts to mere formal freedom of choice. We would, arguably, choose freedom of choice only if we perceived sufficient value in its exercise. But the value of freedom of choice depends vitally on the range or value of options – there is no value for a teetotaler to have a choice between a Margaux and a Pinot Noir from the Russian River Valley (poor fellow). Hence, we can endorse being a person in the Hegelian sense only by moving beyond it. Freedom cannot simply be about freedom of choice.

VALUABLE OPTIONS FOR THE VALUED SELF

Once the range of options is taken into account, it is possible to see how freedom is affected by discrimination, for the latter results in fewer opportunities for the victims of inequality and, *a fortiori*, less freedom for them than for others. As the late Jerry Cohen memorably pointed out, a lack of opportunities – in particular if caused by a shortage of money – implies a lack of freedom.[15]

With that we arrive at a different view of the self-determining self. It presents itself basically as a consumer with plenty of stuff to choose from. The greater the range of options, the greater is the value of freedom. A glimmer of God's almightiness shines into the choosing self.

[12] See Richard Epstein, *Forbidden Grounds: The Case against Employment Discrimination Laws* (Cambridge, Mass.: Harvard University Press, 1992).

[13] I owe this example to Brian Barry, *Freedom and Culture: An Egalitarian Critique of Multiculturalism* (Cambridge, Mass.: Harvard University Press, 2001) at 99.

[14] The reduction of discrimination to irrationality quickly comes to an end if, for example, two groups of persons are equally capable of performing a job and members of one group are not hired owing to widespread prejudice. There is no total loss of social welfare as long as there is enough labor supply from members of the other group. Under these conditions it is not irrational to stick to prejudice (unless the members of the disfavored group were willing to work for less and paying them lower wages would not diminish overall social welfare).

[15] See Gerald E. Cohen, *Freedom, Self-Ownership and Equality* (Cambridge: Cambridge University Press 1995) at 58–59.

But even such a conception of self-determination needs to reach out beyond itself to explain the appeal of choices. Even though the self can now choose everything, the choice still remains formal. A wider range of choices does not really make a difference. A choice from among 1,000 options is just as indifferent to these options as a choice between merely two. For a choice to have value, the chooser has to be able to make out *qualitative* distinctions. In other words, options have to be evaluated.[16]

The value of the choice, however, cannot simply reside in the options either. Otherwise the relevance and value of choice would remain inexplicable. It is important that the chooser actually identify what is of value. Indeed, this is what a choice is all about. It is a relative evaluative identification and endorsement of options. Since any such identification must be determined by the self, it requires relating what is to be chosen to the self for whom something is of value.

We conclude that the value of options would remain unintelligible if it were not for a conception of the self's valuable *practical identity* that accounts for their value.[17] For a vegetarian, for example, the availability of meat is of no value. But this relativity of value demonstrates that the value of options depends on the value of the practical identity that one ventures to enact.[18] If the self – being a vegetarian, for example – were of no value, avoiding meat qua path toward self-perfection would be of no value either. The self would not reflexively endorse its own value through not choosing meat.

THE PLAY OF CHOICES

It pays to proceed with circumspection at this point. If one were to say that the value of choice is entirely derivative of the value of options for a given self, one would clearly create merely a mirror image of a person in the Hegelian sense. It would be equally one sided. While the person in the Hegelian sense actually has no options to identify because of the absence of

16 It is not the case that the value of one chosen option stems from the high quantity of options that were not chosen. The model of the self as a potent chooser does not reckon with opportunity cost.

17 On the concept of "practical identity," see, of course, Christine M. Korsgaard, *The Sources of Normativity* (Cambridge: Cambridge University Press, 1996) at 101, where a practical identity is characterized as a "description under which you value yourself, a description under which you find your life to be worth living and your actions to be worth undertaking."

18 This is, of course, a reference to J. David Velleman, *How We Get Along* (Cambridge: Cambridge University Press, 2009), even though it should be noted that Velleman explores self-conceptions as "descriptions" "under which your actions and reactions make sense to you in causal-explanatory terms" (ibid., 16 footnote 8).

the evaluative dimension, its mirror image would really have no choice but merely have to apply its conception of itself in different situations. The choice would truly be an act of execution or at best amount to an exercise of discretion in cases of doubt.

This misses, however, the value of choice that resides in the fact that it is *oneself*, and not just anybody, who identifies valuable options in an act of endorsement. There is something of value in the choice between and among options that is not inherited from their evaluation in light of some practical identity. There "is" something that precedes this identity, and this something, which is indeed neither something nor nothing,[19] leaves its trace in the process of self-constitution.[20] In fact, it is by virtue of a play[21] between choices and provisional conceptions of who we would like to be that we are self-constituting in actuality. This explains why the range of options is not entirely irrelevant to our freedom. It invites recalibration in the face of discrete "good choices." Options seduce us. Sometimes we yield to temptations and end up asking ourselves "Was this really right for me?" Yet we are only over and above our practical identities if we are free to create puzzles for us and to be ahead of ourselves in our choices.

FREE TO BE WHO YOU ARE

The dependence of valuable options on a positively evaluated practical identity and the dependence of freedom to evaluate on a range of options[22] demonstrate that one can be free only if one is able to attribute value to who one is and is not required to overcome it. If freedom of choice were of value only if one had to "reinvent" oneself before choosing, one may not even choose to have choices.

19 See Gerhard Gamm, *Nicht nichts. Studien zu einer Semantik des Unbestimmten* (Frankfurt aM: Suhrkamp, 2000).

20 See Christine M. Korsgaard, *Self-Constitution: Agency, Identity, and Integrity* (Oxford: Oxford University Press, 2009) at 42. While Korsgaard is quite adamant about the fact that practical identities are not simply adopted and then executed, she does not really elucidate the blind spot that is "you" when you construct your practical identity. See her "Self-Constitution and Irony." In Jonathan Lear, *A Case for Irony* (Cambridge, Mass.: Harvard University Press, 2011) 75–83 at 79: "Your identity is never just a given, but something you are always at work at constructing and – within the limits of the demand for your integrity – how you construct it is really up to you."

21 See Hans-Georg Gadamer, *Wahrheit und Methode: Grundzüge einer philosophischen Hermeneutik* (4th ed. Tübingen: Mohr, 1975) at 98–99.

22 The range of options is valuable for two reasons. First, it is easier for you to find a place for yourself within the world. Second, a great variety of options offers more clues as to what you may want to do with your life.

This is intuitively plausible.[23] Assume that you happen to be a professor of metaphysics and are confronted, by your department, with the choice of teaching either "international trade law" or "evidence." Such a choice would be valuable to you only if you transformed yourself into a law professor with a penchant for technical subjects. Under this condition, each subject matter would provide you with different opportunities to prove yourself. However, there is no reason for you to become a law professor in the first place because teaching either of these two subjects is of no value to you. If the choice is of no value, there is no value in becoming the self for which it would be of value. You can enjoy freedom of choice only if you do not have to change yourself to enjoy it.[24] You may, indeed, venture into new and unchartered territory and open new paths of self-discovery, but this presupposes that you are the person with the courage to confront your own fragility. This does not alter the fact that only if you are *someone*, even if someone whom you have not yet recognized, you are in the position to identify valuable options.[25] "Someonenness" has to be guaranteed to you before you become a chooser.[26] Otherwise, freedom of choice would be reduced to the formal Hayekian spiritual exercise of rising, without any further reason, above desires.

At its most elementary level, then, to be free means to be free to stay who one is or to pursue who one would like to be.[27] We are catching a first glimpse of dignity here. Nobody has dignity to whom it is socially signaled that she is a worthless person unless she turns into someone else.

ANSWERING AN OBJECTION

This analysis must invite an objection. Why do we believe that child molesters have dignity even though they are persons whom we expect to become

23 Here is a transcendental argument (with an eye to Lenin and Lukács): It could be argued that a person after reinventing herself would suddenly perceive the value of options that she had not perceived before. Hence, it may be worth the while to engage in the gamble. This argument, however, presupposes another conception of oneself, namely, that the self has value inasmuch as it creates for itself, possibly through experiment, versions of itself in order to enhance its sphere of experience. Choosing to reinvent oneself to perceive valuable choices is valuable for a conception of the self that must not itself be reinvented or abandoned in this process. If the result of the gamble were a conception of the self that is resistant to reinvention, the valuing self would have disappeared. Hence, one must be allowed to stay the same.

24 Otherwise, you would remain in a state of infancy. But in a state of infancy you do not choose.

25 For a similar argument, see Korsgaard, note 17 at 121.

26 See ibid. at 120–121: "For unless you are committed to some conception of your practical identity, you will lose your grip on yourself as having any reason to do one thing rather than another – and with it, your grip on yourself as having any reason to live and to act at all."

27 The pursuit of the ambition, however, already changes you. You have made yourself into the means to be who you would like to be. For a similar observation, see Korsgaard, note 20 at 41.

different from who they have been before? The explanation is that we share our identity as moral beings with them. This demands that we ascribe to them a desire to rid themselves of a practical identity – or at least a part of it – that they must experience as besetting them as if it were an affliction. We ascribe to them the ability to realize, upon reflection, that there is something deeply troubling and wrong with their self. This presupposes, however, that underneath the troubling practical identity, there is an indelibly valuable part of their self, namely, the moral subjectivity that makes them amenable to practical reason.[28]

But being a member of the kingdom of ends is human dignity's last resort. As we shall see, if what gives us dignity is our amenability to moral insight, we settle on a rather thin version of dignity. First, it opens the gate to universal agility and adaptability. Second, it does not really pay attention to the *play* between choices and constructs of our practical identity. If anything it is the play between accounting and bewilderment that reveals why we are ultimately of value. Acts of self-constitution may expose us as erratic, while our moral identity would force us to be flexible, for it would exhort us to "fit in" and "do our bit."

We expect the child molester to engage in self-repair, not least because we posit that from a moral point of view he must experience the relevant drives as foreign to himself. But should not people, when confronted with their moral identity, feel the same way about their laziness, their lack of discipline, slacking ambition, and outlandish idiosyncrasies? This question raises the broader question of how far the expectation of morally indicated self-repair might legitimately extend. The answer to this question depends on the qualities that we are morally obligated to embrace as our own.

TRADING OFF FREEDOM AND EQUALITY

Any predictable inequality is an invitation to engage in self-repair. Inequality means less or no access to goods for some. Lack of access means that potentially valuable options remain out of reach. Since selves assert reflexively in their choices their own value, sustaining inequality signals that some have no or lesser value than others. They are not "good enough" to partake of some goods or opportunities.

This explains what makes signs such as "No Irish need apply" or "Whites only" so patently offensive. Strategies of segregation affect freedom because they instil in people a sense that they are mistaken about their worth. They

[28] See Korsgaard, note 17 at 121.

suggest that some people have to be fixed or, if that is not possible, that they remove themselves from the places where the "better sort" interacts. Not surprisingly, people wearing the badge of second-class status gladly stay among their peers, for this allows them to zoom out their irreparability. They do not show up at the places that matter. They are ashamed of themselves. A free person, by contrast, is free to be incorrigible (incidentally, a sweet fruit of aging) and flamboyant.

Living with the impression that one is somehow defective is constraining. Invariably, people – at least as long as they have not given up on themselves – engage in efforts of self-repair; if this option is unavailable, their life is restricted to what is accessible to second-class people. Conceivably, life is then lived with an attitude of detachment. Perhaps people experience a lingering sense of loss, that they have missed their "real" life, that they have never made an appearance in their own biography. Not by accident, some victims of discrimination seem to compensate this loss by developing a sardonic sense of irony.

Hence, discrimination creates unequal freedom not only in a quantitative sense (a narrower range of choices). The freedom is also qualitatively unequal. Freedom is invested into repair efforts or in the detached pursuit of limited opportunities.[29] Having to pass as someone who one is not, nor wants to be, forces people into a trade-off between freedom and equality. They either recalcitrantly enact who they are told they have to be or pay the price for being who they are. In the former case, they "reinvent" themselves. They trade presence – at the table of privilege – for internal absence, or, rather, the absence of their own self in the social sphere. This introduces a decidedly undignified element into behavior. Sycophancy, bootlicking, and servile alacrity are part of one genre of self-enactment. Ostensible self-repair efforts infuse inequality with indignity.

ANOTHER OBJECTION

Provisionally, we conclude that self-determination is free if it takes place in the interplay between practical identity and opportunity. This is where human beings can become their own builders. In an important sense, however, they are the subjects of their freedom only by being outside of themselves or, rather,

[29] In the latter case, as Marx famously noted, all doing becomes enduring. See Karl Marx, *Ökonomisch-philosophische Manuskripte* (ed. M. Quante, Frankfurt aM: Suhrkamp, 2009) at 94. Rahel Jaeggi, *Entfremdung: Zur Aktualität eines sozialphilosophischen Problems* (Frankfurt aM: Campus, 2005) at 30.

by being ahead of themselves in their choices. This explains why freedom of choice is an essential element of freedom. By contrast, the moral identity that we share with all reasonable beings explains that we may have to regard certain aspects of our personality as strange afflictions that we should shed.

It may be objected that the observations have already branched out into a terrain that is far too general to be relevant to the topic of discrimination. From the perspective adopted earlier, anyone who feels disrespected in a social context could claim to have been discriminated against. Such a result is, to say the least, overblown, if not outright absurd.

Replying to this objection requires, indeed, raising the problem of self-repair to the level at which it has to be addressed, namely, social cooperation in general.[30] As is well known, discrimination is either behavioral or systemic. In the first case, there is a perpetrator (*e.g.*, a racist shopkeeper); in the second case, disadvantage results from a variety of acts that have not been designed to exclude or to demean (*e.g.*, the job market simply has an unequal impact on women).

Social coordination on markets generally creates and adversely affects opportunities. Being a composer of avant-garde contemporary music, such as Helmut Lachenmann, is not easy in a world that listens to Justin Bieber. Lachenmann is the composer of *musique concrète instrumental*. His works invite listeners "to hear the conditions under which a sound- or noise-action is carried out."[31] The resulting sonorities are such that the large majority of ordinary people would not even recognize them as music. Lachenmann is the embodiment of what it means to be a law unto oneself. But would it be wrong if he were expected to compose, say, country music if, as a result of an apparent lack of broad popularity, his complex scores did not earn him a living? He may well find writing country music unbecoming. Should society care? Would not talk of discrimination be out of place in cases where society legitimately expects adaptation? Why should Lachenmann not repair himself and compose for the Grand Ole Opry? Or would even merely to suggest this constitute an offense to his dignity?

This hypothetical example shows that it makes sense to allow the concept of discrimination to sweep broadly, at least *par provision*, and to include systemic discrimination in it even without paying attention to any particular "forbidden ground." In Lachenmann's case, it concerns systemic discrimination against contemporary music. It is inherent in allowing the shallow tastes of consumers to determine the viability of artistic pursuits.

30 Discrimination, as a topic, is fascinating only if one allows the concept to sweep broadly.

31 https://slought.org/resources/musique_concrete_instrumentale

AGILITY AND ADAPTABILITY

Nevertheless, arguing that Lachenmann falls victim to indirect discrimination is an uphill battle. A competitive society expects everyone to be flexible and to save for another day many matters that people consider essential to their life. Arguably, various forms of hiding one's self and a great deal of actual self-denial are even essential to individual success. Perplexingly, however, in many cases these attitudes can even provide a path toward self-discovery. We may have no clue who we are and what we are good for. All that is left to us is experimentation with the world to determine our place within it. Nothing appears to be better suited for engaging in experiments of this type than a competitive market economy. It creates various and numerous opportunities.

Admittedly, a competitive world is not hospitable to the depressed and the inflexible. In such a world, individual *agility* and *adaptability* are virtues that individuals are generally expected to develop. Whoever struggles with espousing these in his or her conduct is sooner or later eligible to receive some form of "empowering" coaching.

But where would we draw a line given that our identities are not fixed but subject to our own reconstruction in the interplay between already existing practical identities and new opportunities? It must become very difficult to make sense of the concept of discrimination developed here, notably in its systemic form.[32] Why could temporary self-denial or overcoming stubborn idiosyncrasies (or weakness of the will when it comes to the writing of country music) ever pose a normative problem if we are essentially either unfinished or indeterminate and if agility and adaptability are both cardinal virtues of social cooperation and keys to unlocking the secret of a meaningful life? Why should the individual responsibility to adjust to market demand not be the universally shared prime directive that we have to recognize from the perspective of our moral identity?

IMMUTABLE CHARACTERISTICS

When it comes to identifying such a limit, legal reasoning seems to provide us with a clue, even though, as we shall see, it is one of these clues that can easily lead us astray. It directs our attention to so-called immutable characteristics. The complexion cannot be changed, nor can be the country of birth. One is

[32] We could still try to defend it in the context of direct discrimination with regard to some animus on the part of the perpetrator.

stuck with them. Some of these characteristics, such as complexion, are stereotypical markers of lesser social fitness. Owing to widespread social prejudice, they constitute insurmountable obstacles to adaptation for whoever happens to bear them. It makes good sense, therefore, to declare them forbidden grounds of discrimination, at any rate, so long as the relevant characteristic is socially visible, widely used, and unrelated to individual performance.

Hence, even though our practical identity may well be one of these postmodernist entities celebrated in modern literature departments – fluid, pliable, or even "hybrid" – we must be immune from suffering disadvantage if we count as someone whom we may have never chosen to be.

Thus stated, however, protection from discrimination changes its point. It no longer protects against being shamed, shunned, or worse off on the ground of who we are; rather, it turns out to be a type of social insurance against counting as someone if one does not have the power to alter that fact. If there is widespread dislike of Poles in a society, judicial protection from discrimination is designed to remove the obstacle associated with counting as Polish. Some Poles may have abdicated all loyalty to their country. This does not matter. For purposes of protection from discrimination, they are still Poles because socially they count as such.

FROM THE BURDEN ON INDIVIDUALITY TO INDIVIDUALITY AS A BURDEN

In addition to providing an insurance against some stereotypes, the focus on immutable characteristics implicitly harbors a certain view of the individual self. It is at least perfectly compatible with casting the self primarily in object form, namely as a human resource coupled with a set of preferences (which are basically social facts). What is subjective about the self – thinking, willing, judging – is reduced to the exercise of economic rationality. Ideally, the self is a preference-driven human resource in the hands of an impersonal planer. Such an impersonal planer is capable of making smart choices for any given set of preferences in light of individual endowments (Ronald Dworkin). Individual rational selves would be best off if they were mere replicas – indeed, replicants – of the impersonal planner. Whatever imperfection might leave its mark on the planning process, it would reveal the influence of mere personal factors (bad breeding, lack of training, interference of emotions, myopia, risk aversion, confidence bias, etc.).

Such a view of the self is consistent with a certain view of obstacles to achievement. External obstacles result from a lack of resources or unequal opportunities caused by the social relevance of immutable characteristics. Internal obstacles stem from being imperfect at personal planning. The individual self is thus cast as a root of deficiency. Like a disability, it poses the risk of underperformance. Moreover, in a competitive environment imperfect selves need to overcome their internal obstacles themselves. Every single action must therefore always also be an attempt at self-improvement. All doing is supposed to be taking one more step toward "growth." The goal of growth is the infinitesimal approximation to the mind of the impersonal planner.

Interestingly, seen in this way, a competitive market economy overcomes discrimination by *discriminating against everyone equally*. It casts everyone in a state in which we have to be permanently self-repairing. Actual protection from discrimination is supposed to remove some of the obstacles to integration into society that individuals are simply unable to climb themselves. The rest is perennial self-improvement.

Obviously, this view of the self is not quite consistent with our prior finding that dignity demands that we be recognized for who we happen to be. This view is compatible, however, with how self-repairing selves are supposed to choose their practical identity from a moral point of view.

Identity-choosing subjects understand two things. They realize that if they did not endorse some particular practical identity, they would never be able to enact a real self and fail to be a self-determining person.[33] They would end up "drifting through life"[34] and not be determined by their self in their choices. They would not be able to exercise their practical reason fully. But they also understand that the market is a medium in which people establish mutuality with regard to what they make of themselves so that each is able to benefit from the life projects of all others. With this in mind, Terry Pinkard mocked Hayek – by alluding to Rousseau – that, from this perspective, the market actually forces persons to be *truly* free.[35] Interdependence of supply and demand is a mechanism that constrains people to be free in exactly the manner that is compatible with the equal freedom of all.[36]

Consequently, "fitting in" by virtue of agility and adaptation is not only a matter of prudence. It appears to be a moral imperative. Morality seems to demand that one's practical identity be shaped and made relevant by the market. Whichever we choose to adopt under conditions of constrained

33 See Korsgaard, note 17 at 123.

34 See Joseph Raz, *The Morality of Freedom* (Oxford: Clarendon Press, 1986) at 371.

35 See Terry Pinkard, *Hegel's Phenomenology: The Sociality of Reason* (Cambridge: Cambridge University Press, 2004) at 311.

36 See Lisa Herzog, *Inventing the Market: Smith, Hegel, and Political Theory* (Oxford: Oxford University Press, 2013) at 73–79.

opportunities is morally acceptable so long as one does not, for example, decide to harm people by becoming an assassin.[37]

Opportunities generated by markets count. Morality directs us to identify with what might suit us and, more importantly, feed us. Since morality directs us to attend to the market, the given opportunities for enacting a self have authority over us. They can be regarded as arising from collective private self-determination.[38] Private individuals can count the circumstances of action that are created by others only as expressions of their own will if they identify with the requisite spontaneous forms of cooperation, for it is these forms that allow them to realize identities and to enact selves in a morally legitimate way.

It must seem, therefore, as though we would have to give Helmut Lachenmann, were he in need, the advice to scrap his intriguing pieces of avant-garde music and to write songs for the Dixie Chicks. In other words, morality – his obligation to live up to what is humanity in him – would dictate that Helmut Lachenmann reinvent himself. The Grand Ole Opry it is.

TRAGEDY

But what if you – or Helmut Lachenmann, for that matter – realized that engaging your agility and adaptability did in no manner help you arrive at a practical identity that is congruent with being who you divine to be? The question of self-repair then turns into a matter similar to Kierkegaard's "despair." On moral grounds, you cannot be willing to be enacting what you find yourself drawn to be, for this would possibly make you into a useless person. At the same time, since no socially suitable personal identity suits you, you must be unwilling to be a self at all.[39] No morally approved practical identity would ever be compatible with who you sense to be.

The question must arise, therefore, whether you have failed to embrace your moral identity or, conversely, whether your moral identity actually has failed to embrace you. That the latter is actually the case, is implicitly claimed by Christoph Menke who sees the ancient tragic conflict between family ties and political loyalty recur in modern moral life as a collision between the demands of egalitarian morality, on the one hand, and what may strike you as

37 The example is Korsgaard's. See note 17 at 126.

38 See my "Europe: From Emancipation to Empowerment" 60/2013 LSE *"Europe in Question" Discussion Paper*, www.lse.ac.uk/europeanInstitute/LEQS/LEQSPaper60.pdf.

39 See Soren Kierkegaard, *The Sickness Unto Death: A Christian Psychological Exposition for Upbuilding and Awakening* (trans. H.V. Hong and E.H. Hong, Princeton: Princeton University Press, 1980) at 49–60; Michelle Kosch, *Freedom and Reason in Kant, Schelling, and Kierkegaard* (Oxford: Clarendon Press, 2006) at 154.

your individual good, on the other. Egalitarian morality claims to be prior to whatever you deem to be good for you. It does not recognize as inalienable any conception you may happen to entertain of yourself.[40] Morality only respects your ability to choose between and among practical identities. Your moral identity indeed fails to embrace you – it does not identify with you – inasmuch as you experience who you are as inalienable, not susceptible to choice, or as an outgrowth of your "inner nature."[41] In a word, the inalienable individual self is alien to the moral self. Menke concludes, therefore, that modern moral life gives rise to an antinomy (*Entzweiung*) in the relation of moral autonomy in individual self-realization (*Selbstverwirklichung*).[42] In fact, he could have said that morality collapses because self-determination no longer seems possible. The self appears to be split into a socially compatible "Me" and a relatively unruly "I."[43]

MORAL ESTRANGEMENT AND STOICISM

It might be helpful to summarize the result of our first reading of immutability. The theme became relevant when we began wondering how discrimination could ever be possible in the face of universally required agility and adaptability. All have to adapt. But this cannot mean that black persons must become white to avoid disadvantage. The relevance of immutable characteristics protects against such an absurd consequence. The exemption of characteristics of this kind, however, reinforces a view of the self as a rational, self-activating, and perfectly adaptable agent. The self is completely subordinate to what counts as being a useful member of society for being such a member is prerequisite for enacting a morally permissible form of practical identity successfully.

But this amounts to at least an unflattering view of the self. First, if what makes us distinct from a perfect impersonal planner is our "bounded" rationality, then we are all more or less unfit, and the social persona that we create of ourselves is at best an attempt to cover this up. Worse, still, if what it takes to approximate the powers of the impersonal planner is opaque and eventually

40 See Christoph Menke, "Liberalismus im Konflikt: Zwischen Gerechtigkeit und Freiheit." In *Gemeinschaft und Gerechtigkeit* (ed. M. Brumlik and H. Brunkhorst, Frankfurt aM: Fischer, 1993) 218–243 at 237; see also his magisterial study *Tragödie im Sittlichen: Gerechtigkeit und Freiheit nach Hegel* (Frankfurt aM: Suhrkamp, 1996) at 259, 296–297.

41 See Juliane Rebentisch, *Die Kunst der Freiheit: Zur Dialektik demokratischer Existenz* (Berlin: Suhrkamp, 2012) at 129.

42 See *Tragödie*, note 40 at 241.

43 Readers of American pragmatist philosophy may recognize the reference to Mead.

manifest only in "success," then those who have demonstrated their ability to be more successful than others have also established their relatively higher worth. The competitive market society thus leads directly to a society that recognizes unequal worth and unequal rank. Not by accident, American oligarchs are increasingly outspoken about how greater wealth bespeaks higher personal worth.

Second, from the moral point of view, any practical identity is as good as any other. What matters is the success in enacting one. Not unsurprisingly, many young Americans if asked about the goal in their life reply by saying they want to be a celeb. It does not matter who you are and what you do as long as you are rich and famous. Such an attitude toward your own self reflects a deep indifference[44] toward the world of action. It results in a twofold alienation. First, you are alienated from your moral identity, which turns out to be the cousin of the impersonal planer. In no way does it particularly represent you. Second, you are also alienated from the practical role that you "responsibly" put up with. The result is Stoicism. The disengagement from our roles translates into disengagement from the world. It may seem as though you remained "internally free" vis-à-vis both moral and practical identity, but this freedom can never be realized in practice.[45]

IMMUTABILITY, TAKE TWO

Fortunately, there is a more appealing way of eliciting the meaning of immutability. It assumes that people are *entitled* to have certain matters treated as though they were unchangeable because they, but not others, experience them in this way. This involves, evidently, paying respect to the perspective of the first person. In Rawlsian parlance, it means to regard individuals as "self-authenticating sources of valid claims."[46] Immutability, thus understood, creates immunity from agility and adaptability. In contrast to the impersonal planner model, it does not indirectly reinforce these principles.

Religious freedom is a case in point. Religious belief, unless it is shallow, indicates that one has succeeded at becoming a receptacle of insight, revelation, or even – lucky you – grace. From within a religious perspective, "choosing" a religion means demonstrating one's ability to commit oneself to what one recognizes to be the *right* faith. A choice of this kind is very

44 See Rahel Jaeggi, *Entfremdung: Zur Aktualität eines sozialphilosophischen Problems* (Frankfurt aM: Campus, 2005) at 174.

45 All that, however, if it is conceded that there is a way of accounting of "inner nature" that does not lead to either essentialism or reification. See Rebentisch, note 41 at 126.

46 See John Rawls, *Political Liberalism* (New York: Columbia University Press, 1991) at 32.

different from the type of choice under conditions of substitutability. If the pastry shop is out of one's desired doughnuts and one chooses a cupcake instead, this does not pose a problem since both are exemplars of "something sweet." No such substitution would be reasonable in the case of religion ("Sorry, we are out of Judaism, but we give you a choice between Catholic and Protestant Christianity"). Nobody chooses a religion just to have some. In a case such as this, self-determining beings are fully invested in what they believe. Owing to their intentionality, they make themselves into the passive carriers of what they have to rest their faith on. They are free by giving themselves to what they are not and, thereby, realize who they are.[47]

Many of our freedoms expose us publicly as choosing subjects. They suggest that we could, at any time, choose differently. In fact, some of our most important freedoms, – such as the right to marry, the right to profess one's faith, or the right to express one's opinion – preserve our ability to hand us over to our emotions and reasons. We enjoy freedom of choice in order to have our self-chosen ties respected and not scrutinized before some social tribunal.

That what is at stake in our reason-responsiveness leads back to the value of choice. It was pointed out earlier that we constitute ourselves from within the play between choices and shaped practical identities. The builder who pulls ourselves together is someone who is not someone but also not nobody. It is we in the state of being ahead of ourselves. This impersonal and yet personal someone is also the voice of "good reasons." We have to regard it as our own voice. If we, therefore, did not earn social respect for what we regard as indispensable or compelling, we would never be able to appear in our actions.

PROTODISCRIMINATION

Where does this leave us with regard to Helmut Lachenmann? The answer to this question is like any answer to a legal question: it depends. We have seen earlier that discrimination develops its full force – comes, in a sense, to full fruition – as soon as its victims participate, either by engaging in self-repair or by hiding away in socially segregated places. Indeed, discrimination exists pervasively in a prototypical format in which it is not yet really constituted owing to the pervasive acquiescence on the part of its victims. Protodiscrimination easily passes as rational conduct so long as nobody rebels.

This changes as soon as the victims begin to assert their own worth through their commitments. No privileged insight into a determinate substantive self is

47 See Jaeggi, note 44 at 243.

needed for that, just the experience that, as things stand, one is not part of one's life since one is either forced into hiding or shamed for who one is. Going through Hayek's "tough school of the market" may make people realize that the hard labor of interdependence denies them an outlet in this world. But as soon as they are confident that who they struggle to be is of value, they have determined a case of discrimination. In more than one subtle sense, the victims of discrimination are also doers. In a first step, they bring about protodiscrimination through their acquiescence and, in a second step, turn it into discrimination by reclaiming their equal worth.

The rest is straightforward. The rebellion against disadvantage can be successful if a life form is amenable to its claims. The validation of "self-authenticating sources" of claims is a social practice. More is needed, to be sure, than the trite appeals to respect persons or not to deny them their "self-esteem," which are notoriously filling the pages of contemporary analytic philosophy. Respecting persons is not enough because it is abstract. What matters is the esteem for various aspects of a form of life.

Lachenmann's lachenmanliness would be diminished had he to make money as a doorstep salesman flogging off magazine subscriptions and if he wrote music only during evening hours to see it never performed. Nevertheless, engaging in his compositorial pursuits appears to be compatible with expecting him to earn a living as, say, a scholar, a teacher, or a conductor. It leaves room for his pursuits and is not too far removed from his calling. This type of flexibility is compatible with what he has "chosen" to be. Its realization, however, not only presupposes support and subsidization by others but also a cultural format that they find accessible. The existence of lachenmanliness has to be part of what they value about their world even if they do not understand it.

In more somber words, this means that freedom in dignity presupposes a shared social world. This rather Hegelian conclusion suggests that being a law unto oneself is invariably both social and contingent. It is social because rising above the interdependence of markets presupposes a common commitment to a variety of human achievements. What sustains us, as scholars, is a culture that esteems what we are doing. If it were not for the solidarity of others, we would already be extinct. Cultures are, however, particulars. Not everyone can find his or her place in them. As Rawls wisely realized, there can be no social world without a loss.

CONCLUSION

Prohibited grounds of discrimination are attempts to reconcile our most personal experiences of inalienability with our moral identity. Not surprisingly, they respect the principle of universalization. Everyone has to have his or her sexual orientation, religious beliefs, or political opinions respected because they make the person into what he or she is. Such universalizations result from historical struggles. Not by accident, the law has a history. It emerges from the lives of real people.

The validity of the proposed reconstruction of discrimination does not presuppose that people discover their pre-given essence before they can go about claiming respect. Self-constitution in the medium of the play between choices and tinkering with identities may give rise to what Lear has rather enigmatically described as moments of "ironic disruption."[48] These are moments at which we wonder if what we believe to have enacted is indeed what we take it to be (*e.g.*, "What does anything of what I have done in my life have to do with being a man?").[49] But self-constitution continues also when we realize that our belief in who we are has concealed from us someone whom we would really like to be. No fixed entity is needed to be self-constituting in these moments.

It may be objected that the proposed understanding of discrimination may well fit cases when people proudly assert their identity. This is a theory of discrimination for life-affirming gays and lesbians, for fervent religious believers, or for culturally recalcitrant foreigners. But what about victims of race discrimination who could not care less to which race they belong? Does not the rejected meaning of immutable characteristics capture more adequately the indignity involved in counting as someone, and suffering disadvantage, even though one has never identified with one's social persona?

It is indeed the case that the proposed understanding of discrimination invites us to view victims of race discrimination as people who want to be respected for who they are even if carrying a specific social trait would not matter to their practical identity under more favorable circumstances. But this exaggerated respect is necessary to protect them against a situation in which a trait is likely to count as a stain on their practical identity.[50]

Often, paying respect for the sake of indifference is mistaken for involving the recognition of pride. The celebration of "diversity" is based on such a mistake. But perhaps it is a minor flaw of cultures that are trying to cope with deeply entrenched patterns of discrimination.

48 See Lear, note 20 at 21, 31, 56, 61.

49 The practical identity is thus measured against itself. See Korsgaard, note 20 at 76.

50 For an exploration of the concept of discrimination from this narrow perspective, see Sophia Moreau, "What Is Discrimination?" (2010) 38 *Philosophy and Public Affairs* 144–179 at 149.

The final point of the analysis is the most important one and lies beyond the work that has been done here. Living a life in dignity requires more than the narrow legal protection from discrimination. We have not even opened the whole chapter of how slower and more contemplative forms of life are to be insulated against the eroding effects of the functional imperatives of universal agility and adaptability.

Our age has gone wrong in perceiving violations of dignity most paradigmatically expressed in practices of physical abuse. Dignity can only be secured when we understand that the full package of human rights – social, economic, civil, political, cultural – is indivisible.[51]

[51] See also Alexander Somek, *The Cosmopolitan Constitution* (Oxford: Oxford University Press, 2014).

6

The Quest for Agency

The horizontal realization of the legal relation among individuals who enjoy the rights to private property and freedom of contract gives rise to alienation. Individuals, to be able to engage in trade and barter, have to generate economic power, which is the social power to make others want what you offer to exchange. If, in this context, people are confronted with a choice between what constitutes a greater and a lesser evil for them, then alienation is a product of the coercion that a system of private transactions permits. In a situation of widespread alienation and softer or harder coercion, people develop conceptions of agency that indirectly reflect their disempowerment. This can be shown for two forms of "despair" discussed by Kierkegaard. The chapter sketches how relations of social freedom might offer a reprieve by moving beyond the legal relation proper.

INTRODUCTION

The legal relation is a relation among choosers who choose within limited spheres. Paradigmatically, this sphere is private property, for the legal freedom of persons is most strongly manifest in the exclusive use of, and control over, things. The freedom that is limited vis-à-vis other persons is unlimited vis-à-vis your belongings. You can treat them *ad libitum*. Things don't care. Reflexive universalization reaches its most extreme expression in the freedom epitomized by the right to private property. It signifies the sphere in which the will – and nothing but the will – rules.

Political arrangements aside, property owners would not allow anything to affect their property without their consent. Consequently, freedom of contract is the legal institution that complements private property. Both institutions fit the interactions of abstract persons. While private property allows persons to be persons, freedom of contract allows them to benefit from one another.

It is the central paradox of the legal relation that the realization of external freedom involves a loss of internal freedom. This loss is manifest in how alienation and coercion reside in certain situations of choice. We have already seen that coercion is written into the structure of the legal relation. It withholds from each participant the freedom to ignore demands made by others. They have rights. One ends up, consequently, being confronted with the alternative of conformance or of disrupting the reciprocity on which the recognition of one's own choices depends. Legal sanctions play the dual role of representing the impending disruption and of substituting it with penalties.

The task of the following analysis is to demonstrate that the legal relation among abstract persons engenders alienation. This also raises the question whether the choices made under the condition of alienation have to be regarded as coerced choices. To the extent that this is considered to be the case, the structure of the legal relation has to be expanded into a web of relations of social freedom.

AN OUTDATED TOPIC?

Ours is the age of anxiety and of depression. We worry about our weakness and are afraid to discover that we have already surrendered to it. We need to be strong. It is secondary, at best, whether our strength also serves us in being who we are.

The notion of alienation, by contrast, seems to belong to an age when people must have harbored different beliefs and sensibilities. The concept suggests that human beings could in some way be authentically who they are or somehow be whole without being deformed by their circumstances. We, however, find it hard to endorse the requisite beliefs. Any quest for being true to oneself or to have an unmistakable voice[1] is difficult to reconcile with the premise that everything social and psychological is somehow "constructed." This premise reflects a very smart stance. How should from an array of forces that have defined me emerge something that is authentically my own? Any belief in such a something must smack of "essentialism," which we warily suspect of being a sibling of intolerance and fanaticism.

We no longer believe we have a soul. That's too obscure. We have an "ego" or, at best, a "self." The notorious fragility of this residual something that is we has become the object of coaching and a target of the pharmaceutical industry. The ego has no essence. What existentialists called "self-choice" has no direction. The self is a shell and armor. It lends strength to the maximal

[1] See Charles Taylor, *The Ethics of Authenticity* (Cambridge, Mass.: Harvard University Press, 1999) at 15, 29.

satisfaction of wants. Against such a background, concerns about alienation appear to be out of place.

But what if our empiricist or postmodernist wits and smarts are part of the phenomenon that they reject? If people have no essence then nothing makes them distinctively human. Inhuman treatment becomes a conceptual impossibility. There can be only pain and suffering, and – yes – there would be nothing wrong with either as long as we had pills against it. Without a soul, there is no subtle interaction between what is inconvertible and what is intelligent in us. We would then be reduced to our intelligence, which makes us adaptable. If there is nothing over and above our power of adaptation, there is nothing beyond our control that is also we and legitimately dead set against haphazard adaptation to circumstance. Indeed, if exercising control is all that matters to us, then we are all the more who we are the more we control ourselves. Reduced to egos, we are replicas of one and the same type of rational agent that we embody more or less perfectly.

This chapter explores two themes that are closely associated with alienation. The first is taken from Marx and concerns why self-alienation necessarily has both a personal and a social dimension. It is argued that self-alienation is experienced as a *lack or loss of agency*.[2] It would be misleading to conceive of it as something that is caused by obstacles posed in the course of the realization of a self's substance. Nevertheless, there remains an "essentialist" element in the experience of self-alienation since it presupposes a certain understanding of who we ought to be.

The second theme is closely associated with the first. We associate the second theme with the fallen way of being human that a "Heidegger Marxist" such as Herbert Marcuse identified to provide a fresh account of the lack of agency designated by Heidegger's concept of the *Man*.[3] In the medium of the *Man*, social life is experienced as a series of events in which nobody is acting, everything is just happening, and nothing is amenable to change. From Marcuse's Marxist perspective, in such a situation "the individuals identify themselves with the existence which is imposed upon them."[4] While at first glance all talk of alienation must appear to be out of place because the identification with the situation of life is real, the social reality that results from it "constitutes a more progressive stage of *alienation*" in which we are confronted with the "disappearance of the inner space" and the

[2] For an excellent phenomenological account, see Rahel Jaeggi, *Entfremdung: Zur Aktualität eines sozialphilosophischen Problems* (Frankfurt aM: Campus, 2005) 73–90.

[3] See Martin Heidegger, *Sein und Zeit* (14th ed., Tübingen: Max Niemeyer Verlag, 1977) at 126.

[4] See Herbert Marcuse, *One-Dimensional Man: Studies in the Ideology of Advanced Industrial Society* (Boston: Beacon Press, 1964) at 11.

"streamlined containment of centrifugal tendencies."[5] It will be argued that alienation is the emotional recognition of both elements of social experience.[6]

THE DEAD AMONG THE LIVING

The *locus classicus* of Marx's elaboration of alienation are the philosophical-economic manuscripts of 1844.[7] The topic can be most easily introduced on the basis of a brief and somewhat improvised contemplation of one of Marx's most famous statements. It reads in German (and in my own English translation) as follows:[8]

> Der Gegenstand, den die Arbeit produziert, ihr Produkt, tritt ihr als ein *fremdes Wesen*, als eine, von d[em] Produzenten *unabhängige Macht* gegenüber.

> The object produced by labor, its product, appears vis-à-vis labor as an *alien* being, as a power that is *independent of the producer*.

If read somewhat outside of Marx's own theoretical framework, this sentence captures the gist of the overall situation of labor to this day. It has not changed even after people have been told that work offers opportunities for self-realization.[9]

First, the product is alien to the producer. In an elementary sense, this means that, paradoxically speaking, it is *essential* to the product to have an *inessential* nexus to the producer. It is in the nature of the commodities to be the output of potentially anyone. If the product is such that it does not matter who has produced it, it is alien to the producer. It is, indeed, alien to all producers alike. All producers encounter in their work something that could have been produced by anyone else. They encounter their own powers and skills as alien powers because these powers do not belong to themselves in particular.

Second, and more disturbingly, while a piece of work is actually the work of someone in particular – for example, an appellate brief authored by a law firm associate – it is simultaneously only potentially the work of that particular

5 Ibid. at 10–11, 38, 64.

6 For a more recent account of alienation that – in spite of its focus on processes of social acceleration – also focuses on the loss agency, see Hartmut Rosa, *Alienation and Acceleration: Towards a Critical Theory of Late-Modern Temporality* (Aarhus: NSU Press, 2010) at 82–83.

7 I have used the excellent edition prepared by Michael Quante. See Karl Marx, *Ökonomisch-philosophische Manuskripte* (Frankfurt aM: Suhrkamp, 2009).

8 Marx, note 7 at 84.

9 See Franco "Bifo" Berardi, *The Soul at Work: From Alienation to Autonomy* (trans. F. Cadel and G. Mecchia, Cambridge, Mass.: MIT Press, 2009).

person because it could equally well be the product of someone else. The actual relation between product and producer is essentially potential. Severing the tie to a particular producer is essential to the product. Thus understood, the "made in" label attached to clothes signifies the indifference of commodities to the place and person of production. It symbolizes the substitutability and dispensability of particular producers. "Made in" says that it may as well have been made somewhere else and by someone else. Indeed, it is quite inessential to products that a particular producer is alive. Assuming that labor lends expression of the "life energy" of the producers (is a *Lebensäußerung* as Marx would have put it),[10] then the producers encounter in the product their own death. Or, put differently, they perceive the society of producers as a society that is composed of the undead. Everyone is too dispensable to see his or her life energy expressed in a product (and, hence, not really alive) and yet too busy to be already defunct and deceased.

Finally, the product appears alien because it appears as a power that is independent of the producer. The producers have to adjust to demand, for otherwise they would have nothing with which to engage in trade or barter. Aggregate demand, in turn, is not of human design. It is the side effect of countless individual choices. It is a by-product, not planned. Nevertheless, it exercises power over human life because producers have to adjust to supply and demand. Ideally, they are prize takers. The operation of the market does not take heed of individual plans. It is a power that is independent of the producers. They have to surrender to a machinery that is not driven by human purposes.[11] It is a web of natural interdependence (*Naturzusammenhang*).

This is the situation of labor under the condition of the division of labor. Whatever someone does could equally well be done by someone else. Some get to do the job only because they were lucky enough to secure it, even though this job itself could have easily gone to someone else. Jobs are created in the context of managing tasks with an eye to demand. In the large scale of things, every job occupies a special niche, which is, again, not of human design.

The experience of alienation is an experience of individual disempowerment and also of disillusionment. The unmasked illusion is the belief, acquired as a result of familial love, that one matters to others as well as to oneself. The experience of alienation reveals, by contrast, that the sphere of production and consumption is indifferent to individual lives. We are as abstract as the labor that goes into products.

[10] See, for example, Marx, note 7 at 207. [11] See Marx, note 7 at 151.

Experiencing alienation, however, is a mode of recognizing this bitter truth. It is insight in emotional form. What is more, it represents how society reflects on itself because people feel alienated inasmuch as they are members of society. The feelings of being detached from what one does, of not mattering to the world in general, and of being driven by forces that, even though of human origin, are not of human design have cognitive import. The social situation recognizes itself objectively by giving rise to certain "subjective" feelings: emptiness, betrayal, and a sense of profound disempowerment.

ECONOMIC POWER

The previous sketch seeks to capture a situation that emerges from more elementary relations among persons. Marx's analysis of these relations is nothing short of masterful. It begins with the legal relation. The relation between and among producers is one of property-owning persons. They enjoy freedom of contract.

The use of brute force aside, property ownership and freedom of contract are indispensible for building up economic power. Such power would not exist if it were not for these institutions. The person who owns what you want has power over you because your respect for the person's private property forces you to produce what that person wants and to trade your product for hers on the basis of contractual dealings. The economic power of the property-owning person is derivative of its legal position. The legally constituted control of one's property and the legal power to agree to a transfer constitute economic power over others as long as these others want to have what one owns. Freedom of choice is essential to economic power because it requires the freedom to abstain from exchanges.

Against this background, a situation can arise in which the property-owing class is free to coerce the propertyless class. This coercion is effected by forbearance from entering into agreements.[12] The effect of the omission is deprivation and ultimately death by starvation. The propertyless class cannot act as though it were free to pick and choose transactions in the manner in which the property owners can. Since all they possess is their human resource, they have to adjust their labor power to the demand of the employment market. Strategically they have to give the property owners an incentive to enter into an exchange of labor in return for wages. This incentive represents their modicum of economic power. While other property owners among

[12] See Robert L. Hale, "Coercion and Distribution in a Supposedly Non-Coercive State" (1923) 38 *Political Science Quarterly* 470–494.

themselves produce commodities to whet mutually their appetite for stuff, members of the propertyless class have to resort to "self-improvement" for their subsistence.

The remainder of the story is straightforward with regard to the effects that the economy has on the human life. The propertyless have to transform their life into a mere means to sustain life.[13] That which is potentially superior to mere self-preservation – a productive life – is effectively subordinated to the reproduction of bare life. This is an inversion of the teleology of human self-realization.

AN ASIDE ON HALE

To arrive at an analytically even more accurate description of the operation of economic power, it pays to examine briefly Robert Hale's[14] famous view of the market as a network of mutual coercion.[15] Hale's various analyses build upon Oliver Wendell Holmes's realization that duress properly so-called always involves a choice.[16] Coercive acts do not supersede the will in the sense of replacing it with mere causation; rather, they make the will behave as though it were a pinball of impulses. The explanation for this fact is that by virtue of a coercive threat, a reason-based choice is reduced to a choice between or among unequal evils.[17] Having to choose in such a situation is bad in itself. A choice has to be made from among a set of unwanted options. Invariably, when confronted with a set of unwanted options, a rational chooser is quite naturally disposed to choose the lesser evil. It is for that reason that the coercing person can effectively control the conduct of the victim.

The matter is trivial. For the average sporty driver, complying with speed limits is a lesser evil than having to pay a fine; but an evil it is, at least in the sense of an unwanted option. The coercive act consists in removing what people believe to be entitled to, falsely perhaps – in this case, driving at any speed without being fined for it. The person feels that she is coerced into what she is doing.

[13] See Marx, note 7 at 90.

[14] For a highly useful introduction into Hale's work that locates Hale in the broader context of American legal realism, see Neil Duxbury, "Robert Hale and the Economy of Legal Force" (1990) 53 *Modern Law Review* 421–444.

[15] See note 12. See Barbara H. Fried, *The Progressive Assault on Laissez Faire: Robert Hale and the First Law and Economics Movement* (Cambridge, Mass.: Harvard University Press, 1998) at 56.

[16] See Robert L. Hale, "Bargaining, Duress, and Economic Liberty" (1943) 43 *Columbia Law Review* 603–628 at 618.

[17] See Union Pacific Railway v Public Service Commission of Missouri 246 US 67, 70 (1918).

Disturbingly, Hale's analyses often ignore the fact that the options are unwanted and simply focus on how one person relies on the preferences of another to control her conduct.[18] Consequently, a narrower and a broader view of coercion is reflected in his writings of which only the former is intriguing and, indeed, helpful in elucidating the experience of alienation. The narrower view is concerned with unwanted options that arise because something that she is legally or morally entitled to is withheld from a person. The economic power is hard. The broader view pays no heed to whether the options are unwanted and whether something is illegitimately withheld. The economic power is soft.

HARD ECONOMIC POWER

Hale's narrower view of the coercive nature of market dealings – or of any act of influencing a person's choosing by affecting her options – focuses on omissions, more specifically, on the right to withhold one's property from others.[19] Generally, such an act of withholding presupposes legal or raw power. The potential employer who refuses to employ the employee for a living wage abstains from exercising the legal power to enter into a contractual agreement. Freedom of contract includes the liberty not to enter into an agreement.

To perceive the coercive quality of such *hard* economic power, one merely needs to see that the employer agrees to a bargain only on the basis of a transfer. The transfer consists of the wage that is lower than the living wage that the employee supposedly rightfully expects to receive. The extraction of the lower wage is possible in light of the even less pleasant alternative of having no employment at all.

The existence of an even more unpalatable alternative and the expectation that the employee will choose the lesser evil constitute the power of economic coercion. The employer can extract wages below the subsistence level because employees might harbor vague hopes that they could avail of one or the other additional source of income.

Hale's point may become even clearer if one casts the paradigmatic robber situation into one in which something is being withheld whenever a person is confronted with the alternative of "money" or "life." The robber withholds respect for life. Indeed, she makes the respect for life dependent on a transfer. Similarly, the employer withholding consent to a contract that pays a living wage makes wage payments dependent on a transfer. It consists of the part of

[18] See Hale, note 12. [19] For a helpful reconstruction, see Fried, note 15 at 46, 55.

the living wage that is virtually "paid back" by the employee. It represents the fee collected by the employer for offering employment. Likewise, viewed from a purely economic perspective, collecting fines for exceeding a speed limit makes the respect of free movement dependent on a similar transfer.

These comparisons show clearly that the identification of the coercive force of hard economic power requires a *normative baseline*.[20] Respect for life is the norm transgressed by the robber; the living wage is the principle breached by the employer. Coercive acts withhold something that is – at least *prima facie* – owed to a person. At the same time, coercion can only work if as a result of a withholding the remaining alternatives are at least subjectively unpalatable, even though not equally unpalatable. Only if one option is worse than another is it possible to exercise social control (which may indeed amount to something like economic government).[21]

DEMEANING THE PERSON

Upon closer inspection, it turns out that Hale's narrower account covers two slightly different situations. While it is the case for both situations that the coercer withholds or withdraws something that is supposedly owed, the situations differ with regard to whether the remaining options consist of either merely unwanted options or unwanted options and the withdrawn option plus a surcharge. Since the withdrawn option is then both wanted and not wanted (like an overprized commodity), it is still preferred over the unwanted options. This second situation is epitomized by extortion. The abductor promises to return the child on the condition that a ransom payment is made. The first situation is different. Imagine, for example, that a legislature declares the consumption of cannabis illegal. Possibly, hence, users of this recreational drugs do not avail of what they want. Various forms of alcohol may offer a substitute pleasure. Only if cannabis users regard the consumption of alcohol as a lesser evil than the abstention from consuming any drug is it plausible to say that they are being "forced" into the consumption of alcohol.

The second situation reveals quite vividly what coercion does to the will. First, it makes people want what they would not want if it were not for the withdrawal of what they consider themselves to be entitled to. Second, it makes people want what they would not want on the ground of *who they are*. After all, they choose the lesser evil because of their evaluative outlook.

20 See ibid. at 58–59.

21 See Robert L. Hale, "Force and the State: A Comparison of 'Political' and 'Economic' Compulsion" (1935) 35 *Columbia Law Review* 149–201; Duxbury, note 14 at 434–435.

A parent cannot abandon a child to the cruelty of an abductor. The evaluative outlook is part of the practical identity of a person. Without it they would not exercise their very own moral judgment.[22] People who identify with consuming recreational drugs – for whom leading a sober life would be decidedly "uncool" – resort to alcohol to stay true to themselves. More seriously perhaps, a parent will raise any amount of money to rescue a child. Ordinarily, the practical identity explains why and how a person rises above conflicting desires. If the committed father is confronted with doing something that will help his career or taking care of his sick child, he will choose the latter because he is a committed father. He can rise above conflicting inclinations and choose by virtue of his practical identity. Coercion reverses this picture. It turns the practical identity into an instrument to make the person want what she can only want because it is a lesser evil. The person is made wanting what she would not want on the ground of who she is. Instead of rising above options, the person is driven by them. The will of the person is turned against itself by means of the willing person. Coercion undermines the personhood of persons. This explains why it is so mean.

THE EYE OF THE BEHOLDER

Against this background, it can be seen why the broader use of coercion in Hale's work actually robs the analysis of much of its force.[23] If the marketing of a new electronic gadget makes you want to buy it and therefore to spend a certain amount of your savings on it, nothing is withheld from you to which you are believed to be entitled. We do not, at least not ordinarily, consider ourselves entitled to be immune from the lure of commodities. Hale's broader use of "coercion" ignores this tacit normative dimension. Moreover, while you may give in to the shallow appeal of technology, it may not be your practical identity that is used to make you want what you do not want. Perhaps this is a case of weakness of the will. For it would strike us as odd to say that you acted

[22] See Christine M. Korsgaard, *The Sources of Normativity* (Cambridge: Cambridge University Press, 1999) at 100: "When you deliberate, it is as if there were something over and above all of your desires, something which is *you*, and which *chooses* which desire to act on. This means that the principle or law by which you determine your actions is one that you regard as being expressive of *yourself*."

[23] See Robert L. Hale, *Freedom Through Law: Public Control of Private Governing Power* (New York: Columbia University Press, 1952) at 131 (cited in Duxbury, note 14 at 433): "Each party to a bargain is forced by the bargaining power of the other to surrender certain property in the form of money or otherwise or a certain portion of his freedom to act as he pleases or to be idle. The economically strong retain a considerable residuum of liberty and property; the economically weak, very little."

in an unprincipled manner if you did not avoid the greater evil of not possessing the commodity by sacrificing some of your savings. The economic power holding sway over you is *soft*. It is, at any rate, for the reason that it does not withhold something from you to which we consider you to be entitled.

Returning to hard economic power, on several levels, the actions by the robber and the employer involve the difference between commission and omission. The robber actively issues a threat. The employer merely decides not to enter into an agreement. In the case of the robber – and of the state issuing the speeding ticket – it is the perpetrator who imposes the sanction. By contrast, in the case of the employer, the sanction lies in the situation. The situation itself constitutes the threat. The deontological element of directly aiming at evil is absent.[24] This does not necessarily render it soft assuming that employees are entitled to a living wage. Nonetheless, the hard economic power exercised by the employer does not involve the use of coercive threats.

Such differences explain why Hale's claims concerning the ubiquity of coercion are both revealing and misleading. They are revealing as soon as one shares certain normative background assumptions. Actually, the strength of Hale's narrower analysis depends on its implicit appeal to beliefs concerning fairness. Nevertheless, the ubiquity thesis is also misleading because it allows any use of leverage to count as "coercive" even where it does not strike us as illegitimate.[25] Incentives, for example, induce certain behavior not by withholding something that ought not to be withheld, but by offering an additional reward. There is no coercion in play because the resulting set of choices is not composed of two or more evils.[26] Contrary to Hale's exuberant rhetoric, not every appeal to the preferences of persons, even though undoubtedly an attempt to control the behavior of others, is also coercive. It is economic power working with carrots rather than sticks. It is soft. Only the withholding of something that is owed and the extracting of a transfer for its provision is coercive, even if the evil avoided resides in the situation.

It must be conceded, though, that the narrower account of coercion can be used widely to articulate one's subjective experience. Whoever *feels* to be entitled to a new gadget and considers not having it as an evil will claim to be forced into spending money for its acquisition. People may harbor various

24 On this, see Thomas Nagel, *The View from Nowhere* (New York: Oxford University Press, 1986).

25 Hale left the normative question open concerning the desirablity of this or that relation of "coercion." This undermines the force of his analysis considerably. The concept has explanatory value only if something is illegitimately withheld.

26 This is overlooked by Duxbury, note 14 at 436.

normative expectations and hence experience the conduct of others as coercive. But this does not imply that their claims are correct. The normative baseline has to be the right one.[27]

What Hale, however, recognized with equal force as Marx did is that acting within a market economy is about augmenting economic power. Moreover, by juxtaposing Hale and Marx, it becomes clear that a system of transactions that systematically withholds due recognition to needs and replaces it with recognition of property rights is coercive, at least as long as the recognition of needs is made dependent on transfers that involve choices of lesser evils. Hale, of course, would have never claimed that these lesser evils encapsulate alienation. What his analysis indirectly shows, nonetheless, is the *diminution of agency* involved in wanting only a lesser evil. It also explains why subordinating a person to what she cannot but want is demeaning. It demotes the person to a slave of herself.

MONEYMAKING

While the focus of Marx's analysis undoubtedly rests on labor, it would be mistaken to conclude that alienation only affects the propertyless class. On the contrary, Marx ingeniously demonstrates that alienation is inherent in economic exchanges that are conducted in the shadow of economic power (both, as analyzed earlier, in hard and soft form). The root cause of alienation is that it is inherent in economic power to transform all economic relations into struggles over economic power.

If you, as a property-owning individual, strategically contemplate exchanges with another property-owning individual, you thereby recognize this person's property and freedom of contract.[28] You recognize this person, that is, as a person *in abstracto*, namely, as someone who is entitled to act on desires that happen to affect him. Marx will later come to call the resulting relation as one between and among "character masks."[29] The important point is that the (mutual) recognition does not extend to human beings and their needs directly. It only extends to persons in the Hegelian sense. Indeed, people who only have needs, but no property, and are not considered to be a valuable human resource do not even appear on the scene of commerce.

27 It should be added that coercive acts can be *justified*. They interfere with what people are *prima facie* entitled to enjoy, but the interference is carried out for a good reason.

28 See Marx, note 7 at 190.

29 For a valuable analysis, see Georg Lohmann, *Indifferenz und Gesellschaft: Eine kritische Auseinandersetzung mit Marx* (Frankfurt aM: Suhrkamp, 1991) at 259 (Marx, Kapital I 100).

They are kindly referred to as "the needy." Quite possibly, they are deemed eligible to handouts on moral grounds.

Of course, for those who engage in trade and barter, the demand for commodities indicates needs.[30] But the recognition of needs is conditional upon the recognition of exchange value and, indeed, quite inessential for the determination of the latter. If you produce no commodities or if your commodities do not exercise any economic power over me, your need for products remains utterly irrelevant to me. Your need of my commodity is of value – and has "dignity" – only inasmuch as I regard your product as the equivalent of my product.[31] Our mutual value is the value of our commodities:[32]

> Also ist der Mensch selbst uns wechselseitig *werthlos*.
>
> Hence, the human being itself is mutually of *no value* to us.

Property owners who need or want what others produce have to come up with what these others want and induce them to trade. This implies that the recognition of the needs of property owners depends on their building up of economic power. Marx states that the mutual recognition of needs is mediated by the mutual power exercised by commodities.[33] From this follows, in turn, that property owners only seemingly produce their own commodities. Their products are only a token used to receive what they want in return. In a sense, their products are merely the *money* they use to obtain other things. Thus understood, everyone is a moneymaker.[34] Commodities are the alternates of themselves.[35] Your commodity is merely the sensual shroud (*sinnliche Hülle*) of my commodity because your production of your commodity means and "wishes to express" the acquisition of mine.[36]

Under conditions of reciprocity, every producer makes himself into that as which his counterpart perceives him.[37] He transforms himself into a means to an end. The end is to build up economic power, for it provides access to goods. To attain that objective, producers have to serve as the instruments of their commodities. They have to organize the competence and skill requisite for its production. The shoemaker is the instrument of shoes that allows him to wield economic power just as the attorney is the instrument of the claims that he files in a court of law.

Marx goes so far as to say that producers become the servants of their commodities, by which he indeed suggests a relation of *intrapersonal servitude*.[38] It is manifest in working toward distant rewards, postponing the

30 See Marx, note 7 at 197. 31 See Marx, note 7 at 205–206. 32 Marx, note 7 at 206.
33 See Marx, note 7 at 204. 34 See Marx, note 7 at 201. 35 See Marx, note 7 at 198–199.
36 See Marx, note 7 at 206. 37 Ibid. 38 Ibid.

satisfaction of wants, and doing work that is indifferent to who you are and what you want.[39] Like a slave, the producer is working to satisfy the wants of others to stay alive or possibly even to prosper.

SELF-ALIENATION AND ALIENATION FROM OTHERS

This explains why Marx can claim that we become the property of our property.[40] If you have to use your property to generate economic power, then the commodity is yours only inasmuch as it is a means that allows you to wield control over others. This means, according to Marx, that you are excluded from "true property" qua enjoyment of things and true production qua self-realization for its own sake (including the realization, as we shall see, of your species being).[41]

At this point, Marx points to the nexus between self-alienation and the alienation from others:[42]

> Wir selbst sind von dem wahren Eigentum ausgeschlossen, weil unser Eigentum den anderen Menschen ausschließt.
>
> We ourselves are excluded from true property,[43] for our property excludes the other human being.

While Marx's analysis seems to suggest that the alienation from others follows from self-alienation, the relation between ground and consequence is actually the reverse. The alienation from others is the root of self-alienation.[44] Only if everyone is indifferent to the needs of others – that is, does not focus on these directly – everyone has to aim at generating economic power for the purpose of exchange. One has to produce exactly that which makes one relatively powerful in relation to others. Since this is determined by the anonymous mechanism of the market, the pursuit of economic power forces one to be indifferent to one's own needs, abilities, or desire for self-realization. The alienation from others logically precedes the alienation from the self.

Since the point of economic activity is the generation of economic power, it is essential that one take advantage of others. If producing for exchange necessarily entails maximizing your economic power, then ripping off others is a maxim of prudent behavior. In a like manner, every good produced and sold is an investment in one's own market position. Every professional

39 See Lohmann, note 29 at 310–315. 40 See Marx, note 7 at 94.

41 See Marx, note 7 at 87–88. 42 Marx, note 7 at 288.

43 "True property" in Marx's analysis is the use of material to realize one's individual potential. This is how I, at any rate, read his remarks on p. 207.

44 But see Marx, note 7 at 92.

achievement is an entry on the scoreboard of the "resume." Yet, what counts as an achievement is determined by circumstances beyond individual control.

THE COMMUNITY IN ALIENATED FORM

Under the conditions of the struggle for economic power, human beings are not the subjects of their life, neither individually nor collectively. They do not lead it. The interactions driven by the struggle over economic power come first, and human beings simply adapt to the resulting constellation of forces without ever rising above it.

Yet, even under this condition we realize what Marx calls, following Ludwig Feuerbach,[45] our "species being." It is manifest in any acts in which we implicitly recognize that we live among – and with – others.[46] Buying and selling are such acts. Were we to take cognizance of our social existence explicitly, each of us would view him- or herself as one human being with needs among equal others. We would realize that our social nature – our mutual dependence and complementation[47] – represents what is universal about us. Through our explicit embrace of our sociality, the true community (das *wahre Gemeinwesen*) would appear before us by virtue of reflective insight.

But this is not how the community – qua relations of interdependence – is actually brought about. The community is not constituted in acts involving the mutual recognition of our humanity but, rather, on the basis of a mutual recognition of our abstract personhood. As Marx puts it, the community appears on the ground of the need (*Not*) and egoism of individuals, that is, from the midst of their competitive struggle for economic power. The bases of recognition are private property and freedom of contract. Hence, buying and selling are indeed acts with which we realize and implicitly recognize our species being (qua being among equal others); but we do so in a manner that does not involve the direct recognition of needs. With these acts we realize the community in alienated form. What appears, thus, is the "*Gemeinwesen* unter der Form der *Entfremdung*."[48]

The community in alienated form is a "caricature"[49] of the true community,[50] not least because its constitution involves the inversion of the true human species

45 See Ludwig Feuerbach, Das Wesen des Christentums (1841), *Werke in sechs Bänden*, vol. 5 (ed. E. Thies, Frankfurt aM: Suhrkamp, 1968) at 18.

46 See Marx, note 7 at 195. 47 See Marx, note 7 at 207. 48 Marx, note 7 at 195.

49 Marx, note 7 at 196.

50 It should be noted that Marx uses the term *Gemeinwesen* deliberately in both literal and metaphorical form. *Gemeinwesen* stands for the community, but also for the essence of human

being. Activity turns out to be suffering. One's own creation is experienced as an alien power and the affluence of society means poverty for most. What is more, the essential bond among human beings is considered to be quite inessential to humans. Living separately from others is espoused as being part of human nature. Living as such is taken to involve sacrificing the enjoyment of life. In a word, living a life means having no life.

Marx contrasts this constitution of community with how the community would appear if people acted upon the mutual recognition of their species being. First, from the perspective of individual agents, labor would be experienced as a manifestation of their very own powers and capabilities. Work would be, as Marx puts it, a free expression of life and not the alienation of life (*Lebensäußerung* in lieu of *Lebensentäußerung*).[51] Second, if the individual agent works for the satisfaction of her own needs, she experiences the work as serving its purpose. Third, if others enjoy the product, the agent realizes that she has actualized the sociality of human beings, which consists of benefiting others (and to be benefited by them). From this follows, fourth, that the agent understands that the people who are benefited by her regard her existence as a complementation of their own. They could not be who they are if the agent's work were not an integral component of their life. Marx captures this last manifestation of the species being in the following poetic image:[52]

> Unsere Productionen wären eben so viele Spiegel, woraus unser Wesen sich entgegen leuchtete.

> Our productions would amount to as many mirrors out of which our essence shone toward itself.

Less exuberantly stated, our species being is manifest in intentional actions in the sphere of production and reproduction, that is, when people engage in production and exchange in recognition and anticipation of the needs of others. Clearly, the intentions of the species being must reflect love of humanity. This explains why such a being must appear to be out of place in civil society.

The mutual recognition of needs in the context of designing social arrangements was, however, a prominent theme of John Rawls's theory of justice. Rawls characterized society as a system of cooperation for the benefit of all.[53] The subject of social justice is the distribution of "primary goods."[54] These

beings inasmuch as it involves living among others. Every human being is communal in the sense of having or being a *Gemeinwesen*.

51 See Marx, note 7 at 207. 52 Ibid.

53 See John Rawls, *A Theory of Justice* (Cambridge, Mass.: Harvard University Press, 1971) at 4.

54 See ibid. at 62.

were understood to be, at least in Rawls's later works, legitimate representations of human needs.[55] From this angle, which is undoubtedly not Marxian, it is possible to contrast the horizon of the species being with the mind-set of the species being in what would be the caricature of a system of cooperation. In the first case, people would use their sense of justice to design arrangements leading up to a just distribution of primary goods. In the second case, they pursue their self-interest in a competitive economy, which is a community in alienated form. In a community of that kind, the generation of universally beneficial social output is not a common aim. The species being is not realized directly because people do not transact for the sake of satisfying the needs of others. Actually, a market economy demotes the pursuit of this social objective to the level of a by-product. What could potentially be controlled becomes a side effect of operations that, in the aggregate, are deemed to be beyond human control. Society becomes alien to its members. The theologians of this alienated form of existence call it "catallaxy"[56] and profess belief that this *Être suprême* is superior to anything of human design.

ESSENTIALISM?

The previous analysis suggests strongly that Marx's reference to the "species being" invokes an essence that provides the criterion for any finding of alienation. Hence, the belief in alienation seems to presuppose some form of "essentialism."

This point may even have to be conceded inasmuch as a certain structure of interaction is deemed appropriate to human flourishing. But it does not entail the belief that individuals are the owners of some inner essence that becomes eclipsed by forms of system integration. The experience of alienation is not epitomized by the person who was born to be a concert pianist and ends up preparing tax returns for others.

Alienation is above all a sentiment. It is by virtue of this sentiment that individuals become aware of the *false* realization of human sociality. Moreover, it is through alienation that social cooperation on markets becomes conscious of itself in the medium of an emotional state or *Befindlichkeit*. Society thereby recognizes its false actualization within something that gives rise to a cluster of social phenomena such as widespread boredom,

55 See John Rawls, *Political Liberalism* (New York: Columbia University Press, 1991) 187–190.

56 See F.A. Hayek, *Law, Legislation and Liberty*, vol. 3 (Chicago: Chicago University Press, 1979).

absenteeism, *paresse*, shallow consumerism, drug abuse, and so on. Whoever experiences alienation therefore already rises above the mere interplay of economic power and perceives it – internally – from the outside. Thus understood, the sentiment is a proto-political act.[57]

Rising above mere interdependence is what common action is all about. Hence, experiencing alienation is already an *epiphany of emancipation*. But it does not amount to action, or, rather, it is action only in a state of being inhibited by the powerlessness that is emotionally recognized.

This explains why the recognition of alienation does not, contrary to its appearance, presuppose an essence, perhaps not even the species being. It merely requires recognition that one's own agency is really not what it appears to be.[58] It is not agency of the self. Marx describes this situation in quite drastic terms. Doing is experienced as suffering, strength as impotence, and procreation as castration.[59] It is the experience of passivity, that is, of being an onlooker of one's own life.[60]

Viewed from this angle, the experience of alienation can be reconstructed as reflecting unconscious self-determination. It is self-determination of a reflexive kind, namely a determination of what counts as one's own action. It sets the social norm on the ground of which a person can judge whether she can find herself in her actions or is, instead, a pinball tossed around by economic circumstance. More precisely, the experience of alienation involves a critique of an understanding of collective self-determination that is inherent in the horizontal transactions of abstract persons. Assuming that the decentralized operation of the market can count as a form of collective private self-determination,[61] the outcome of market transactions represents the *volonté de tous* of the community in alienated form. This form of self-determination is challenged through the anticipation of a community in non-alienated form. What collective self-determination would have to amount to in its case is notoriously difficult to pin down. Historically, at any rate, its demands have been articulated by establishing negative liberty from collective private self-determination through various forms of de-commodification.

[57] One needs to be particularly circumspect at this point. Remarks of this type are darlings of an aesthetically enchanted left that is easily disposed to mistake feelings for a political action. It is important, therefore, to stress the *proto*-political nature of emotional social self-knowledge.

[58] See Marx, note 7 at 88.

[59] See Marx, note 7 at 89.

[60] On the contemplative character of the self-relation of the subject under capitalism, see Georg Lukács, *Geschichte und Klassenbewusstsein: Studien über marxistische Dialektik* (10th ed., Neuwied: Luchterhand, 1988) at 191.

[61] See Alexander Somek, *The Cosmopolitan Constitution* (Oxford: Oxford University Press, 2014) at 32, 159, 162.

FROM ALIENATION TO DESPAIR

At this juncture, a remarkable convergence can be observed in the relation of the two grand alternatives of post-Hegelian philosophy.[62] Marx's account of alienation and Kierkegaard's analyses of despair reflect the same situation, however from different angles. Marx reconstructs the social causes of a widespread sense of disempowerment, while Kierkegaard can be read as examining how the disempowered self rationalizes this effect by developing two alternative outlooks on life. These rationalizations – which can be called, loosely speaking, "aesthetic" and "ethical" – lend expression to impoverished understandings of human agency. The social prevalence of these understandings is integral to the community in alienated form. That is, the understandings are manifest in maxims that people act upon. As a result, they experience in more than merely sentimental form the loss of agency that originates from alienation. Despair can be alienation's progeny. It represents an emergent insight into the deceptiveness of agency rationalized under alienated conditions.

Assuming that Michelle Kosch's fresh interpretation of Kierkegaard's pseudonymous writings[63] is correct, then the two conscious forms of despair identified by Kierkegaard are vain attempts to restore the power of individual agency. They are unpromising, for their view of agency is mistaken.[64] Read against a Marxian background, this suggests that the false relation toward others, epitomized by the horizontal realization of the legal relation, carries over into the relationship of the self toward itself. Not by accident, the falsity of the conceptions of agency lies precisely in what is at stake in alienation, namely, the experience of not acting oneself, that is, of being acted upon while purportedly acting. The false conception of agency reflects this experience in the attempt to conceive of oneself as an agent.

The first conscious form of despair that Kierkegaard identifies in *The Sickness unto Death* concerns "not wanting to be oneself."[65] Whatever the deeper ramifications of such an attitude of self-rejection might be, it is consistent with an alienated life in which one experiences one's accidental

62 See Karl Löwith, *Von Hegel zu Nietzsche: Der revolutionäre Bruch im Denken des neunzehnten Jahrhunderts* (reprint: Stuttgart: Kohlhammer, 1950) 162–168.

63 See Michelle Kosch, *Freedom and Reason in Kant, Schelling, and Kierkegaard* (Oxford: Oxford University Press; Oxford: Clarendon Press, 2006).

64 See ibid. at 143, 154, 204.

65 See Søren Kierkegaard, *The Sickness unto Death: A Christian Psychological Exposition for Upbuilding and Awakening* (ed. and trans. H.V. Hong and E.H. Hong, Princeton: Princeton University Press, 1980) at 49.

make-up and "natural endowments"[66] as constituting a risk to well-being or success.[67] Your abilities and inabilities may turn out to be obstacles, paradoxically, either to your well-being or to what society requires in order to create a presence for yourself.[68] It is best for you to be what is most conducive to the satisfaction of wants or what passes as socially apposite. But even if you do not succeed at transforming yourself into who you are not, you at least have to be adept at playing some role that carries the promise of success. This infuses agency – the agency that you observe in yourself as well as in others – with theatricality.

This is of relevance for the socially generalized conception of agency. It posits that the self has no substance and is, in its relation to itself, not dependent on relations to others. The self has to conceive of itself as capable of taking on any shape that is conducive to the satisfaction of wants and the successful projection of a persona. It is immaterial what the self might be outside of the roles that it performs. This irrelevance is the core of not wanting to be oneself.

The conception of agency is, however, flawed. The self is driven by two forces, namely, the desires that the self happens to be thrown into, on the one hand, and the anonymous mechanisms for the allocation of social esteem, on the other.[69] The self does not choose itself; it has itself chosen by the circumstances of want-satisfaction and recognition. It is drifting through life.[70] The self finds itself in what it does *as if* it were genuinely present in its acts even though this presence is in fact the work of heedless yielding to impulses and appetites. There is no self-determination and therefore no sensible way to establish the self's responsibility for action.

The other form of conscious Kierkegaardian despair arises from the attempt to restore self-determination. Hence, it results from wanting to be oneself. Being oneself vis-à-vis wants and conventions of social recognition presupposes that one rise above fleeting affections.[71] Over and above various drives

66 See Ronald Dworkin, *Sovereign Virtue: The Theory and Practice of Equality* (Cambridge, Mass.: Harvard University Press, 2001).

67 See Chapter 5.

68 From a Rousseauvian perspective, we are clearly confronted in this case with a more pathological manifestation of amour-propre. For an illuminating commentary, see Frederick Neuhouser, *Rousseau's Theodicy of Self-Love: Evil, Rationality, and the Drive for Recognition* (Oxford: Oxford University Press, 2008) at 74–75.

69 It is a Hegelian critique of Romantic irony that is repeated in Kierkegaard's work. See Juliane Rebentisch, *Die Kunst der Freiheit: Zur Dialektik demokratischer Existenz* (Berlin: Suhrkamp, 2012) at 156–160.

70 See Kosch, note 63 at 149.

71 See, generally, Christine M. Korsgaard, *Self-Constitution: Agency, Identity, and Integrity* (Cambridge: Cambridge University Press, 2009).

and wants resides, supposedly, a self-legislating being. Selfhood is possible only by virtue of autonomy.[72] An idea of who one is and ought to be in order to be true to oneself – a conception of one's character – represents the law that the self is to itself. This idea informs and guides particular choices.

Such autonomy would not be satisfactorily grounded if the self found itself thrown into a particular character without being able to change it. The self can count as autonomous only if it is able to transcend itself and to recalibrate its character "from above." In other words, it must partake of universal selfhood by virtue of which it is capable of rising above heteronomous forces.[73] This accounts for its moral existence.[74] The self can be true to itself if it respects the moral law, which is nothing but the law that the self is to itself inasmuch as it rises above all particular desires and characteristics. Rising above such heteronomous forces is the effect of a cause that is not mired in the necessity of nature.

To enact this causality, the self must strive to overcome its dependence on mere nature and to control impulses and inclinations in the face of objectives.[75] It is through the control of urges and enticements that the self can realize itself as a self-determining being. In marked contrast to the "aesthetic" attitude with which the first despairing self surrenders itself to pleasure and convention, its second, "ethical" counterpart aspires to take total control of itself because this is what it believes to be required to be true to itself.[76]

The form of despair that emerges from this ambition is a relative of the paradox of autonomy.[77] The law that the self is supposedly to itself is revealed only in the control of inclinations and impulses. The transcendence of impulses, however, also exhausts what the self is. The self lacks substance. It is pure negativity. Since, by stipulation, no substance is within the self, any substantive determination of the self can only originate from the outside. Consequently, to stay true to itself, the self constantly has to reinvent itself.[78]

72 See, in particular, Johann Gottlieb Fichte, *Das System der Sittenlehre nach den Prinzipien der Wissenschaftslehre* (1st ed. 1798, ed. H. Verweyen, Hamburg 1995) at 49.

73 See Kierkegaard, note 65 at 67–68.

74 See Fichte, note 72 at 55.

75 See Immanuel Kant, *Kritik der reinen Vernunft* (ed. H. Klemme, Hamburg: Meiner, 1998) at 622 (A 534/B 562).

76 See Kosch, note 63 at 204.

77 On the paradox that the self-given law appears to be given by a lawless self, see the helpful introduction by Thomas Khurana, "Paradoxien der Autonomie." In *Paradoxien der Autonomie: Freiheit und Gesetz I* (ed. T. Kurana and C. Menke, Berlin: August Verlag, 2011) 7–23.

78 See Roberto Mangabeira Unger, *Passion: An Essay on Personality* (New York: Free Press, 1984).

Such a conception of the self is, however, literally self-defeating.[79] In any moment in which the self controls one impulse or inclination, it has to suspect itself of being vulnerable to the influence of another. Exercising control in one respect involves relinquishing it in another. Since the self is substantively empty, it is systematically vulnerable to external determination, which it must try to shed in the next act.

What one arrives at, in the end, is a strangely heteronomous form of autonomy, the social face of which is well known. Many ascetic selves take their cue from social norms that target various dangerous dependencies. They quit smoking cigarettes. They ingest fat-free yogurt and drink nonalcoholic beer. They follow social norms while patting themselves on their backs and taking pride in willpower that flatters their self-love.[80] Asceticism is a form of narcissism.[81] Substantively, however, it may be entirely conventional.

This demonstrates that wanting to be oneself is eventually subsumed under not wanting to be oneself. Self-control can be a technique mastered by a self living entirely outside of itself. The second form of despair falsely suggests self-mastery. Any self that is consumed by this idea must mistake its own self as the epiphany of the universal self. But since it cannot rise above particularity and heteronomy by virtue of its substantive emptiness, it turns out to be an embodiment of evil.[82]

Kierkegaard attributes the second misconstrual of agency to a false sense of independence. The self does not realize that the relation that it entertains to itself is established by something outside of itself.[83] As a religious thinker, Kierkegaard conceives of this dependence of the relation that relates to itself as recognition of external normative authority that is revealed to human beings. Even though religious belief is irrational – it cannot be deduced on theoretical or practical grounds – Kierkegaard believed that it "fits" the situation of human agency better than any aesthetic or ethic attempt to break away from it.

BEYOND THE LEGAL RELATION

Kierkegaard's conclusions concerning the dependent nature of free agency do not necessarily entail a move toward religion. They merely recognize that

79 On forms of despair as self-defeating constructions of human agency, see Kosch, note 63 at 154, 204.

80 See Sigmund Freud, "On Narcissism: An Introduction." In *Complete Psychological Works*, vol. 14 (trans. J. Strachey, London: Hogarth Press, 1957) 73–102 at 74–75.

81 See Robert Pfaller, *Die Illusionen der anderen: Über das Lustprinzip in der Kultur* (Frankfurt aM: Suhrkamp, 2002).

82 See Kosch, note 63 at 212–214.

83 See Kierkegaard, note 65 at 79.

individual self-determination depends on something outside of it and that it cannot be accounted for so long as it is spelled out only formally, either as "weak"[84] role-play or as obsessive permanent reinvention.

The dependence, of course, has to be adequate to self-determining agency. Hence, only another free agency can be a candidate for what the self depends on.[85] Otherwise, the relation of dependence would not generate another free agent. The dependence *of* freedom has to be a dependence *on* freedom. Stated differently, dependence is the equivalent to independence if every dependent agent embraces the free selfhood of others on which his particular selfhood depends. This dependence is not merely formal. It is substantive. One discovers who one is only in interactions with others. It is written into a historically grown structure of interdependence. This is how we can share our particularity and attain the independence – the universality – that is unattainable for anyone considered in isolation.[86]

We have begun with various analyses by Marx and Hale that have helped us realize that alienation is first and foremost about the loss of individual agency. Hale's analysis has shown that acting under economic duress involves

[84] Kierkegaard also called the first form of despair "despair in weakness." See note 65 at 49.

[85] This, at any rate, is the lesson that can be drawn from Fichte's *Aufforderung* qua summons to engage in free activity. See Johann Gottlieb Fichte, *Grundlage des Naturrechts nach Prinzipien der Wissenschaftslehre*, in his *Werke: Auswahl in sechs Bänden* (ed. F. Medicus, Leipzig: Meiner, 1912) vol. 2 at 36–37. Darwall has recently discovered Fichte's work for analytical moral philosophy. See Stephen Darwall, *The Second-Person Standpoint: Morality, Respect and Accountability* (Cambridge, Mass.; Harvard University Press, 2006) at 246–247 and, most recently, his "Why Fichte's Second-Personal Foundations Can Provide a More Adequate Account of the Relation of Right than Kant's" (2014) 90 *Grazer Philosophische Studien* 5–20. Darwall's reading of Fichte appears to be often entirely correct, in particular when he emphasizes that the *Aufforderung* ("summons") invites a person to regard herself as being seen as a free and rational being. See Stephen Darwall, "Because I Want It" in his *Morality, Authority, and Law: Essays in Second-Personal Ethics* I (Oxford: Oxford University Press, 2013) 93–113 at 108–109. Yet, at times Darwall seems to assimilate the "invitation to free effective activity" implicit in the making of second-personal demands. This is too specific. Rather, Fichte has one paradigm for the *Aufforderung*, namely, acts of education that are presupposed to elicit the autonomous insight on the part of the pupil. See, for example, Ludwig Siep, "Naturrecht und Wissenschaftslehre" in *Fichtes Lehre vom Rechtsverhältnis: Die Deduktion der §§ 1–4 der Grundlage des Naturrechts* (ed. M. Kahlo et al, Frankfurt aM: Klostermann, 1992) 71–91 at 84. Honneth is of course right in concluding that the *Aufforderung* is implicit in every speech act that expects a rational reply by the addressee. Hence, the *Aufforderung* is one attempt to explain subjectivity on the basis of intersubjectivity. See Axel Honneth, "Die transzendentale Notwendigkeit von Intersubjektivit*ät* (Zweiter Lehrsatz: § 3)" in *Johann Gottlieb Fichte: Grundlage des Naturrechts* (ed. J. C. Merle, Berlin: Akademie Verlag, 2001) 63–80 at 76.

[86] We need, in a sense, to embody the particularity of all others in our own life. And this is possible within a structure of social action in which we mutually share our particularity with others. What this means is the great riddle of political philosophy.

choosing a lesser evil, which, by definition, cannot be embraced wholeheartedly. Rather, one is *made* to want what one does not want. The most elementary point of Marx's observations was that the struggle for economic power demotes work to working for a living (*Erwerbsarbeit*) and human life into a means of its own subsistence. The coercive force of economic power, even though backed up by law, resides in the broader situation of action. One is forced to transform oneself into the human resource that the market requires one to be. One ends up doing what one does following the dictates of self-preservation. All actions are acts of yielding. They are basically passive and, in a sense, forms of suffering.

Kierkegaard's hermeneutics of despair can be read as rationalizations of how the self relates to itself as an agent under conditions of a lack of agency. The self is then cast as either capable of enacting a role or as firmly controlling its impulses. In both cases, however, the substantive emptiness of the self indicates that agency exists only in a highly diminished way. While both conceptions suggest empowerment, the requisite power is that of someone who merely adapts to the circumstances that drive him.True agency, by contrast, would have to overcome two dimensions of indifference that prevail in the situation of alienation and its reflexive coping in despair. First, there is indifference toward what could be our own life. Put in Marxian terms (prefiguring Harry Frankfurt), people follow outer rather than inner necessity.[87] Self-realization is indefinitely postponed. This indifference is a systemic but not a necessary feature of market relations. It is a systemic feature because its emergence is inherent in the operation of markets as such. At the same time, it does not necessarily arise. It is conceivable that market relations actually involve a mutual interest in the free self-realization of others. The latter is quite consistent with our "species being." Whether or not self-realization is possible is left to chance.[88]

Second, alienation bespeaks indifference toward what could be achieved through common action. The experience of alienation teaches actually that you cannot be free if you are left to your own devices. You cannot all by yourself rise to the level at which you are capable of controlling your circumstances and to rise above the level at which the dictates of self-preservation force you into certain choosings. You cannot, in other words, lift yourself up to

87 See Marx, note 7 at 207.

88 It is an intriguing fact, of course, that an alienated life offers an equivalent to self-realization, namely the "career." The social psychology of the career is intricate, not least because it is deeply entangled with *amour-propre*. It is about being by means of shining in the eyes of others. Perhaps the career is the interface at which the analysis of alienation has to yield to the analysis of Kierkegaardian despair.

the level where you no longer live the life of a slave. Real freedom is a common achievement, something that human beings have to bring about together.

If, therefore, alienation is about a loss of individuality in one's action, the key to its transcendence has to be sought in a form of individuality that is inherently social or, put differently, in a form of personal self-realization that is reciprocally concerned with others.

COMMUNISM OR SOCIAL FREEDOM

Conceivably, there are at least two ways of overcoming alienation. The first requires that humans collectively rise above markets and control their social cooperation on the basis of an interpretative assessment and determination of their needs. Establishing common control thereby supersedes economic power. We associate this step with socialism or communism. Both have had a bad press since 1989, and we do not need to enter into a discussion of the requisite failed projects here.

There is, however, one presupposition of the communist project that has been contested, surprisingly, by critical theorists. It is the presupposition that the common coordination and control of production and distribution reconcile people with what they do. If that were the case, drudgery would lose its alienating character as long as it was carried out with the awareness that it is for the good of others whom one thereby benefits. A communist society would in and of itself offer good work for everyone. There is reason to be skeptical that the alienation of labor can ever be overcome. It explains, for example, why Habermas shifted the emphasis of a critical theory from labor to the creation of less dominated structures of communication.[89]

From a different angle, Menke perceives an enduring tragic conflict between the right and the good,[90] which also provides a profound challenge to any communist project. For even if it were possible to create a world in which tasks, resources, and goods were allocated justly, there would still be no guarantee that people could lead lives that they regarded as authentically their own. The tragic conflict between family loyalty and loyalty to the polity, which is a topic of antiquity, is thus replicated within a polity that supposedly reconciles this conflict through a social contract. Yet, the conflict is replicated

89 See Jürgen Habermas, *Technik und Wissenschaft als "Ideologie"* (Frankfurt aM: Suhrkamp, 1968) at 46.

90 See Christoph Menke, *Tragödie im Sittlichen: Gerechtigkeit und Freiheit nach Hegel* (Frankfurt aM: Suhrkamp, 1996).

in the relation between the legitimate demands of the community and the aspiration of individual self-realization.

There is, however, a second way of addressing the predicament of alienation. It is essentially conservative, not only because it leaves the market principally in place but also because it looks back to traditions of de-commodified human dealings. It aims at protecting parcels of social freedom against erosion. Authors of different persuasion have opted for it under different names, most famously Michael Walzer under the heading of "Spheres of Justice."[91]

Keen interpreters of Hegel's social philosophy, such as Frederick Neuhouser and Axel Honneth, have reinvigorated the category of "social freedom."[92] This freedom is, essentially, not only about having a choice but also about being present in activities and goods that one cares about. Simply put, it concerns not the possibility ("choice") but the actuality of freedom.

Arguably, the presence of persons in their own doings depends on two conditions. The first condition has made Hegel's philosophy of law perennially controversial even though Hegel began with a relatively uncontroversial premise. One is not really free – or one is only *formally* free while substantially alienated from oneself – if one's status or action is experienced as resigning oneself to a foreign force or will. People can through their own choices relinquish themselves to fate. This is not terribly controversial. Hegel's views become divisive when we are told that individuals can overcome a state in which they are detached or alienated from their own lives by reconciling themselves with traditional social roles. The explanation for this proposition, which must smack of conformism, is that individual freedom can be "actual" only if it fits into an already existing social world.

Hegel had at least one reason for his belief. The freedom of moral self-legislation may result in aloof detachment. For example, it is perfectly consistent with the categorical imperative to live without private property, since it would not be immoral to have a socialist society. If one were to choose to live on the basis of this maxim, however, one can scarcely establish a connection with others whose lives are calibrated to a property-owning world. Therefore, individuals can live among others only if they identify with a social role. But not just any social role: the role has to be coherent with the role and interests of others. If they did not so identify, they would, as some utilitarians and Kantians

91 See Michael Walzer, *Spheres of Justice: A Defence of Pluralism and Equality* (Oxford: Blackwell, 1983).

92 See Frederick Neuhouser, *Foundations of Hegel's Social Theory: Actualizing Freedom* (Cambridge, Mass: Harvard University Press, 2000) at 33–37; Axel Honneth, *Das Recht der Freiheit: Grundriss einer demokratischen Sittlichkeit* (Berlin: Suhrkamp, 2011) at 81–110.

undoubtedly do, live in a moral fantasy world. Freedom has to have "substance," in Hegel's words. This is not to say, however, that the slave is expected to identify with his status. Relationships of social freedom are constituted by a *mutuality* that serves as a test for the adequacy of roles. If whatever one is or does is of value to others, it has to be reciprocated by doings or attitudes that are of value for oneself and must leave one with a set of valuable options.

The second condition of social freedom says that the participants in such an institutional setting recognize their mutual dependence and embrace it either affectionately or in a spirit of loyalty and solidarity. Their relationship would be altered profoundly if it became asymmetrical and one person took advantage of the weakness and vulnerability of others. The attitude of this one person toward others would no longer be that of a genuine appreciation of what these others are or what they do; he would rather use them and their needs as mere tools for his own advantage. The whole relationship would change, for those who fall victim to extortion or exploitation would no longer be fully invested in what they do. They would grudgingly yield to demands. Remarkably, the beneficiary's freedom would no longer be extended into the freedom of another. In Hegel's terms, the beneficiary would no longer encounter someone like himself, but an unfree person, in the others who serve him.

EPILOGUE

The theory developed in this book tries to remain faithful to the original constructivist ethos of modern legal positivism. Constructivism is committed, first, to minimizing the moral idealization of law and, second, to developing the point of law from the bottom up. The basis thereto is the analysis of the legal relation. Within the legal relation, people are cast as choosers. They expect from one another normatively to have their choices respected. Their freedom of choice is bounded.

In contrast to legal positivism, constructivism does not put "norms" or "rules" at the center of legal theory. Actually, it views rights and obligations as more central to the idea of law. The legal relation is necessary to create and to sustain our presence in the social world. This presence is mediated by agency.

The most fundamental condition of agency is explicability. One can pass as the author of one's acts as long as one can pass as a sufficiently reason-responsive being. This does not require acting for what others would view as the right reason. It requires merely that one's choices must not transgress universally acceptable limits. Explicability has to stay within the bounds of moral justifiability.

Bad acts are explicable. Our actions are still explicable in terms of reasons, but the reasons are bad. Doing something bad also creates presence for us, but it is presence of someone who is not good at being human. Some, perversely, delight in that. This does not alter the fact that being bad at what we are is a deficient way of being that.

The legal relation is a constructive response to the predicament that – along the social dimension – moral justifications cannot promise more than to amount to explicability. The explanation of this impossibility is the actual or conceivable plurality of evaluative outlooks. They infuse universalization with particularity.

In giving rise to the legal relation, moral universalization becomes reflective. It carves out the spaces within which people may legitimately stay merely explicable to one another even if they intend to universalize. Their conclusions are thus rendered as choices and their claims as mere wants.

Law thereby supersedes mere morality. But it also makes it possible. Ironically, the moral determination of action, which is supposedly based upon insight in the first- and third-personal relation, is made authoritative by law in the second-personal relation. Morality is less serious from a second-personal perspective than it must appear from the other perspectives.

The law, however, does not supersede morality in one fell swoop. Resolving matters legally is the activity of taking the step toward reflective universalization repeatedly by supplanting the question of what ought to be done with the question of who ought to decide what. Law, in a sense, is the repeated move to the reflective level. This move, nonetheless, always needs to draw on moral ideas.

The second-personal authority that originates from the legal relation is political and not private. It would be private if – as in the case of the service conception – authority were a device for making you yield to reasons that apply to you under conditions where you encounter an obstacle to perceive them or to have them (lack of expertise and collective action problems, respectively).

Politics is, by contrast, about dealing with and yielding to the reasons of others. It is about creating a space in which I encounter reasons in a state in which they could be mine only if I were another person invested with a different moral outlook (*Veranderung*).

Within the legal relation, valid claims made by others are represented as sources of law. Sources contain "disclaimed claims" to legal knowledge. They are asserted as mere social facts ("We believe that . . . "). The validation of these claims requires another source (*e.g.*, laws are valid for the judiciary).

The operation of sources is based upon a necessary form of recognition. Its point is to render the law clear. Sources can be arranged in a sequence with an eye to how successfully they contribute to the attainment of this objective.

The reasons underpinning positive law are in principle the reasons of others. This fact colors the manner in which we reason legally. The distance toward the reasons that one encounters in legal materials is properly matched with irony. This irony is bitter when one needs to succumb to pointless conventions of legal reasoning; it is serene when one works with the reasons of others productively. One is then in the business of letting "the law" speak.

The reciprocity inherent in moral universalization appears within the legal relation as the equality principle. Its meaning is best drawn out by elaborating what constitutes discrimination. Such an elaboration presupposes an appealing idea of self-determined action through which agents assert their presence in this world. This presence would be denied to them if they had to resort to social strategies of hiding and ducking or to engage in self-repair to avoid disadvantage. Since social cooperation nevertheless requires universal agility and adaptability, the question must arise to what extent individuals may legitimately defy pressures of adaptation. The protections against discrimination that emerge from requisite struggles over "protected grounds" are, however, historically contingent.

The realization of the legal relation also gives rise to the experience that one's freedom can be worthless if it does not provide avenues for self-realization. Such an experience of alienation is rationalized in two forms of despair.

In addressing the problems of discrimination and alienation, the reciprocity inherent in the legal relation can be further developed into structures of social freedom.

Such structures merely make explicit what is already anticipated in the legal relation. The legal relation makes people yield to the second-personal authority of others. You consider handguns obnoxious. You would never buy one yourself and find it wrong for others to own one. If you had your moral way, all handguns would be confiscated. The right to private property, however, not only makes you respect the choices of others; your yielding to their choices makes your actions (*e.g.*, paying higher taxes for public safety precautions) part of the realization of their freedom. Thus understood, social freedom is written into the "genetic code" of the legal relation.

The freedom of this type, however, exists fully only in relations of mutual dependence if the action of one contributes reciprocally to the realization of the freedom of another. Structures of social freedom are the answer to the question of what is necessary to create the conditions under which one can be plausibly the author of one's own life. Within them the operation of hypothetically taking the place of another in the process of universalization becomes real in relations of actual interdependence. A can agree to B's action if A's life is enhanced by it (and the other way round).

Such a view of freedom is not individualistic. It makes one view one's own life as part of a larger whole to which this life is taken to belong. It makes the self-realization of one person dependent on the self-realization of others.

Bibliography

Arendt, Hannah. *The Human Condition* (Chicago: University of Chicago Press, 1958)

Austin, John. *The Province of Jurisprudence Determined* (Amherst: Prometheus Books, 2000)

Barry, Brian. *Freedom and Culture: An Egalitarian Critique of Multiculturalism* (Cambridge, Mass: Harvard University Press, 2001)

Behler, Ernst. *Klassische Ironie – Romantische Ironie – Tragische Ironie: Zum Ursprung dieser Begriffe* (Darmstadt: Wissenschaftliche Buchgesellschaft, 1972)

Bentham, Jeremy. *An Introduction to the Principles of Morals and Legislation* (Oxford: Clarendon Press, 1789)

Berardi, Franco "Bifo." *The Soul at Work: From Alienation to Autonomy* (trans. F. Cadel and G. Mecchia, Cambridge, Mass.: MIT Press, 2009)

Besson, Samantha. *The Morality of Conflict: Reasonable Disagreement and the Law* (Oxford: Hart Publishing, 2006)

Bix, Brian H. "Natural Law Theory." In *A Companion to Philosophy of Law and Legal Theory* (ed. D. Patterson, Oxford: Blackwell, 1996) 223–240

Bix, Brian H. *A Dictionary of Legal Theory* (Oxford: Oxford University Press, 2004)

Bix, Brian H. *Jurisprudence: Theory and Context* (7th ed., Durham: Carolina Academic Press, 2015)

Bochenski, Joseph Maria. *The Logic of Religion* (New York: New York University Press, 1965)

Böckenförde, Ernst-Wolfgang. *Geschichte der Rechts- und Staatsphilosophie: Antike und Mittelalter* (2d ed., Tübingen: Mohr Siebeck, 2006)

Brandom, Robert B. *Making It Explicit: Reasoning, Representing and Discoursive Commitment* (Cambridge, Mass.: Harvard University Press, 1998)

Brandom, Robert B. *Tales of the Mighty Dead: Historical Essays in the Metaphysics of Intentionality* (Cambridge, Mass.: Harvard University Press, 2002)

Cohen, Felix. "Transcendental Nonsense and the Functional Approach" (1935) 35 *Columbia Law Review* 808–849

Cohen, Gerald E. *Freedom, Self-Ownership and Equality* (Cambridge: Cambridge University Press, 1995)

Colebrook, Claire. *Irony* (Abingdon: Routledge, 2004)

Coleman, Jules L. "Negative and Positive Positivism" (1982) 11 *Journal of Legal Studies* 139–164

Coleman, Jules L. *The Practice of Principle: In Defence of a Pragmatist Approach to Legal Theory* (Oxford: Oxford University Press, 2001)

Coleman, Jules L. and Leiter, Brian. "Legal Positivism." In *A Companion to Legal Philosophy and Legal Theory* (ed. D. Patterson, 2d ed. Oxford: Wiley-Blackwell, 2010) 228–248 at 228

Coleman, Jules L. and Shapiro, Scott (eds.), *The Oxford Handbook of Jurisprudence and Philosophy of Law* (Oxford: Oxford University Press, 2002)

Corpus Iuris Canonici, vol 1: *Decretum Magistri Gratiani* (ed. A. Friedberg, Leipzig: 1879)

Coyle, Sean. *Modern Jurisprudence: A Philosophical Guide* (Oxford: Hart Publishing, 2014)

d'Almeida, Luís Duarte. "Legal Statements and Normative Language" (2011) 30 *Law and Philosophy* 167–199

Darwall, Stephen. "Because I Want It," in his *Morality, Authority, and Law: Essays in Second-Personal Ethics I* (Oxford: Oxford University Press, 2013a) 93–113

Darwall, Stephen. *Morality, Authority, and Law: Essays in Second-Personal Ethics I* (Oxford: Oxford University Press, 2013b)

Darwall, Stephen. *The Second-Personal Standpoint: Morality, Respect, and Accountability* (Cambridge, Mass.: Harvard University Press, 2006)

Darwall, Stephen. "Why Fichte"s Second-Personal Foundations Can Provide a More Adequate Account of the Relation of Right than Kant's" (2014) 90 *Grazer Philosophische Studien* 5–20

Davidson, Donald. "A Nice Derangement of Epitaphs." In *Truth and Interpretation* (ed. E. LePore, Oxford: Blackwell, 1986) 433–446

Davidson, Donald. *Inquiries into Truth and Interpretation* (Oxford: Oxford University Press, 1982)

Dickinson, Julie. "Interpreting Normativity." In *Properties of Law: Essays in Honour of Jim Harris* (ed. T. Endicott, J. Getzler, and E. Peel, Oxford: Oxford University Press, 2006) 22–42

Duxbury, Neil. "Robert Hale and the Economy of Legal Force" (1990) 53 *Modern Law Review* 421–444

Dworkin, Ronald. *A Matter of Principle* (Cambridge, Mass.: Harvard University Press, 1985)

Dworkin, Ronald. *Justice in Robes* (Cambridge, Mass.: Harvard University Press, 2006)

Dworkin, Ronald. *Justice for Hedgehogs* (Cambridge, Mass.: Harvard University Press, 2011)

Dworkin, Ronald. "Law as Interpretation." In *The Politics of Interpretation* (ed. W.J.T. Mitchell, Chicago: Chicago University Press, 1982) 249–270

Dworkin, Ronald. *Law's Empire* (Cambridge, Mass.: Harvard University Press, 1986)

Dworkin, Ronald. *Sovereign Virtue: The Theory and Practice of Equality* (Cambridge, Mass.: Harvard University Press, 2001)

Dworkin, Ronald. *Taking Rights Seriously* (2d ed., Cambridge, Mass.: Harvard University Press, 1978)

Emerson, Ralph Waldo. *Essays: First and Second Series* (New York: Vintage Books, 1990)

Epstein, Richard. *Forbidden Grounds: The Case Against Employment Discrimination Laws* (Cambridge, Mass.: Harvard University Press, 1992)

Esser, Joseph. *Vorverständnis und Methodenwahl in der Rechtsfindung* (Frankfurt aM: Athäneum, 1970)

Feuerbach, Ludwig. Das Wesen des Christentums (1841), *Werke in sechs Bänden*, vol. 5 (ed. E. Thies, Frankfurt aM: Suhrkamp, 1968)

Fichte, Johann Gottlieb. *Das System der Sittenlehre nach den Prinzipien der Wissenschaftslehre* (1st ed. 1798, ed. H. Verweyen, Hamburg: Meiner, 1995)

Fichte, Johann Gottlieb. *Grundlage des Naturrechts nach Prinzipien der Wissenschaftslehre* (ed. F. Medicus, Hamburg: Meiner, 1979)

Fichte, Johann Gottlieb. "Grundlage des Naturrechts nach Prinzipien der Wissenschaftslehre," in his *Werke: Auswahl in sechs Bänden* (ed. F. Medicus, Leipzig: Meiner, 1912) vol. 2

Finnis, John. *Natural Law and Natural Justice* (2d ed., Oxford: Oxford University Press, 2011a)

Finnis, John. *Reason in Action: Collected Essays: Volume 1* (Oxford: Oxford University Press, 2011b)

Fish, Stanley. *Doing What Comes Naturally* (Oxford: Oxford University Press, 1988)

Frank, Jerome. *Courts on Trial: Myth and Reality in American Justice* (Princeton: Princeton University Press, 1949)

Freud, Sigmund. "On Narcissism: An Introduction." In *Complete Psychological Works*, vol. 14 (trans. J. Strachey, London: Hogarth Press, 1957) 73–102

Fried, Barbara H. *The Progressive Assault on Laissez Faire: Robert Hale and the First Law and Economics Movement* (Cambridge, Mass.: Harvard University Press, 1998)

Fried, Charles. *Saying What the Law Is: The Constitution in the Supreme Court* (Cambridge, Mass.: Harvard University Press, 2004)

Gadamer, Hans-Georg. *Die Aktualität des Schönen: Kunst als Spiel, Symbol und Fest* (Stuttgart: Philipp Reclam Jun., 1979)

Gadamer, Hans-Georg. *Wahrheit und Methode: Grundzüge einer philosophischen Hermeneutik* (4th ed., Tübingen: Mohr, 1975)

Gamm, Gerhard. *Flucht aus der Kategorie: Die Positivierung des Unbestimmten als Ausgang der Moderne* (Frankfurt aM: Suhrkamp, 1994)

Gamm, Gerhard. *Nicht nichts. Studien zu einer Semantik des Unbestimmten* (Frankfurt aM: Suhrkamp, 2000)

Gardner, John. "Legal Positivism: 5½ Myths" (2001) 46 *American Journal of Jurisprudence* 199–227

Gardner, John. "The Legality of Law" (2004) 17 *Ratio Iuris* 168–181

Gardner, John. *Law as a Leap of Faith: Essays on Law in General* (Oxford: Oxford University Press, 2012)

Goffman, Erving. *The Presentation of Self in Everyday Life* (New York: Anchor Book, 1959)

Green, Leslie. "The Concept of Law Revisited" (1997) 94 *Michigan Law Review* 1687–1717

Green, Leslie. "Positivism and the Inseparability of Law and Morals" (2008) 83 *New York University Law Review* 1035–1058

Grey, Thomas C. "Langdell's Orthodoxy" (1983) 45 *University of Pittsburgh Law Review* 1–45

Guinier, Lani, Michelle Fine, and Jane Balin, *Becoming Gentlemen: Women, Law Schools and Institutional Change* (Boston: Beacon Press, 1997)

Habermas, Jürgen. *Technik und Wissenschaft als ‚Ideologie"* (Frankfurt aM: Suhrkamp, 1968)

Habermas, Jürgen. *Theorie des kommunikativen Handelns, vol. 1: Handlungsrationalität und gesellschaftliche Rationalisierung* (Frankfurt aM: Suhrkamp, 1981a)

Habermas, Jürgen. *Theorie des kommunikativen Handelns, vol. 2: Zur Kritik der funktionalistischen Vernunft* (Frankfurt aM: Suhrkamp, 1981b)

Habermas, Jürgen. *Zur Logik der Sozialwissenschaften* (5th ed. Frankfurt aM: Suhrkamp, 1982)

Habermas, Jürgen. *Faktizität und Geltung: Studien zur Diskurstheorie des Rechts und des demokratischen Rechtsstaats* (Frankfurt aM: Suhrkamp, 1992)

Habermas, Jürgen. *Between Facts and Norms: Contributions to a Discourse Theory of Law and Democracy* (trans. W. Rehg, Cambridge, Mass.: MIT Press, 1996)

Haferkamp, Hans-Peter. *Georg Friedrich Puchta und die "Begriffsjurisprudenz"* (Frankfurt aM: Klostermann, 2004)

Hale, Robert L. "Coercion and Distribution in a Supposedly Non-Coercive State" (1923) 38 *Political Science Quarterly* 470–494

Hale, Robert L. "Force and the State: A Comparison of 'Political' and 'Economic' Compulsion" (1935) 35 *Columbia Law Review* 149–201

Hale, Robert L. "Bargaining, Duress, and Economic Liberty" (1943) 43 *Columbia Law Review* 603–628

Hale, Robert L. *Freedom Through Law: Public Control of Private Governing Power* (New York: Columbia University Press, 1952)

Hamish, Stewart. "Incentives and the Rule of Law: An Intervention in the Kramer/ Simmonds Debate" (2006) 51 *American Journal of Jurisprudence* 149–164

Hare, R.M. *Moral Thinking: Its Levels, Method, and Point* (Oxford: Oxford University Press, 1981)

Harris, James W. "Kelsen"s Pallid Normativity" (1996) 9 *Ratio Iuris* 95–115

Hart, H.L.A. "Positivism and the Separation of Law and Morals" (1958) 71 *Harvard Law Review* 593–621

Hart, H.L.A. "Kelsen Visited" (1963) 10 *UCLA Law Review* 709–728

Hart, H.L.A. "Bentham and the Demystification of Law" (1973) 36 *Modern Law Review* 2–17

Hart, H.L.A. *The Concept of Law* (2d ed., Oxford: Clarendon Press, 1994)

Hayek, Friedrich August von. *The Road to Serfdom* (London: Routledge, 1991; first edition 1944)

Hegel, G.W.F. *Elements of the Philosophy of Right* (H.B. Nisbet tr, Cambridge: Cambridge University Press, 1991)

Hegel, G.W.F. *Philosophie des Rechts: Die Vorlesung von 1819/20 in einer Nachschrift* (ed. D. Henrich, Frankfurt aM: Suhrkamp, 1983)

Heidegger, Martin. *Sein und Zeit* (14th ed., Tübingen: Max Niemeyer Verlag, 1977)

Hellman, Deborah. *When Is Discrimination Wrong?* (Cambridge, Mass.: Harvard University Press, 2008)

Herget James E. and Wallace, Stephen. "The German Free Law Movement as the Source of American Legal Realism" (1987) 73 *Virginia Law Review* 399–442

Herzog, Lisa. *Inventing the Market: Smith, Hegel, and Political Theory* (Oxford: Oxford University Press, 2013)

Hill, Christopher. *The World Turned Upside Down: Radical Ideas During the English Revolution* (London: Pelican Books, 1975)

Himma, Kenneth Einar. *The Nature of Law: Philosophical Issues in Conceptual Jurisprudence and Legal Theory* (New York: Foundation Press: 2011)

Hobbes, Thomas. *Leviathan* (ed. I. Shapiro, New Haven: Yale University Press, 2010)

Hogrebe, Wolfram. *Prädikation und Genesis. Metaphysik als Fundamentalheuristik im Ausgang von Schellings "Die Weltalter"* (Frankfurt aM: Suhrkamp, 1989)

Hollerbach, Alexander. *Der Rechtsgedanke bei Schelling: Quellenstudien zu seiner Rechts- und Staatsphilosophie* (Frankfurt aM: Klostermann, 1958)

Holmes, Oliver Wendell. "Law in Science and Science in Law" (1899) 12 *Harvard Law Review* 443

Honneth, Axel. "Die transzendentale Notwendigkeit von Intersubjektivität (Zweiter Lehrsatz: § 3)." In *Johann Gottlieb Fichte: Grundlage des Naturrechts* (ed. J.-C. Merle, Berlin: Akademie Verlag, 2001) 63–80

Honneth, Axel. *Unsichtbarkeit: Stationen zu einer Theorie der Intersubjektivität* (Frankfurt aM: Suhrkamp, 2003)

Honneth, Axel. *Das Recht der Freiheit: Grundriss einer demokratischen Sittlichkeit* (Berlin: Suhrkamp, 2011)

Horn, Christoph, Mieth, Corrina, and Scarano, Nico. *Immanuel Kant: Grundlegung zur Metaphysik der Sitten* (Frankfurt aM: Suhrkamp, 2007)

Horn, Christoph. *Nichtideale Normativität: Ein neuer Blick auf Kants politische Philosophie* (Berlin: Suhrkamp, 2014)

Jaeggi, Rahel. *Entfremdung: Zur Aktualität eines sozialphilosophischen Problems* (Frankfurt aM: Campus, 2005)

Jhering, Rudolph von. *Der Geist des römischen Rechts auf den verschiedenen Stufen seiner Entwicklung*, vol. 2.2 (5th ed. Leipzig: Härtel, 1899)

Jhering, Rudolph von. *Geist des römischen Rechts auf den verschiedenen Stufen seiner Entwicklung* (6th ed. Leipzig: Breitkopf and Härtel 1907), vol. 1

Kant, Immanuel. "Grundlegung der Metaphysik der Sitten" in *Kants gesammelte Schriften* (Royal Prussian Academy edition, reprint, Berlin: de Gruyter 1963) vol. 4, 385–463

Kant, Immanuel. Die Metaphysik der Sitten, *Werkausgabe* (ed. W. Weischedel, Frankfurt aM: Insel, 1968) vol. 8

Kant, Immanuel. *Kritik der reinen Vernunft* (ed. H. Klemme, Hamburg: Meiner, 1998)

Kelsen, Hans. *Hauptprobleme der Staatsrechtslehre entwickelt aus der Lehre vom Rechtssatz* (2d ed., Tübingen: Mohr, 1923)

Kelsen, Hans. *Das Problem der Souveränität und die Theorie des Völkerrechts. Beitrag zu einer reinen Rechtslehre* (2d ed., Tübingen: J.C.B. Mohr, 1928a)

Kelsen, Hans. *Der soziologische und der juristische Staatsbegriff: Kritische Untersuchung des Verhältnisses von Staat und Recht* (2d ed., Tübingen: J.C.B. Mohr, 1928b)

Kelsen, Hans. *Pure Theory of Law* (2d ed., trans. M. Knight, Berkeley: University of California Press, 1967)

Kelsen, Hans. "Recht und Moral." In *Die Wiener Rechtstheoretische Schule* (ed. H. Klecatstky, R. Marcic, and H. Schambeck, Vienna: Europaverlag 1968) vol. 1 797–810

Kelsen, Hans. *General Theory of Norms* (trans. M. Hartney, Oxford: Oxford University Press, 1991)

Kelsen, Hans. *Introduction to the Problems of Legal Theory* (trans. B. Litschewski Paulson and S.L. Paulson, Oxford: Clarendon Press, 1992)

Khurana, Thomas. "Paradoxien der Autonomie." In *Paradoxien der Autonomie: Freiheit und Gesetz I* (ed. T. Kurana and C. Menke, Berlin: August Verlag, 2011) 7–23

Kierkegaard, Søren. *The Sickness unto Death: A Christian Psychological Exposition for Upbuilding and Awakening* (ed. and trans. H.V. Hong and E.H. Hong, Princeton: Princeton University Press, 1980)

Kierkegaard, Søren. *Fear and Trembling* (trans. S. Walsh, Cambridge: Cambridge University Press, 2006)

Kirchmann, Julius Hermann von. *Die Werthlosigkeit der Jurisprudenz als Wissenschaft* (Berlin: Julius Springer, 1848)

Kletzer, Christoph. "Absolute Legal Positivism" (2013) 42 *Netherlands Journal of Legal Philosophy* 87–99

Korsgaard, Christine M. *The Sources of Normativity* (Cambridge: Cambridge University Press, 1996)

Korsgaard, Christine M. *Self-Constitution: Agency, Identity, and Integrity* (Cambridge: Cambridge University Press, 2009)

Kosch, Michelle. *Freedom and Reason in Kant, Schelling, and Kierkegaard* (Oxford: Clarendon Press, 2006)

Kramer, Matthew H. *In Defence of Legal Positivism: Law Without Trimming* (Oxford: Oxford University Press 1999) 128–192

Kramer, Matthew H. "Introduction." In M. Kramer et al. (ed.), *The Legacy of H.L.A. Hart* (Oxford: Oxford University Press, 2008) xiii–xviii

Kripke, Saul A. *Wittgenstein on Rules and Private Language: An Elementary Exposition* (Cambridge, Mass.: Harvard University Press, 1982)

Lafont, Cristina. "Meaning and Interpretation: Can Brandomian Scorekeepers Be Gadamerian Hermeneuts?" (2008) 3 *Philosophy Compass* 17–29

Langdell, Christopher Columbus. *Selection of Cases on the Law of Contracts* (Boston: Little Brown, 1871)

Lear, Jonathan. *A Case for Irony* (Cambridge, Mass.: Harvard University Press, 2011)

Leiter, Brian. "Legal Realism and Legal Positivism Reconsidered" (2001) 111 *Ethics* 278–301

Leiter, Brian. *Naturalizing Jurisprudence: Essays on American Legal Realism and Naturalism in Legal Philosophy* (Oxford: Oxford University Press, 2007)

Leiter, Brain. "The radicalism of legal positivism," *University of Chicago Public Law and Legal Theory Working Paper* No. 303, 2010

Leiter, Brian. "Why Legal Positivism Again?" http://papers.ssrn.com/sol3/papers.cfm?abstract_id=2323013

Llewellyn, Karl N. *On Legal Realism* 104–106 (Birmingham, Ala.: Legal Classics Library, 1986)

Locke, John. *A Letter Concerning Toleration* (ed. J. Tully, Indianapolis: Hackett, 1985)

Lohmann, Georg. *Indifferenz und Gesellschaft: Eine kritische Auseinandersetzung mit Marx* (Frankfurt aM: Suhrkamp, 1991)

Löwith, Karl. *Von Hegel zu Nietzsche: Der revolutionäre Bruch im Denken des neunzehnten Jahrhunderts* (reprint: Stuttgart: Kohlhammer, 1950)

Luhmann, Niklas. *Rechtssoziologie* (Reinbek: Rowohlt Taschenbuch, 1972)

Luhmann, Niklas. "Law as a Social System" (1989) 83 *Northwestern Law Review* 136–150

Luhmann, Niklas. "Operational Closure and Structural Coupling: On the Differentiation of the Legal System" (1992) 13 *Cardozo Law Review* 1419–1442

Luhmann, Niklas. *Social Systems* (trans. J. Bednarz Jr and D. Baecker, Stanford: Stanford University Press, 1996)

Luhmann, Niklas. *Law as a Social System* (trans. R. Nobles and K. Ziegert, Oxford: Oxford University Press, 2004)

Lukács, Georg. *Geschichte und Klassenbewusstsein: Studien über marxistische Dialektik* (10th ed., Neuwied: Luchterhand, 1988)

Lyotard, Jean-François. *The Differend* (trans. G. Van Den Abbeele, St. Paul: University of Minnesota Press, 1989)

Mackie, J.L. *Ethics: Inventing Right and Wrong* (Harmondsworth: Penguin Books, 1977)

Man, Paul de. *Aesthetic Ideology* (ed. A. Warminski, Minneapolis: University of Minnesota Press, 1996)

Marcuse, Herbert. *One-Dimensional Man: Studies in the Ideology of Advanced Industrial Society* (Boston: Beacon Press, 1964)

Marmor, Andrei. *Philosophy of Law* (Princeton: Princeton University Press, 2011)

Marx, Karl. *Ökonomisch-philosophische Manuskripte* (ed. M. Quante, Frankfurt aM: Suhrkamp, 2009)

Mead, George Herbert. *The Philosophy of the Present* (ed. A.E. Murphy, Chicago: University of Chicago Press, 1932)

Mead, Georg Herbert. *Mind, Self, and Society from the Standpoint of the Social Behaviourist* (Chicago: University of Chicago Press, 1934)

Menke, Christoph. "Liberalismus im Konflikt: Zwischen Gerechtigkeit und Freiheit." In *Gemeinschaft und Gerechtigkeit* (ed. M. Brumlik and H. Brunkhorst, Frankfurt aM: Fischer, 1993) 218–243

Menke, Christoph. *Tragödie im Sittlichen: Gerechtigkeit und Freiheit nach Hegel* (Frankfurt aM: Suhrkamp, 1996)

Menke, Christoph. *Die Gegenwart der Tragödie: Versuch über Urteil und Spiel* (Frankfurt aM: Suhrkamp, 2005)

Menke, Christoph. *Kraft: Ein Grundbegriff ästhetischer Anthropologie* (Frankfurt aM: Suhrkamp, 2008)

Menke, Christoph. *Die Kraft der Kunst* (Berlin: Suhrkamp, 2013)

Merkl, Adolf Julius. "Prolegomena zu einer Theorie des rechtlichen Stufenbaus" In *Gesellschaft, Staat und Recht: Untersuchungen zur reinen Rechtslehre* (ed. A.J. Verdross, Vienna: Julius Springer, 1931) 252–294

Merkl, Adolf Julius. "Das doppelte Rechtsantlitz. Eine Betrachtung aus der Erkenntnistheorie des Rechts" reprinted in *Die Wiener Rechtstheoretische Schule* (ed. H. Klecatstky, R. Marcic and H. Schambeck, Vienna: Europaverlag 1968a) vol. 1, 1091–1113

Merkl, Adolf Julius. "Das Recht im Lichte seiner Anwendung" reprinted in *Die Wiener Rechtstheoretische Schule* (ed. H. Klecatstky, R. Marcic and H. Schambeck, Vienna: Europaverlag 1968b) vol. 1, 1167–1201

Mirandola, Pico della. *Oratio de hominis dignitate* (ed. A. Buck, Hamburg: Meiner, 1990)

Montesquieu, *The Spirit of the Laws* (trans. A.M. Cohler et al., Cambridge: Cambridge University Press, 1989)

Moreau, Sophia. "What Is Discrimination?" (2010) 38 *Philosophy and Public Affairs* 144–179

Nagel, Thomas. *The View from Nowhere* (New York, Oxford University Press, 1986)

Neuhouser, Frederick. *Foundations of Hegel's Social Theory: Actualizing Freedom* (Cambridge, Mass.: Harvard University Press, 2001)

Neuhouser, Frederick. *Rousseau's Theodicy of Self-Love: Evil, Rationality, and the Drive for Recognition* (Oxford: Oxford University Press, 2008)

Nietzsche, Friedrich. *The Dawn of Day* (trans. J.M. Kennedy, New York: Russell and Russell, 1964)

O'Neil, Onora. *Acting on Principle: An Essay in Kantian Ethics* (2d ed., Cambridge: Cambridge University Press, 2013)

Oakeshott, Michael. "The Rule of Law." In his *On History and Other Essays* (Indianapolis: Liberty Fund, 1999) 129–179

Oliphant, Herman. "A Return to Stare Decisis" (1928) 14 A.B.A. 71

Parsons, Talcott. *Sociological Theory and Modern Society* (New York and London: Free Press, 1967)

Patterson, Dennis. "Explicating the Internal Point of View" (1999a) 52 *Southern Methodist University Law Review* 67–74

Patterson, Dennis. *Law and Truth* (Oxford: Oxford University Press, 1999b)

Paulson, Stanley L. "Hans Kelsen's Earliest Legal Theory: Critical Constructivism" (1996) 59 *Modern Law Review* 797–812

Paulson, Stanley L. "A 'Justified Normativity' Thesis in Hans Kelsen's Pure Theory of Law? Rejoinders to Robert Alexy and Joseph Raz." In *Institutionalized Reason* (ed. M. Klatt, Oxford: Oxford University Press, 2011)

Peirce, Charles S. Lectures on Pragmatism (ed. E. Walther, Hamburg: Meiner, 1973)

Peirce, Charles S. *Reasoning and the Logic of Things* (ed. K.L. Ketner, Cambridge, Mass.: Harvard University Press, 1993)

Pfaller, Robert. *Die Illusionen der anderen: Über das Lustprinzip in der Kultur* (Frankfurt aM: Suhrkamp, 2002)

Pinkard, Terry. *Hegel's Phenomenology: The Sociality of Reason* (Cambridge: Cambridge University Press, 1994)

Pippin, Robert. *Hegel's Practical Philosophy: Rational Agency as Ethical Life* (Cambridge: Cambridge University Press, 2008)

Postema, Gerald J. *Bentham and the Common Law Tradition* (Oxford: Clarendon Press, 1986)

Puchta, Georg Friedrich. *Cursus der Institutionen*, vol. 1 (Leipzig: Breitkopf and Härtel, 1841)

Radbruch, Gustav. "Statutory Lawlessness and Supra-statutory Law (1946)" (2006) 26 *Oxford Journal of Legal Studies* 1–11 (translated by Bonnie Litschewski Paulson and Stanley L. Paulson)

Rawls, John. A *Theory of Justice* (Cambridge, Mass.: Harvard University Press, 1971)

Rawls, John. *Political Liberalism* (New York: Columbia University Press, 1991)

Raz, Joseph. *The Authority of Law: Essays on Law and Morality* (Oxford: Clarendon Press, 1979)

Raz, Joseph. *The Concept of a Legal System: An Introduction to the Theory of Legal System* (2d ed., Oxford: Clarendon Press, 1980)

Raz, Joseph. *The Morality of Freedom* (Oxford: Oxford University Press, 1986)

Raz, Joseph. *Practical Reason and Norms* (2d ed., Princeton: Princeton University Press, 1990)

Raz, Joseph. *Ethics in the Public Domain* (2d ed., Oxford: Clarendon Press, 1995)

Raz, Joseph. *Between Authority and Interpretation: On the Theory of Law and Practical Reason* (Oxford: Oxford University Press, 2008)

Rebentisch, Juliane. *Die Kunst der Freiheit: Zur Dialektik demokratischer Existenz* (Berlin: Suhrkamp, 2012)

Ricoeur, Paul. *Freud and Philosophy: An Essay on Interpretation* (New Haven: Yale University Press, 1970)

Rorty, Richard. *Contingency, Irony, and Solidarity* (Cambridge: Cambridge University Press 1988)

Rosa, Hartmut. *Alienation and Acceleration: Towards a Critical Theory of Late-Modern Temporality* (Aarhus: NSU Press, 2010)

Sander, Fritz. "Die transzendentale Methode der Rechtsphilosophie und der Begriff der Rechtserfahrung" (1920) *In Die Rolle des Neukantianismus in der Reinen Rechtslehre: Eine Debatte zwischen Sander und Kelsen* (ed. S.L. Paulson, Aalen: Scientia, 1988) 75–114

Savigny, Carl Friedrich von. *Of the Vocation of Our Age for Legislation and Jurisprudence* (New York: Arno Press, 1975)

Scanlon, T.M. *What We Owe to Each Other* (Cambridge, Mass.: Harvard University Press, 1998)

Schelling, F.W.J. *Philosophie der Offenbarung*, vol. 1 (reprint, Darmstadt: Wissenschaftliche Buchgesellschaft, 1955)

Schelling, F.W.J. *Über das Wesen der menschlichen Freiheit* (ed. W. Schulz, Frankfurt aM: Suhrkamp, 1975)

Schelling, F.W.J. *Philosophical Investigations into the Essence of Human Freedom* (Albany: State University of New York Press, 2006)

Schlag, Pierre. "Normativity and the Politics of Form" (1991) 139 *University of Pennsylvania Law Review* 801–932

Schlegel, Friedrich. Philosophische Lehrjahre I (1796–1806), *Kritische Werkausgabe*, vol. 18 (ed. E. Behler, Munich: Verlag Ferdinand Schönigh, 1963), II 668

Schlink, Bernhard. *The Reader* (trans. C. Brown Janeway, New York: Vintage Books, 1999)

Schmitt, Carl. *Der Leviathan in der Staatslehre des Thomas Hobbes: Sinn und Fehlschlag eines politischen Symbols* (Stuttgart: Klett Cotta, 2012)

Schmitt, Carl. *Gesetz und Urteil* (Berlin: Otto Liebmann, 1912)

Schopenhauer, Arthur. "Preisschrift über die Grundlage der Moral." In *Werke in fünf Bänden*, vol. 3 (ed. L. Lütkehaus, Zurich: Artemis, 1988)

Schulte, Joachim. *Wittgenstein: Eine Einführung* (Stuttgart: Reclam, 1989)

Sedwick, Sally S. "Hegel's Critique of the Subjective Idealism of Kant's Ethics" (1988) 26 *Journal of the History of Philosophy* 89–105

Shapiro, Scott J. "The Bad Man and the Internal Point of View." In *The Path of the Law and Its Influence: The Legacy of Oliver Wendell Holmes Jr.* (ed. S. Burton, Cambridge: Cambridge University Press, 2000) 197–210

Shapiro, Scott J. "What Is the Internal Point of View?" (2006) 75 *Fordham Law Review* 1157–1170

Shapiro, Scott J. "The 'Hart-Dworkin' Debate: A Short Guide for the Perplexed." In *Ronald Dworkin* (ed. A. Ripstein, Cambridge: Cambridge University Press, 2007) 22–55

Shapiro, Scott J. "What Is the Rule of Recognition (and Does It Exist)?" In *The Rule of Recognition and the U.S. Constitution* (ed. M. Adler and K. Einar Himma, Oxford: Oxford University Press, 2009) 235–268

Shapiro, Scott J. *Legality* (Cambridge, Mass.: Harvard University Press, 2011)

Shklar, Judith. *Legalism: Law, Morals, and Political Trials* (Cambridge, Mass.: Harvard University Press, 1986)

Siep, Ludwig. "Naturrecht und Wissenschaftslehre." In *Fichtes Lehre vom Rechtsverhältnis: Die Deduktion der §§ 1–4 der Grundlage des Naturrechts* (ed. M. Kahlo et al., Frankfurt aM: Klostermann, 1992) 71–91

Simmonds, Nigel. *Law as a Moral Idea* (Oxford: Oxford University Press, 2007)

Solum, Lawrence B. "We Are All Originalists Now." In Robert W. Bennett and Lawrence B. Solum, *Constitutional Originalism: A Debate* (Ithaca: Cornell University Press, 2011) 1–64

Somek, Alexander. "The Emancipation of Legal Dissonance." In *Europe: The New Legal Realism* (ed. H. Koch et al., Copenhagen: DJØF Publishing, 2010) 670–713

Somek, Alexander. *Engineering Equality: An Essay on European Anti-Discrimination Law* (Oxford: Oxford University Press, 2011a)

Somek, Alexander. "The Spirit of Legal Positivism" (2011b) 12 *German Law Journal* 729–756

Somek, Alexander. *The Cosmopolitan Constitution* (Oxford: Oxford University Press, 2014)

Somek, Alexander. "Europe: From Emancipation to Empowerment" 60/2013 *LSE "Europe in Question" Discussion Paper*, www.lse.ac.uk/europeanInstitute/LEQS/LEQSPaper60.pdf

Taylor, Charles. "What"s Wrong with Negative Liberty." In his *Philosophy and the Human Sciences* (Cambridge: Cambridge University Press, 1985) 211–229

Taylor, Charles. *The Ethics of Authenticity* (Cambridge, Mass.: Harvard University Press, 1999)

Teubner, Gunther. *Law as an Autopoietic System* (Oxford: Blackwell, 1993)

Theunissen, Michael. *Der Andere: Studien zur Sozialontologie der Gegenwart* (2d ed., Berlin: de Gruyter, 1977)

Theunissen, Michael. *Sein und Schein: Die kritische Funktion der Hegelschen Logik* (Frankfurt aM: Suhrkamp, 1980)

Unger, Roberto Mangabeira. *Passion: An Essay on Personality* (New York: Free Press, 1984)

Vaihinger, Hans. *Die Philosophie des Als Ob: System der theoretischen, praktischen und religiösen Fiktionen der Menschheit aufgrund eines idealistischen Positivismus* (9th and 10th ed., Leipzig: Felix Meiner, 1927)

Velleman, J. David. *How We Get Along* (Cambridge: Cambridge University Press, 2009)

Velleman, J. David. *Foundations for Moral Relativism* (Open Book, 2013)

Velleman, J. David. "Reading Kant's Groundwork" http://ssrn.com/abstract=2088330

Waldron, Jeremy. *Law and Disagreement* (Oxford: Oxford University Press, 1999)

Walzer, Michael. *Spheres of Justice: A Defence of Pluralism and Equality* (Oxford: Blackwell, 1983)

Wendell, Oliver. Holmes, "The Path of the Law" reprinted in (1997) 110 *Harvard Law Review* 991–1009

Wilde, Oscar. *The Picture of Dorian Gray* (1891)

Winch, Peter. *The Idea of a Social Science and Its Relation to Philosophy* (London: Routledge and Kegan Paul, 1958)

Wittgenstein, Ludwig. *Über Gewissheit* (Frankfurt aM: Suhrkamp, 1984)

Yoshino, Kenji. "The Assimilationist Bias in Equal Protection: The Visibility Presumption and the Case of 'Don't Ask, Don't Tell'" (1989) 108 *Yale Law Journal* 485–571

Index